LOST IN WYOMING

KENNETH J WEIMER

Trilogy Christian Publishers
A Wholly Owned Subsidary of Trinity Broadcasting Network
2442 Michelle Drive
Tustin, CA 92780

Cover design by: Cornerstone Creative Solutions

For information, address Trilogy Christian Publishing
Rights Department, 2442 Michelle Drive, Tustin, Ca 92780.
Trilogy Christian Publishing/ TBN and colophon are trademarks of Trinity Broadcasting Network.

For information about special discounts for bulk purchases, please contact Trilogy Christian Publishing.

Manufactured in the United States of America

10 9 8 7 6 5 4 3 2 1

Library of Congress Cataloging-in-Publication Data is available.

ISBN 978-1-63769-218-9 (Print Book)
ISBN 978-1-63769-219-6 (ebook)

DEDICATION

This book is first dedicated to my mother, C. Joan Aldrich Weimer. She was not a rebel but detested people that would follow one another like dumb sheep for no good reason or purpose. She would often say to my older brother, who was terrible for following the crowd in whatever current fad, thought, or action was taking place, "If everybody wore a horse turd on their head, I guess you would too!"

Mom had drifted away for years from the Lord after meeting and marrying my father. However, in her later years, she became a wonderful Christian that was dearly loved by her church and family. She was full of the love of God for all.

I also dedicate this book to my wonderful wife, Brenda. If not for her urging and support, I would never have recorded these many true stories and events in this work, though I would often enjoy relating them around a campfire or gathering to those who requested to hear them.

Finally, and foremost, this work is dedicated to the Lord Jesus Christ (the anointed one). Without Him and all that He has done for me, these works would never have existed.

ACKNOWLEDGMENTS

My thanks to Rick Bluel of Meeteetse, Wyoming. He is a fine Christian friend that, like myself, very much enjoys trout fishing in Park County, Wyoming. It was on one of these trips that Rick took a photo of me. With no plans for the photo at the time, it has now become the photo for the author's biography for *Lost in Wyoming*.

INTRODUCTION

Lost, lost, it is a terrible thing to be lost. Going along when it becomes obvious that something is amiss. Something is out of whack. How could this be? What is to be done now? The feeling of being lost is gut-wrenching, terrifying, and very confusing.

The events in *Lost in Wyoming* are all true. Some names of individuals have been changed or excluded, but every effort is made to include them in the stories of which you will find a wide variety of events and human interest. Humor, history, sorrow, danger, miracles, and a vast array of colorful characters living in the rugged mountain west cowboy state of Wyoming and the Last Frontier state of Alaska are but some of the emotions and experiences you will find in *Lost in Wyoming*.

BOOK 1

Rock Springs was always a rough town. It came about mostly because of coal, trona, ranching of cattle, and herding and raising of sheep. It was settled by tough people that came there as pioneers, explorers, independent-minded folks, and even "end of the road" characters. Chinese were brought into the town to work in the mines at a reduced cost of what the whites would work for. This caused a great deal of tension, which led to the white people taking up violence against the Chinese. Killing and injuring them. Running them out of the community and destroying what little wealth they had accumulated. Eventually, the United States government had to send troops into the area at that time to protect the Chinese and bring peace to the area.

It was an area rich and diverse in culture. People came there over the Oregon/California Trails. Over the Mormon, Lander Cutoff, and Overland Trails. The city (town) is located south of Boar's Tusk, southeast of Pilot Butte, and east of White Mountain. It sits near the Green River and, of course, now the Flaming Gorge Reservoir. The pony express came through Rock Springs when it transported the mail.

It was full of all types of customs and different races of people, but we were all Americans. We were all Wyomingites. We all knew and understood our differences and appreciated that in the years I recall. That is not saying that we all got along just peachy all of the time. There were plenty of tensions and troubles among the races and the diversities, but for the most part, folks got along pretty well. Generally, we could call a person by slang names for their nationality. It was usually without ill intent. It was simply describing the nationality of a person or in conversation with or about a person or something related to them. Oftentimes the terms were used by those nationalities as well to describe themselves or others in their own race.

For instance, we might say, "Oh, that old dago owns that store. Be careful, or he'll Jew you out of your money." Or we might say, "Those japs own the flower store, and they are really nice people." Well, you get the idea, I think, I hope. Things have sure changed.

There were lots of nationalities in Rock Springs, and it certainly was not your typical Wyoming town. It was into this town that I was born on a hot summer day in August 1955. Born at the old hospital of Sweetwater County at 6:25 in the evening. In fact, my two younger sisters were also born in the same room, as well as a nephew, many years later until the new hospital was built up on College Hill and the old hospital became a courthouse and all different offices and that type of thing.

Depending on how you look at it. The fact that my mother had more than one child, that being Chuckie, it was a miracle or answer to prayer that she had more children. The doctors sternly warned her after the birth of Chuckie that she was not to have any more children. Her health would be in great peril if she did otherwise, and they eluded that there might be other serious problems as well.

Right across the street from the hospital set the cemetery. My mother used to joke that it was only a short distance to your final resting place if you didn't make it out of the hospital. Folks had a great view of the boneyard out of the back windows of the hospital. I often wondered what they thought of that. It probably scared "the soup" out of some of them or made them focus on their eternal destiny.

Rock Springs and Sweetwater County were some of the few areas that were of Democratic persuasion in the days I was growing up. Wyoming was mostly a very conservative Republican state and is even more so that way today. Of course, the Democratic Party then was nothing like it is today and was pretty conservative at that time, compared to the Democratic Party of the current day. I vividly recall being old enough to vote and casting my first presidential vote for

Jimmy Carter for a president. I do not have many regrets in my life, but of one I do have, it is casting that vote for Jimmy Carter.

We were basically really kind of a poor family, but we lived pretty well. I joined my family at our little house on A Street. We rented a house from two old ladies who lived nearby. One of them was said to capture and drown cats that came into her yard. I do not know if that was true, but I didn't have a cat anyway. One of the ladies' names was Vennis, but I thought it was Dennis. I thought that strange, but I still thought, *Wow, pretty neat for a lady to have a boy's name!*

Living at the house were my grandpa Joe, who I received my middle name from, and my grandmother Frances. Grandpa's first name was really Joseph, and grandma's first name was really Mary, and Frances was her middle name. They came from farms in the state of Missouri, came to Wyoming to work in the coal mines and get their fortune, I guess. They first lived in Sheridan, Wyoming, and then eventually came to Rock Springs, working in the coal mines, of course. Grandma worked really hard in a laundromat that was owned by Jewish people. She worked there till she nearly dropped and loved it.

Grandpa used to joke that he might be Joseph and grandma might be Mary, but in regard to my father, they sure did *not* have baby Jesus. Grandpa went to work in the trona mines later when the coal mines petered out in the area.

Grandpa Joe was tall and lean and was really a good grandpa. He loved to hunt and fish. He especially loved to fly fish, had some really neat fly rods and all equipment, and went with it. He also loved to make things look nice, and in the front of the little house we rented too. He planted a very nice large lawn and flowers and just made it look really beautiful. The place had kind of a ramshackle wooden wire fence, as I recall, and grandpa Joe later put in a really nice black rod iron fence that is still there to this day.

I especially remember the old ramshackle fence that has long been gone because of an incident that took place with me and my older brother Chuckie. Chuckie was six years older than me and had been born in Sheridan, Wyoming, before the family moved to Rock

Springs. He was named after my father, Charles Wesley Weimer, Sr., of course, he was junior as my father was senior. Both of them were hellions in numerous ways. Anyway, I was probably about four years old, and I and my brother filled water balloons to throw at each other in the front yard. We had a great time for a while, but Chuckie, easily bored, soon decided we might want to throw them at people walking by on the street or at passing cars or anything otherwise of great interest. Well, it was not long before here came this dumpy-looking, heavyset girl walking down the sidewalk. She was large, and she was packing a whole bunch of stuff in her arms like books or something. We clobbered her with water balloons. I think I missed my shot, but Chuckie beaned her with at least one good one. She had on a white shirt, pants and wore those black-rimmed glasses that were so popular back then. It is rather funny. You see people wearing those kinds of glasses again now. My dad always said, "Don't throw your clothes away that are out of date, and in a few years, they will be back in style." Anyway, when the balloon hit the girl, she began to scream, and then here she came at us full speed on the run. I learned then that fat girls can run pretty fast if they want to. Chuckie took off full speed for the house with me in tow. We tore through the front screen door and into the house. The big girl came right over the ramshackle fence and finished, knocking it down into the yard, and was hot on our heels. She tore right through the screen door and into the house, screaming all the way, my poor shocked mother met all three of us as we charged into the front area of the home. When my mother finally sorted out the mess, she found out that the girl was complaining that we had ruined all of her recent high school yearbook photos. I do not know who my mother was the angriest at, the girl for charging into our home or us for soaking her with a water balloon. Well, my mother offered to pay for the pictures if she would produce them. She never did, and it was a hot day in a little water that really didn't hurt the old gal. Anyway, that is the way we have not figured. My mother was not happy with us, but as I recall, we only got a tongue-lashing, and, from my kindly mother, it was mild. However, if my mother was angry with me, she then called me by my first full name. That and in formal settings or by people that didn't know me are really the only times that I was usually called Kenneth.

We got a few spankings over the years, but it was not too bad for a while. Mom had this new cowboy belt she would use on us, didn't hurt a bit. It was so stiff that it did not matter how hard she hit with it; it just did not have a wallop to it. Well, we did not want that to stop, so we soon figured out that all we had to do was whoop and holler, scream and yell and plead for mercy when she whipped us with the belt. Then after the punishment was over and mom was out of the area, we would chuckle at how clever we were. Mom never said anything about it, but at some point, the jig was up. The cowboy belt disappeared, and a razor strap took its place. Now that thing hurt! I do not know where that implement of torture came from, nobody in our house ever had a need to sharpen a razor on the thing.

We lived only about a block away from a little Assemblies of God church, but we seldom went to it. I am told that on one occasion, when we went to a service, an offering was taken. I had a dime or some other small token to put into the offering basket as it came by, and so I deposited the coin into the basket. I apparently did not understand the process, and as the usher walked away, I began yelling at the top of my lungs, "Here, bring my money back here," much to the embarrassment of my mother and grandmother.

There had been a Peeping Tom going around the neighborhood at night. One late night, he got careless and apparently made too much noise. This drew my father's and the neighbor's attention, and they both ran out in the dark to try to catch the guy. Dad had on a housecoat, but the neighbor was only in his underwear. The Peeping Tom eluded them. But the police showed up and caught dad and the neighbor. The police thought they had caught the Peeping Tom, or Toms, in this case. They were calling the neighbor the underwear man. After it was all sorted out, they let them go back home. Dad came in the house laughing about it, it was pretty funny. Our neighbor being called the underwear man, the dreaded Peeping Tom! The Peeping Tom never showed back up, and that was the end of that, as they say.

When you think of it now, things have really changed in just a short period of time. There used to be old tradesmen show up at the house that were professional sharpeners. For a dollar or two, they would sharpen all your scissors and knives or anything else you needed sharpened. I remember they were usually older men with long beards, flop hats, and old jeans or bib overalls and kind of sorrowful-looking. They were friendly old guys, and I felt sorry for them, why I am not sure. They seemed pretty content with their life.

Just a few years later in our next house. We had an insulated aluminum box on the step landing. You would fill out a paper form and leave it in the box, and the milkman would leave you milk, eggs, or whatever you wanted. You burned your garbage in a fifty-five-gallon barrel in the yard, a paperboy delivered your paper, and then would come around monthly to collect the fees due. The telephones had dials and were usually black and heavy things. Televisions were black and white and with small screens. Fridges that we called iceboxes from an age passed were small and had an even smaller freezer section. We would buy a quart of ice cream and thought that was a big deal. They had ice trays in them that you filled with water and then froze in the freezer for ice cubes. Dishes were washed and dried by hand, and things actually had to be cooked on the stove or oven. We had a big old coal cooking stove in the house on A Street. The heavy lids had to be lifted off the top of the stove and the coal put into the stove from those openings. The coal would be carried up from the basement in a big heavy coal bucket. Clothes were dried on the clothesline outside after they were washed in a tub with the wringer.

On one of our trips to visit relatives in Washington State, I think it was my cousin Sharon that had a rocking horse. The really neat kind on a metal stand with springs and all. I loved that rocking horse and wanted one with all that was within me at the time. I rode the horse every chance I had while we were visiting. For several years after that, I pleaded and begged my parents to buy me one for my birthday or Christmas. I do not know if they just did not want one in the house. Or they thought it was too much to pay for a toy, but I never got it. Finally gave up on the idea when I turned about eighteen—ha-ha!

Another time, we were visiting in Missouri. I think we were in St. Louis, and I went with my mother and father to some kind of a store downtown. I thought it was like a camera or jewelry store, but I am not sure. While we were all standing at the glass counters and my dad was dealing with store personnel about something he was trying to buy there, I spotted some plastic red-colored fireman hats they had for sale. They were on a high shelf at the back of the wall, and I began asking mom to buy me one. She quietly said no. Being the persistent little devil I was, I kept on. She was firm about this. I was not going to get the fireman's hat. Well, I kept on, and I got louder and louder, and I could tell dad was really annoyed with me while he was still trying to do his deal. But he didn't stop, and I did not either. Pretty soon, I began to wine and blubber, and my pleadings grew louder. Oh, I was headed for real trouble, but I was willing to risk it. As they say, nothing risked, nothing gained! Well, my folks were not going to buy me a hat. But all was not a loss, a kindly old lady that was also in the store trying to do business either became annoyed with my loud rantings and just took pity on the poor kid, or maybe both. Anyway, she had the man get a hat down and bought and paid for it for me. I was grateful to his poor old soul. I had that hat for a lot of years. It finally got broken up and had to be thrown away.

Things were going pretty well, I guess. Mom was a stay-at-home mother. Grandpa and grandma were working, and my dad had taken up house painting for a bishop in the Mormon church that had his own small painting business. I was about five years old, and we packed up and moved several miles away to Elias Avenue in Rock Springs. The family bought a large old house on the corner of Elias and Soulsby Street. The plan was for my grandparents to live downstairs and the rest of us upstairs, but we all ended up living upstairs.

It was a very nice neighborhood in those days, located at the north end of Bunning Park. We lived next door to a Japanese family. They were people that could not be beat. A justice of the peace lived up the street and conducted court out of his house. The Traveler's Lodge was on one section of the street that rented apartments by the month and also provided night rooms to the passenger bus drivers that had layovers. There was also kind of a plush apartment house near our home that we called the pink apartments because they were pink in color. The owner and operator of the apartment house complex was a snobby older French couple with little yappy Pekingese dogs. There were a large Catholic church and a Catholic school nearby, and on the church, property were old homes that had been the barracks of the troops that had been stationed in Rock Springs during the Chinese uprising (uprising against the Chinese) that I mentioned earlier. These homes were now mostly occupied by Spanish and Mexican families, and the rest of the area was a mixture of apartments and pretty nice homes. Some of the more uppity neighbors must have thought, *Well, there goes the neighborhood* when they saw our clan move in. Maybe they were not completely wrong about that!

We took up residence that summer, and grandpa Joe soon had beautiful flowers planted all in front and alongside the house near the sidewalk. We had our first television at that house, although we did not watch it much. It had a small screen with black and white pictures. When everybody was at work and grandpa Joe had a day off, I would set to watch baseball games with him in the daytime. I did not really understand the game, but it was fun to set with grandpa. Sometimes on hot afternoons, we would lay on their bed and take a nap. I cherished my grandpa and dad, although grandpa was really much closer to me during this young period of my life.

One day grandpa was doing minor work on a car at the front of our house. I was standing on the sidewalk, watching him. Vehicles were parked in parallel fashion all along the street. For some reason, I decided to run between the parked cars and across the street. I never checked for traffic. I just darted out. I do not really remember it, but grandpa says I ran right in front of an oncoming car. It was too late for him to do anything, and he figured the car that was going about twenty to twenty-five miles an hour was going to run me over. All he could do was watch in horror as somehow the car missed me. Grandpa swore that I must have had an angel that kept me from disaster, for he did not know how in the world the car could have avoided me but did. I scared the soup out of poor grandpa. Of course, he related this incident to my mother right after it happened, and she was upset. Grandpa was always kind and gentle and did not say much about it, except he just kept repeating his account of how an angel must have saved me from disaster as there was no way that the car could have missed me otherwise.

The summer ended, and the fall came on, and my brother and I went off to Washington school, which was only a few blocks away. The school was an ancient wooden building that is located where the playground is now. Thus, I began my educational career in Mrs. Mooney's kindergarten class.

It was Halloween, and we had a Halloween party at school. Mom made some special cookies with the little candy pumpkins on top of them, and grandpa walked me to the class that day. I went in with the box of cookies that I had to share with everyone and my grandpa in tow. I was so proud of my grandpa. I had to show him off just as if it was a show-and-tell day. I think he was a little embarrassed to get all of the attention, but he never complained about it.

With the exception of holidays, we seldom ate family dinners at the table. The custom was generally to sit around in the living room and eat off TV trays, visit with one another and watch television. That is the way it was on one cold stormy night in February. We were all there, except for Grandpa Joe. He had not made it in from work yet that evening. We were not overly concerned at the time, even though it was very bad weather. Grandpa was working in the trona mines, which were about thirty to forty miles away from Rock Springs. It was expected that travel would be slow with the bad road conditions, and he was expected home at any time.

Then it was that the storm really hit. There was a knock on the front door of the house. Dad and grandma answered the door, and when it opened, you could see a sheriff's vehicle setting out in front of the house with the red bubble light flashing. On that cold night at the door were the sheriff or one of his deputies and the county coroner Peter Vase. The news they had for our family was far more bitter than the cold weather of that night. A terrible accident had occurred about five miles out of town on the state highway involving my grandfather's vehicle, a bus coming from the trona mines, and a

PIE eighteen-wheeler truck. Many were injured, some were killed. Grandpa Joe would never come home again.

Dad would not have grandpa to depend on anymore. A major income was lost to make the payments on the property, even though we retained it. These were sad, sad times. Who can make sense out of such a sudden tragedy? Grandpa Joe had been a vibrant, healthy man not yet sixty years old, and now in a flash, he was gone. It brought home the scripture that tells us our life is like a vapor that appears for a while, and then it is gone. It is all temporary, Job said it well. Naked we come into this world, and naked we'll leave it.

Grandpa and grandma also had a daughter. Her name was Mary Lou. She was a handsome young lady. She was married and living in Colorado, around Pueblo, as I recall. We drove down one time to visit them. I don't remember too much about it, except it was the long trip by car, or so it seemed to a little boy. She and uncle Wayne came back for the funeral with their little wiener dog Brandy. I had other aunts and uncles on my mother's side, but Mary Lou is my favorite. She called me Keek and sometimes playfully Keeky go-go. Even though we were never around each other all that much, she seemed to favor me. I think she liked my independent spirit and can-do attitude.

Grandpa's mangled white car was taken to a local garage, and we were told that he and the eighteen-wheel truck collided. His vehicle was knocked from the highway, and he went out the back window and was thrown onto the trunk of the car. Conditions were terrible. It had been a terrible blizzard that day, Mr. Vase told us that grandpa was killed instantly. Aunt Mary Lou was a Catholic when she lived in Rock Springs or was persuaded to that religion due to her friendship with a family in which at least the mother of the family was a strong Catholic, and they owned the other mortuary in town. Grandpa's body did not go to Vases, it went to the Rogan mortuary.

About the same time, I became desperately ill with a bad case of the measles. Kindly people were coming to the house in droves and bringing all kinds of food, visits, well wishes, and all the comfort possible for such a terrible tragedy. I became so tired of all the company that I just tried to hide out; at one point, I got onto my grandma and grandpa's bed and hid under a huge pile of coats from all the visitors that had been placed on the bed.

I was allowed to go out on one cold wintry day to see grandpa at the mortuary. Mom asked me if I wanted to touch grandpa's hand as he lay in the open coffin. Here he was in a suit and tie. Seldom had I seen grandpa dressed that way. He was the "ball cap, plaid shirt, and blue jeans" type of guy. I held the cold, stiff hand of grandpa and told him goodbye. I remained so ill that that was the last that I saw my grandpa.

Dad now had responsibilities that I do not think he really wanted. Grandma had white hair. She said it had been that way since she was seventeen years of age. She was only in her 50s too, younger than grandpa, but now she looked older than ever. She had a sadness about her that I had never seen before and that lasted for a long time. She was a worrywart, always more of a serious type, and didn't joke around much. Years later, we always said of grandma that if she did not have something to worry about, she would manufacture something in the meantime.

We would watch some TV. As a family, it was usually cops and robbers, *The Jimmy Dean Show, The Real McCoy's, The Beverly Hillbillies, Mutual of Omaha's Wild Kingdom, The Rifleman, Have Gun—Will Travel* (I always thought it was *Half Gun Will Travel*), westerns, war movies, and boxing. For me, it was *Sky King, The Three Stooges, Highway Patrol, The Sheriff of Cochise, Superman*, and *The Lone Ranger*, with the few cartoons thrown in for good measure.

Actually, we spent most of our time outside. I learned and knew the neighborhood like the back of my hand. I knew all the escape routes and all of the shortcuts. Spent countless hours in Bunning Park, which is great, except they wouldn't let us play on the grass. The park was full of old retired men that sat on benches talking about everything imaginable. They wore dress hats in those days, even to sit on a park bench. Large wooden signs, black-and-white in color, were posted at both entrances into the park, warning all evildoers, "Keep Off the Grass." By order of the chief of police. The park had a number of crab trees in it as well. We loved to climb the trees and get the apples. Of course, you had to go on the grass to get to the trees. So, at the risk of life and limb, we would dash across the grass, hurry into a tree and shake down and pull all the apples we could. Stuff all the little apples you could into your pockets or paper bag and run for your life. Probably at this very instant, somebody was calling the police from the caretakers' shack in the park. But worse than that, those old guys were the caretakers who would try to catch you, and some of them were out for blood. One little guy, we called him the funny little clown, would get so mad that, while he was chasing after you, he would throw rakes, hoes, shovels, or anything that was handy at you. We could easily outrun them. But sometimes they would try to double-team you and catch you before we could get over the wire fences or through the few gates that enclosed the park. Sometimes the police would actually show up, and you had better be gone by then. Most of the police were middle-aged to older guys, and you had better not mess with them.

We would get a salt shaker and eat the apples with salt. Strangely enough, you could return to the park the next day, and as long as you kept your nose clean, those guys never said a word to you. Only hours ago, you had been in a life-and-death pursuit with the caretakers, and now here they were watering and cutting grass, and tending flowers, and acting as if they had never seen you before. The caretakers were all older guys. They were probably retired coal miners, tough men, all of them. They wore wide-brimmed hats, work shirts, bib overalls, and work boots. Then in the late afternoon, there was a regular park guard. His name was Marco, he wore a watchman's badge, a wide-brimmed hat, and he had a stick like a cane that had a metal poker at the end of it. He would stay around until dark and then go home. I copied his uniform, and I would go over and hang out with him and help guard the park. He put up with me and would even give me a nickel or dime at times for being his assistant.

So, it was a mixed and checkered life for me. An apple thief and violator by daytime and a lawman in the afternoon and evening. What a great life! Nobody seemed to complain about it, and it worked for me.

I was careful never to steal or vandalize. We may have been a nuisance, but I would never even think of doing such things. Still today, I do not understand why people get a thrill out of damaging or stealing someone else's property. It amazes me that people will litter and vandalize public property, people of all ages, and all with impunity.

At the end of every school year, we would get a free ticket to go to the local sponsored circus that was held at the high school football field. It came along with your report card with you passed the grade or failed. So, no matter what, it was good news to get the free ticket. This was only in grade school, of course. Mom did not want to go, and she would let me go by myself. So, grandma would offer to take the afternoon off from her job at the dry cleaners and take me. We went for two or three years in a row, and this is one of the few things that she and I ever did together that amounted to much and was something fun. We would set out on the open bleachers in the hot sun and watch the three-ring circus. It was a pretty good circus. And then, of course, there was always cotton candy and stuff like that. Then grandma, who was pretty red from the hot sun, would always complain about being baked at "that old circus." She enjoyed it as much or more than I did, but that was like a high insult for her to call it an "old circus." If there was some girl or woman she did not like or that she had a low opinion of, her most insulting term for them would be "that old thing." Boy, that was pretty low if she called some female that! This description was reserved for what she considered to be the bottom of the barrel or some troublemaker of some sort.

I have always liked older people. A few of them are bitter and nasty, but mostly I have found them to be friendly, kind, and interesting. Many of them are wise (although old age does not guarantee wisdom, for sure, I have met some older folks that were pretty foolish and just plain dumb) and did not mind spending and investing some time on a curious little boy. As a little boy, I would go around the neighborhood and check on and visit with some of the older retired people. There was Mrs. Allen, a widow who lived across the street from us in the old white apartments. She would invite me in, and I would go in for fifteen or twenty minutes and have a little chat with her to cheer her up. It was a sad day for me a few years later when she was carried out of her apartment by the county coroner in a body bag.

Then there was Mr. McCall, who lived down the street. On summer days, he would set out a little bench in front of his little shanty that he rented from the Harvey family. He had no voice, and he had a hole in the front of his throat that he kept covered with a piece of gauze. He had a metal pipe with a rubber tube that he would put on the whole in his throat and talk, and it would vibrate, and you could hear his voice then. Did not bother me. I would always stop several times during the week and visit with him for fifteen or twenty minutes. We especially liked to talk about hunting and fishing, and he would give me his old copies of *Outdoor Life* and *Field & Stream*. He just disappeared one day. I do not know what happened to him. I do not think he moved away. I think it was like General Pershing said of old soldiers, "They never die, they just go away."

The Harveys were three retired old people. They owned the rental that Mr. McCall lived in, as well as a whole bunch of other rentals and their own house all near us around Bunning Park. She was an old retired schoolmarm, one brother was an old retired policeman that was known as Flashlight Willie, and the other brother was ancient. I do not know what he did, but they said he was a crack shot in his younger days. They were not older people that you could visit with. They lived together in their home that looked like something out of the 1920s inside. They had more money than they knew what to do with, but you would never know it. She dressed in simple clothes like it was 1930. Her name was Sarah, but, of course, you called her Mrs. Harvey. Young people rarely addressed older people by their first names. It was always Mr. or Mrs. or miss or ma'am or sir. Sarah ran the show.

When I got to the ripe old age of twelve and thirteen, she solicited me for cutting grass on their property. She had lots of grass to cut, and it all had to be done with old push mowers and manual grass clippers. She would work you all day in the hot sun for twenty-five or thirty cents and then maybe felt like you were overpaid. But there was always a bonus for good and completed work. "Come to the house," she would say when you get done, "and I have something for you." Well, I knew what that was, oh joy! Happily, I collected my coins, but the big bonus was a warm bottle of root beer that you had set on the front step and drink. The reason that you could not leave with the bottle but had to stay there and drink it was because she wanted the bottle back. She was not going to be denied her five-cent deposit back for the return of the pop bottle.

Sarah's brother, Bill, the retired policeman, was not as tight with the money as long as Sarah was not wise to what was going on. He had an old car. He kept it in the garage near our house. He would get all dressed up in a suit and go get his car out of the garage and go downtown for lunch. That was his big outing, I suppose. Of course, he only did that once every couple of weeks. He was not a skinny man.

We knew that he was known as Flashlight Willie, but we never called him that. He got that name when he was a policeman because he was afraid to go into dark places. He would stand at the end of alleys and shine his flashlight down them but never set foot into them. I was told in later years that he would also go berserk if he was in a police car that he judged to be going too fast. By "fast," I mean just a few miles over the speed limit. So poor Flashlight did not have too glorious of a police career, and we knew that, but he was harmless. He had been retired for a long time too.

One day he was getting his car out of the garage, and as he opened the garage door, I was nearby. About that time, this mean teenage boy rode by on his bicycle. I knew the kid; he was from another part of town. Came from a pretty dysfunctional family. As he rode by, he shouted at Mr. Harvey, "Hey, Flashlight Willie!" Good thing he kept on riding. Bill went into an immediate rage. I had never seen a man so gussied up in his suit throw such a fit. He let go of the garage door and began cussing and yelling, running down the street after the kid on the bike. As I said, he was not a skinny man, and it was a pretty short chase. I just stood there watching the whole event and did not let on that I knew anything about his slang name. He came back all huffing and puffing and red in the face and walked up to me. He pleaded with me not to tell his sister Sarah about any of this event. Actually, the thought had never even crossed my mind to do that. He even offered to give me some hush money, but I did not want it. So poor old Bill went on and drove off in his light-blue-colored car and had lunch that afternoon, indigestion, and all from this unsavory event, I suppose.

Bill Harvey needed his tires changed over on his car one day, only two of them, I think. It was only a matter of taking off two wheels and tires and putting two spare wheels and tires back on. He called on my brother Chuckie to do that for him. My brother went down to his garage, changed the tires over in a matter of about twenty or thirty minutes, and was generously paid about twenty dollars. Of course, this came with a warning from Bill, "Don't let Sarah know about this." *A fine thing*, I thought, *my brother works for half an hour and gets twenty bucks. I work and sweat and blister my hands all day in the hot sun and get twenty-five or thirty cents and a warm bottle of root beer.*

My dad was a handsome, healthy man. He sure had some wild streaks in him, though, that he never did away with. My brother Chuckie took after him. My dad catered more to Chuckie because they were more alike than I and my dad were. He was a pretty good provider. Despite everything, he took us on some pretty neat trips and vacations. But oh, he loved to drink and party, and he would disappear for days at a time sometimes. He would go off with a bunch of drunks and miss work. My poor mother would load me and my brother up in a car and go driving around town scouring it for my father. I would hate to tell you how many miles we put on searching for my dad, different times. Fortunately, the Mormon bishop that he painted for would put up with it. He knew that my father needed this job to support his family and that the family had been through a lot of hardships with the loss of my grandpa and so on. So, where other people may have fired my father, the Mormon bishop showed mercy. Eventually, my dad would show up. Come home drunk as could be, sleep it off, and go back to work. Sometimes he would have big black eyes. Sometimes he was really mad. Sometimes he had to be packed into the bed.

My dad spent a fortune on booze and gambling. Gambling was illegal in Wyoming, but it went on in many of the back rooms of the bars in Rock Springs on a regular basis. One of the games that my dad lost money at regularly was one called bar boot. I do not know anything about the game or how it was played, but I know my dad lost lots and lots of money trying to win it. He would also play craps with dice, and that was another loser for him and the other suckers.

When I was about seven or eight, it was against the law to sell alcohol on Sunday, the bars had to be closed. So, they would be closed, but people would be in them, cleaning and stocking and so on. But this made it very convenient to sell alcohol out of the back door of the bars. So, my dad would drive downtown with all of us in the car. He would warn us to wait quietly while he went across the street to buy some beer at the back of the bar. He never failed to score, and he was never caught at this. Most of the time, I believe he really had plenty of beer. It was just a big game that he enjoyed. He just could not help himself from being a bad boy.

My mother put up with a lot over the years with my father and Chuckie, my brother. Dad would lose all or most of his paycheck gambling and drinking and come home in a rage. He would keep all of us up for hours into the night or early morning. He would hang out in the kitchen ranting and raving, cursing, and hollering. I don't know where he got the voice or energy for all of that, but he did.

Sometimes he would get out a .22 pistol and mess with it. Several times he shot it off in the house through the ceiling. Mom and grandma would plead with him to eat something and quit drinking. To quit ranting and raving before the neighbors heard him and called the police. I don't know if the neighbors ever heard him, really, I don't know how they could not have heard him, but no one ever called the police. Back then, you only called the police for serious stuff! Dad would be urged to go to bed and stop his displays, but it fell on deaf ears. When he finally got worn out and done, then he stumbled off to bed.

Dad was good in a lot of ways, though. He had lots of run-ins with the police in his younger days, and he did not have any use for them. Nor did my grandma. Despite that, we ended up with law enforcement officers in our family, and, of course, that was different when they were actually wearing a badge. Maybe some cops were okay!

Dad told some pretty hair-raising stories about his wild times in Jackson Hole, Wyoming, Missouri, and other places. Times of jail and just general wild and reckless behavior that drove my poor easy-going grandparents crazy.

My dad would work hard when he worked, and he would go out and tear a car motor completely apart and fix it and put it back together just for the adventure of it all. Chuckie was right there with him on most of these backyard mechanic jobs.

Dad, to the consternation of most of our neighbors, kept the large yard full of cars in various states of disrepair. He kept all of our cars going, and he would buy and fix cars and sell them at pretty good profits most of the time. He sold lots of cars to the Mexicans and Indians that would be in town working for the railroad. These poor buzzards usually were only in town for a few days, and they had just been paid by the railroad. They spent most of the time in some of the bars and were usually drunk and just having a big wild time. Dad would always sell some vehicles at exorbitant prices to these poor souls. He was sure to help empty their pockets of the cash they had earned. We would sometimes see the vehicles he had sold to these guys a day or two later. They were left at the roadside, broken down. Dad had lots of satisfied customers, though, and sold lots of cars to people over the years.

With grandpa gone, we never had a nice yard again. It was more like a junk-car-lot yard. No more flowers or grass. We began renting the downstairs of the house to families. Most of them were pretty good people, but we did end up with a few real lulus. Dad let us play in some of the cars, and we had a lot of times in those things.

We had two garages on the property. One of them was the nicest that was two-car and sat near the road. It was rented for years to government trappers. I always found it interesting to watch the men come and go with pelts of various critters and traps and all. The other garage was attached to the side of the house and started out nice and orderly. Not for the keeping of vehicles but for tools and equipment. Within a few years, my dad had it so full of stuff that you could barely get inside most of the time. Or you had to crawl around and search for whatever you wanted.

Cars were parked all around the house on the street. Neighbors would complain about the place, but my dad could care less. The police would harass him some about it but not much ever changed. He figured he was paying for the place so he could do what he wanted with it. Sure, made an eyesore for the really nice Bunning Park near us. I wonder what the tourists thought about it when they would stop in there for a picnic on their travels and see our place.

The floors in the house were all linoleum and some bare wood. Dad made some sort of a deal with his boss, Woody Hunter, the Mormon bishop that he painted for, and was able to come up with this used green carpet. We put it down in the living room. It covered the width of the room but not quite the full length. It was probably four feet or so short. We sure liked it that, though. Wow, to have a carpeted room and be able to lay on the floor and play or watch a little television, we felt like we were in hog heaven now! It was an alright carpet, but it had been well used. It made the floor much warmer to be on in the cold weather, and the folks had it on the floor for quite a few years before finally replacing it with new carpeting.

Mom was an easy-going person too. She had to be. She was born in Sheridan, Wyoming, and met my dad there. She had several sisters and one brother. They had all left Wyoming and were living in Washington State as long as I knew of any of them. They were very nice people, and most of them were really fun aunts and uncles. We went and saw them once or twice, and they all came and visited us, most of them several times. I didn't know or really do much with cousins, but I sure liked my aunts and uncles. I liked to sit and visit with them. They were wise and funny. Lots more fun to listen to and visit with than a bunch of whiny kids! Even though I was a kid myself.

Mom was the only one in her family that stayed in Wyoming. Her father was killed in an auto accident, and I never knew him. Her mother was with family in Washington and died when I was probably six or so. I remember the long trip we took by train to go out there and back to the funeral.

Mom was a very pretty woman and kept a clean and orderly home most of her years despite my dad's propensity for bringing in junk of all types and hoarding stuff. She had been raised to be a Christian or to at least have strong Christian influence, maybe I should say. She was nothing like my dad. Somehow, though, he lured her away, and they eventually ran off one day without her family's knowledge or consent and drove the short distance to Harding, Montana. She was too young to be married in Wyoming but could get legally married in Montana. So that is where their union took place. She never said much about it, but I am sure if she could have rethought that decision, she would have made far different choices than she did. My dad could have driven a weaker woman to insanity or worse, but not mom. She was far too strong for that. She never even complained much. Never cried about her situation or lamented about it to others. She would often say about other situations, "You have made your bed, now lie in it." She figured that that applied to her for sure.

Her family could not have been too happy with what had occurred. She did not get to graduate from high school because of the marriage and never did complete high school. She ended up living with my father's family in Sheridan and took on the responsibilities of a wife and mother later.

Like I said, my dad could be a really good guy, but he sure could go wild streaks and tangents. Most of the time, I just ignored his foul-talk criticism. One time he was mad at me, and he made a statement to me in front of my mother in the kitchen at our home that went like this, "You could mess up a beautiful dream." I was a young teenager, and I think there may have been one or two other people present in the room. I am not sure who it may have been now. But this was one time I saw my mother get really angry at my dad and told him so. She lashed him good and said she did not ever want to hear such a thing said again to me. Boy, she was hot, and he knew it. That sure backfired on my dad. He really thought he was being clever when he said that to me. It did not really bother me, and I got quite a kick out of him getting the chewing out.

My dad would take us to all kinds of interesting places in our vehicles and on vacations and trips, hunting and camping. We would go most summers up into the Big Sandy openings and stay at least two weeks, camping out of tents or some other device and fishing, we had great times.

We took several trips on the trains to see relatives and attend funerals and several trips by car as well. The trips on the passenger train were fun, but they would get long and drawn out, and you were eventually glad to get to your destination. To save on expenses, we seldom ate in the dining car. The train would stop at little places along the trip, and you could buy sandwiches and get water, and so on. The car trips were also long and drawn out. I think the train trips were mostly to Washington State, while the car trips were to Colorado and Missouri.

The cars had no air conditioning, so you would have to roll the windows down for air, and the air was pretty hot. There were no rest areas, so you had to wait till he got to a little town and stop at filling stations. We had the old canvas water bags with the Indian Chief painted on the front of them. You would put water in those and put them on the front of the vehicle. The motion of traveling would keep the water somewhat cool, so you did have some water to drink. All the travel was by state highways and routes or little dirt and gravel roads. In fact, I remember some years later, dad taking us out near Rock Springs and showing us this area where they were building the interstate that would be I-80. He tried to explain to us what an interstate was as compared to the old highways and routes. It seemed pretty amazing that such a thing could be built, going clear across the country in different directions.

One time he broke down in a small town somewhere with our car on a trip to Missouri. I remember sitting at a filling station for a long time in the heat, waiting for the part to come in. There was an old guy that sort of worked at this filling station. He kept setting in the shade near our car and kept asking me to come out and set with him. Mom and grandma and Chuckie were in the car with me. Mom repeatedly refused to let me go sit by the man. He may have been harmless, who knows, but mom would have none of that. And that was probably a good thing for me.

We had to stop one night, parked somewhere along the roadside, in the dark and wait for it to get light to continue on our destination. Maybe dad was worn out from driving and wanted to sleep for a while, I am not sure. But it was a long hot night. Everybody sleeping but me, sitting up in the seats of the car. I had a terrible thirst. We only had one bottle of hot pop. This was opened with the bottle opener and given to me to drink. We finally reached our destination in Missouri and stayed with relatives. They lived in a big old house way out in the country. It was sure different than Wyoming. They had a swing fixed to a tree. There were trees and creeks all over the place. They had a huge raised front porch on their house. They had lots of grass, but you could not set on it because the chiggers would bite you to pieces. They did not have toilets that flushed. In the night, you had to use a pot near the bed and an outhouse in the daytime. All my cousins talked funny and ran around in bib overalls and shoeless, but they were good kids, and we had some fun together for a few days. Things were pretty laid-back and really different, even from Wyoming. And people from California and back east thought Wyoming was primitive!

Every so often, he would come home with a vehicle and had usually been drinking, probably mad or upset about something. I am not sure what it was all about most of the time. He would load up all the kids, he and mom included, and we would go for some wild, outrageous drive. He would take off toward the town of Green River or some other nearby direction. It seemed to me had a death wish, and I often wondered if we would make it back home without a terrible crash. He would drive the car just as fast as it would go going both directions. It amazed me that we never ran into a highway patrolman. But he got away with a lot of stuff like that over the years. He sure gave us a lot of white-knuckle rides.

I got him pretty good later when I was a teenager. He had gotten more where he did not like to drive too fast, even though he was not all that old. I had a great big old battleship of a car with a great big engine, it was white in color. It was my death trap on wheels. It really went pretty good for an old used car. It had tires that you could run over a dime and tell whether the dime was heads or tails. That is really no joke, even though it is funny. I could not afford tires, so I would find tires at the dumps, and that is what went on my car. The speedometer did not work in this car, and I had not driven enough years to be good at estimating my speed. I took my dad for a ride to show him what a nice car I had bought not too long ago. We went north out of town and headed up to 14 Mile Hill. I took off in that baby after we left town. I had no idea how fast we were going, but we were flying. My dad's face turned white. He got a grip on the dash and the passenger door handle, and he stuttered out, "How fast are we going?"

I replied, "I don't know, the speedometers are broken."

He blurted out, "Well, for God's sakes, slow down!" I did slow down and turned around, and then I took off back to town at the same high speed. He would comment how fast things were flashing by and ask how fast I thought we were going.

I said, "Oh, not too fast." He never said no more, just sweated and held on for dear life. He never rode with me much after that. I am not a vengeful person, but that was pretty sweet!

My dad was always making deals with shady characters he would call friends or associates. Always buying or trading something. One time he bought a pistol that he knew was stolen from a guy. He bought the pistol for a song and dance, and he was pretty pleased about it. He was not too worried about it being stolen. He sure was not happy when a few days later, a deputy sheriff showed up and took the pistol away from him.

Dad did not care if we drank as long as we stayed in the house or around the house and did not get in trouble with the police. He kept beer and whiskey readily available, and we drank our share. I tried a little whiskey, but I did not care for the hotness of it. We would have wine for some holidays and could drink it if we wanted. I liked it but didn't drink but a glass or two at a time. It had a very good grape flavor. But I did like beer. I was actually only drunk once or twice. I drank beer just because I liked the taste of it. I did not like feeling sick and not being in control of myself. My brother Chuckie was the opposite. He drank because he liked to get drunk.

One hot summer afternoon, we began hearing loud pops in the two-car garage attached to the house. Upon rushing out there, we found that a big quart of bottles of beer was blowing up and throwing brown glass, bottle caps, and beer all over the place. Nearly half of the thirty or more bottles blew before they stopped.

Oh, we knew the beer was there. Dad and a drinking buddy of his, John Parks, had made this home-brewed concoction. John Parks was an odd duck. A single homely red-haired unkempt guy in his 30s. He wore big black-framed glasses and had several teeth missing. He and his mom and dad had moved to Wyoming from somewhere far south. He lived with them in their home on the south side of town. The parents were older and must have been retired. They didn't seem to do much. The father just sort of hung around and wore bib overalls, he was a big quiet guy. The mother was a heavy woman. She was stern but laid-back. She was always after John and my dad for their wicked ways, but this was to no avail. She went to a local church, Church of God, I think it was, and was sort of religious, but that didn't keep her from chewing tobacco where she liked, and she liked!

Their son John and dad hung out quite a bit. They both loved to drink, mostly beer. John tried to avoid work if he could. Well, he and dad got their heads together and figured on making their own beer, which was illegal then. So, they bought recycled Budweiser bottles, the big brown quart type. Dad got an old manual bottle capper device, and they bought the caps and ingredients for their home brew. They were hiding out and making it in a hot room over the garage at the Parks' home. Mom and I had to stay there while they made it, and we had to keep going to the store for more stuff they would need, like yeast or sugar, etc. They were brewing this concoction in big plastic garbage cans. I never went into the room where they were making the beer. I stayed outside and had to entertain myself and be quiet while the process went on for hours. Occasionally, Mrs. Parks would come out and speak to me, but she stayed inside mostly. I think they were big eaters and liked to sit around and watch television and sleep.

This was a big undercover project for dad and Parks. Any moment the local law or worse might sweep down on them and cart them and their brew off, so it had to be hush-hush. They finally completed this mess days later after letting the stuff cure and so on. It was bottled, divided among its two genius makers, and dad took his home and stored it in the garage. Thus, the exploding beer later that summer.

When the beer started exploding, Lord knows it could have been anything in that garage. We were surprised that it was the beer. Dad kept dynamite—some of it leaking nitroglycerin—and all sorts of volatile fluids and gases in the place. It is a small wonder that we and the neighborhood never blew sky-high. He was a little upset over the beer but not especially so. The reason being that the beer tasted awful. I drank some, and I think between dad, Chuckie, and any other unsuspecting soul dad could con into it, that which didn't blow was finally consumed. It was bitter, nasty stuff for sure.

After the measles I had during the death of my grandfather, I had more bouts with the stuff. I had several types of and several repeats of the measles. Then there were several cases of chickenpox. The treatment for these illnesses back then was to put you in a room that was all darkened, and you had to lay there, still and not scratching for days at a time. I was always comfortable by myself, but I think this just aided in me being more comfortable with being alone. Chuckie was always dependent on other people and had to have company around. I was just the opposite.

I missed so much school in the first grade due to these illnesses that I had to repeat the first grade. I had repeat bouts of tonsillitis and ended up at the doctor's office many times over that. Once I finally made it to about third grade, I was a pretty healthy kid. During all of these bouts of tonsillitis, the doctors wanted to take my tonsils out. I wanted no part of that, and I talked my folks out of it. Still have my tonsils to this day and feel fine!

Every time we went to the doctor over tonsillitis, it was penicillin shots. I dreaded those shots. There were two nurses at the clinic, one of them was named Mabel. Mabel was a kindly nurse and wore a regular nurse hat and nurse's outfit. If the shot was from Mabel, there was no big problem. The other nurse wore a pointed nurse's hat. She was not a friendly person. She hated me, and I did not like her. When she bore the duty of having to give me the shot, it took her and my mother a long struggle to get my pants down and give me the shot. I did not go easy! But in the end, they won. But at least I made her earn her money!

I fell over a toy truck and cut my chin wide open one time. Mom and Chuckie rushed me to the clinic for stitches. Nothing doing, but Chuckie wanted to be in the room and see me get the stitches. The doctor started putting the stitches in, and *boom!* Chuckie passed out and hit the floor. He could not take the blood and gore, I guess!

We didn't actually go to the doctor a lot, though. The school usually made us go if we had tonsillitis or strep, but otherwise, we would tough out illness or injury if the blood wasn't spurting too far out! One time mom made us take a big dose of castor oil. Nasty stuff! But usually, she forced a dose of cold medicine down me. This was a red liquid in a glass bottle that had all kinds of healing qualities in it according to the manufactures. She would also put a menthol rub on us and sometimes then a warm cloth on your chest or around your neck. Usually, this, a sterile cover, and some iodine could fix about any illness or injury; otherwise, she did have some Bayer baby aspirins for us too. These tasted great, and if I could, I would eat a few like candy. Also, cough drops. You could buy a box for a nickel or dime. The cherry-flavored ones were good until you ate too many.

My dad had put a large yard light in our yard, so we could play outside at night in the summer. One quiet summer night, I and Chuckie were out in the yard, and he was fixing his bicycle. He was down on his knees fixing the upturned bicycle and facing away from the house. I was standing on the other side of the bike and facing him. To the rear of me was a fence at the end of our property. It was dark and getting pretty late. Chuckie was working away, and we were chatting when all of a sudden, he got quiet. He whispered to me, "Don't turn around." Usually, I would pay no attention to the fool, but I knew he was not joking. He kept on working and whispered to me that there was a really weird, bad-looking guy sitting on the fence watching us. He thought we had better bolt for the house. Sounded like a good idea to me. He whispered to me to take off, and he would follow quick as he could. That was pretty unusual. Normally he would have just run and left me to fend for myself. I took off like a flash, and he right behind me. I could hear somebody jump off the fence and chase us. I never looked back, but we could hear the guy behind us, we bolted into the house, slammed the door shut, and locked it. Chuckie was genuinely scared, and I was too. To this day, I have no idea what that was all about, and we never spoke of it again. The neighborhood was generally safe. But there were some weird characters that would show up around the Bunning Park every once in a while.

We would have bums and tramps and beggars show up at the Bunning Park every summer that were passing through town. Invariably some of them would come to our house begging for food. My mom would never turn anybody away. She would fix some sandwiches and a regular picnic lunch and hand it out to them. She wondered why they would always pick our house out to come to. Grandma told her that they had some way of marking the house, in that way, other bums passing through would know that we were generous people.

There was one couple that showed up at our house one summer and kept coming back for several days. It looked like a man and an ugly woman. My mom was pretty sure it was a man and another man dressed like a woman. She gave them breakfast and lunch. They came back for a couple of days. It was getting to be a bit much, almost to the point that we thought they might just start taking meals with us! Mom finally had her full of this couple the next morning. Not because they came back asking for breakfast to take with them, but because after she gave them coffee, the guy returned and demanded some cream to go in it. She gave him the cream, but she also gave him the boot on that trip.

We were big fans of police shows. I would never miss the afternoon adventures of the Sheriff of Cochise. He drove an old station wagon and packed a rifle. One time my mother took me for one of the infrequent trips to the dentist. The dentist asked me what my name was, and I replied, "I am the Sheriff of Cochise." He thought that was pretty funny.

He chuckled and said, "Okay, Cochise, get up in the chair."

I knew as a little boy I wanted to be a policeman and not just anywhere. I wanted to be a Rock Springs policeman. I was torn, however. I liked to watch religious programs and especially was interested in the priests that had robes and white collars. So, lots of times, if I was not playing policeman or sheriff or soldier or calvary with a mix of Superman thrown in, I would be wearing an old blanket and all the other garb I could find and be playing priest.

Chuckie would play with me some, but if we played sheriff, he always had to be the deputy, I was the sheriff. He would irritate me, though. It was serious business we were in, and he always wanted to mess around. After a short time, I would get mad, and run him off. He got a great kick out of it.

I would play a lot by myself. But I did have a lot of friends. A few other white guys, but most of my friends were Spanish or Mexican, a few Japanese and Chinese and some black guys.

I had one friend of the same age that lived in the pink apartments near us. He had a neat trick that I wished I could have done. We would buy the black cow caramel suckers. After he would get it good and wet and gooey, he would attach it to his top teeth. It was amazing how all of his teeth would come. Not much is said about it, just a lot of laughs. He had some kind of condition that had caused him to lose his teeth, and he had false teeth at that early age, at least on the top.

His family only lived one summer at the pink apartments, and then they moved away. We were probably about seven years old, maybe eight. One particular day we were playing on the sidewalk up and down Elias Avenue. There was this kid that lived in the Traveler's Lodge at the other end of the block that was probably about twelve or thirteen years old. He hadn't been around very long; we did not know much about him. He was a big kid and had a really nice brand-new bicycle. On this particular day, we were going up and down the sidewalk. Not bothering anybody, not looking for trouble. For some reason, he decided that he owned the sidewalk. We were not to go up and down it anymore. He threatened us and warned us that we had better not be on the sidewalk after that. We tried to be nice, did not really want him for an enemy. He was mean and insistent we had better stay off the sidewalk. Well, that did not sit too well, especially with me.

This kid would park his bicycle in front of the building on the sidewalk where he lived. I told my friend that this would not do. We needed to go pick up a bunch of big rocks and fix the new owner of the sidewalk! That is just what we did. Within the hour, we returned and had nearly every spoke broken out of both wheels of the bicycle with the big rocks we had gathered. Justice was served. Not a bad day's work. We both went to our separate homes, pretty pleased with ourselves. About an hour later, there was a knock at the front door of the house. I was called to the door by my parents only to find two uniform policemen at the door, and everybody looked pretty unhappy. Yes, the kid and his mother called the police and reported our terrible act of violence, which the kid assured his mother of. There was absolutely no reason for it. Well, I was pretty scared. Like I said before, you did not mess with these old cops. The cops were known for making people only too happy to make it to jail! They weren't rough on me, but they made me come out onto the sidewalk and give a full accounting of what happened. My parents had no idea that all of this had taken place. I was all on my own, cold sweat pouring down my face. With fear and trembling, I gave my truthful account to these big old cops of what happened only a short time ago. They did not ask many questions once we got started, they just had me tell what happened.

At first, they appeared confused why such an angelic-looking little guy would do such a horrible thing. They looked stern and like I was in for, but eureka, as I gave the painful details of the story, suddenly the cops began to look sympathetic and even smile. See, cops were so bad I knew it all the time! They just wanted justice like I did! They had no quotas to fill, did not care about making a pinch. I knew it all of the time, grandma and dad were wrong about the police.

What a great day it was! The police kindly told me to try not to do that type of thing again, patted me on the head, and told me not to worry about it and to go on in the house. The officers spoke just a few minutes to my folks, and they were gone. Never heard much more about the whole thing from anybody. My friend got in some trouble, and we never played too much together after that, but justice was done!

Oh, there has to be some expense to meting out justice. That is to be expected. I did miss playing with my buddy, but I had plenty of other friends. Like I said, he moved away the next fall or so anyway. But the older kid with the bike, I hardly ever saw him again. He steered clear of me and nearly ran away every time he saw me. He was afoot. I never saw him ride a bike again. I held no ill will toward him, but I sure enjoyed being able to go up and down my sidewalk as I pleased. He also moved away not long after that. I like to think I probably saved him a lot of trouble in his life. He may have learned a valuable lesson about not picking on little guys and hopefully how that the police really are good guys! Judge, you don't need a judge, just some good old reasonable cops!

Unfortunately, I came to the conclusion that sometimes it was in your best interest not to tell the truth. I think it was in the second grade. Teachers in those days were tough like the cops, and you did not mess with them. Most of our grade school teachers were women, but they were tough older women. The principles were even worse. Regressing to this story. I recall when I was in the first grade, one of the boys had done something out on the playground and gotten into trouble. The skinny little principal lady came into the classroom that day, eating an apple. You could tell she was annoyed to have to do this. It was going to interrupt her eating of the apple, and she was not happy about it. She had it in her hand. One of those paddles that they used to attach a little ball to with a rubber band, and you would bounce the ball back and forth with the paddle. Of course, the rubber band and the ball were gone now, and the paddle was painted red. These were the implements of torture used in those days to inflict our punishment. I tell you, they hurt. The principal spoke briefly to the teacher, interrupting our class. The principal got a chair and sat down in front of our class, still eating her apple. The poor little urchin victim was called forward.

He and the principal talked quietly for a moment. All of us boys and girls set horror and suspense with our mouths hanging open. We were about to witness an execution, a public execution. This was not really all bad, as long as you were not a participant and only an observer!

Suddenly, the principal spoke loudly again. In between eating her apple, she told the boy to drop his pants and lay over her lap. The poor kid began this sniffle, but he did as he was told. And then the beatings began, *whack, whack, whack.* She would eat her apple and give the kid a whack. Just as quick as it began, it was over. The blubbering little kid returned to his desk, and the principal left. Nothing more was said about it, and we do not know why he was spanked. But we learned, you do not mess with the warden or the guards at this joint!

Despite all of this, as I said, I made a choice one day not to tell the truth. I was on the playground with a friend of mine that was a Greek kid. I say that because he always made a big deal about being a Greek and how the Greeks are smarter and better, stronger than anybody else like Hercules. Anyway, I and Hercules decided to throw snowballs at kids and junk on the playground. This was strictly forbidden, and we knew it. So, after recess, we were taken into the interrogation room. Not together but alone. Hercules buckled and admitted that, yes, he was involved in throwing snowballs as well as me. I was not going to go that easy. "No," I said, "there must be a mistake. It could not have been me involved in it. I was out on the playground. But no, surely not throwing snowballs. I would never do such a thing." The evidence mounted against me. Both of us got stern warnings to never throw snowballs again. Okay, we had learned our lesson. Hercules (Mike), "You go back to class," me, I got the red paddle not for throwing snowballs but for lying about it. Painful as the truth can be, I learned that it can be considerably less painful than lying!

It was in the second-grade class on the beautiful Indian summer, November day, that was that day that they say that you will never forget where you were. I walked home for lunch. Everybody was upset. The radio was on, the news was that President Kennedy had been shot. I ate my sandwich and listened to the radio reports. People were crying on the radio when they talked about it, and then the sad news came that he was in fact dead. This was terrible, but I did not really know what it meant for us living way out here in the boonies of Wyoming. The president never came out here, but it would surely have some bad effect. I returned to school; everybody was sad crying about President Kennedy. We figured we would have an easy day because of all the sadness and disaster. But this was not to be in Mrs. Harmon's class. She was a big, heavyset no-nonsense lady. No, no, she did not want to hear any more about it. "Get out your class books and let us go to work." Shucks. Other teachers were talking about it. Letting the kids play games and have treats. Sad as it was, it was just another day for Mrs. Harmon. She was a good teacher, and we really all loved and respected her. Each and every one of us little slaves!

Over the weekend, I watched all the continuous reports about the Kennedy incident. I was highly interested in it. The rest of my family, not so much. Especially my dad. He could care less. We went out for an afternoon of rabbit hunting, and while we were out rabbit-hunting, we came back to learn that Oswald had been shot and killed. My grandmother met us at the door, she was excitedly telling us about Oswald. My dad pushed his way on into the house. He could care less, and the rabbit headhunting had not been very good anyway.

If my dad wasn't working, he loved to lay in bed and just relax, read the paper and smoke and what have you. My poor mother would wait on him hand and foot. Sometimes he would do this when we were supposed to leave to go rabbit-hunting or on some other adventure. It would drive you crazy. He would say we were leaving, and then he would lay in bed for hours and keep telling you we would go pretty soon. Sometimes it was almost too late to go. Then suddenly, like Lazarus, he came to life and was up and off like a shot. And you had better be ready to go to. To this day, I do not like to lay in bed once I wake up! Some people really like breakfast in bed. I despise it.

Chuckie and I received a really neat dart gun that had rubber-tipped darts. The trouble was, he wouldn't let me use it much. One summer day, we were out of the neighborhood, playing. We were walking around shooting the darts at stuff, and I kept bugging him to let me shoot the gun. But oh no. He hung on that gun like a miser does his money. Pretty soon, he got tired and sat down on the garden wall of a neighbor's house. I was standing there in front of him, and finally, oh joy, he handed me the gun with a dart in it. I could hold again, but I could not shoot it while he took a breather. I was thinking, *Well, we will see about that.* He sat there blabbering about something, and then all of a sudden, he wanted the gun back. Well, I would not give it back to him. So now it was no more Mr. Nice Guy. He wanted the gun back. *Okay, you'll get it back.* I raised it again and made a quick snapshot. *Pow,* right in the nose. They did not make wimpy little dart guns in those days. Just like somebody turned on the faucet, his nose began to bleed profusely. I mean, blood shot out of his nose, and he began to scream. I dropped the gun and beat it for the house. Mom saw me come running in excitedly and asked where Chuckie was. I said, "Oh, he'll be coming along any time." About that time, here he came crying and yelling, blood all over his shirt. He was wiping blood and told my mom what happened. She had her hands full trying to take care of him. I don't know what all the excitement was about, he was still breathing and, in all likelihood, would continue to do so. Well, mom wasn't too mad at me. She said something like, "Kenny, why did you do that to Chuckie?" Kenny was a keyword. If I was in trouble, it would have been Kenneth, or really bad trouble would have been Kenneth Joe.

I recall one really hard spanking my mother gave me with a razor strap. The people renting the basement from us were having trouble flushing the toilet. So, they came up and borrowed the toilet plunger. I guessed he kept it a little too longer than I thought they should have. I took it upon myself to go to their door a short time later and tell them my mother wanted that plunger back.

They seemed kind of surprised, but they gave me the plunger, and I took it back upstairs to our house. I was so proud of myself. I had our family's prized possession back home. My mother saw me walk in with the plunger, and she asked me what I was doing with that. I knew that she would be pleased with me. The recovery of our treasures! I told her what I had done and was expecting praise. Boy, did she whip me with that razor strap? Once the beatings were over, the plunger was returned to the renters. Sometimes it is better not to get involved in things or worry about worldly possessions!

Grandma did not drink at all. My mother drank very little alcohol, usually only a beer once in a while. Mom and dad both smoked quite a bit in the house, in the cars, everywhere, which was common in those days. They tried to discourage Chuckie from smoking. But he followed in their footsteps, and he smoked like they did. I may have tried between three to half a dozen cigarettes. I thought they were terrible and too expensive. So fortunately, that was a habit I never picked up on.

My first gun, other than cap pistols and toy guns, was a BB gun (a blue steel beauty). It was used but in good shape. It was the lever-action type. I took it when we went out of town and was able to practice shoot with it. I was also allowed to shoot it in the backyard as long as I did not shoot anything that would cause damage. I would shoot bottles and targets of all types in the backyard. It was great fun! Lots of kids would shoot birds and things like that with a BB gun, but I knew better than that. Not that I had been told not to, I just knew that life is too precious to just waste it by shooting things just to watch them die.

I never was even big on shooting gophers and rodents just to kill them. If they were overrunning the place and needed to be thinned out, that was okay. We had a family that rented the downstairs from us. They had two boys about Chuckie's age. These guys would go out with some other boys and use big quantities of water to drown or chase gophers and rodents out of their holes. Once, they ended up with one that was nearly drowned, but they brought it home to our house. It was a young gopher, wet and nearly dead, but kind of cute-looking. We took pity on it. Especially my dad did. And with warm milk and an eyedropper, we began nursing it back to life. Pretty soon, the little fellow was feeling well, and we made him into a dandy little pet. We called him Squeaky. We kept him in a little cage, but we let him out to play around in the house where we were. He was very clean and never bothered anything. He was also very friendly and playful. My dad would lay on the bed with his shirt and pants on, and the little gopher would crawl up his pant leg, up into his pants, his shirt, and come out at the top of my dad's shirt. He would just set that way for a long time looking around. Squeaky was very content to play this game for long periods of time. We took pictures of them, my dad with the little gopher peeking out of his shirt top lying on the bed.

We probably had Squeaky for five or six years before he finally died of old age. We also had parakeets and dogs, never any cats. My first dog was a big brown multicolored hairy dog named Bingo. He was a good dog, but I only had him for about a year. He got hit by a car or something. He made it home and died in the backyard on the patio. After that, we had mostly smaller indoor dogs. I also had a rabbit named Thumper that I received one Easter from my mom and dad. That rabbit sure ate a lot of lettuce. I would go to the nearby stores and get the trimmings from the lettuce and bring them home for his food, and he got an occasional carrot, which he really enjoyed!

My dad gave me my first rifle. It was an old bolt-action .22 rifle. It was so old it did not even have a serial number. It was in good shape and shot well once I learned how to shoot it. Dad probably gave me my BB gun when I was about six or seven and the .22 when I was about eight or nine. The .22, of course, could only be shot when we were out of town. Usually target practicing or rabbit hunting. I had that rifle for many years and eventually passed it onto my son, who still has and uses it.

There was one time I was involved in an incident of vandalism. It involved one of my dad's cars parked in our yard. I was probably about six or seven, and Chuckie thought it would be a great idea for us to bust the taillights and parking lights out of the vehicle. So that is what we did with rocks and sticks, and shortly afterwards, my dad found out about it. In fact, it was the very afternoon. We actually did quite a bit of damage to the vehicle, which was not too bad of a car. Dad was pretty unhappy about it, but he did not really do too much to us. Maybe because there was company over at the time. I learned that Chuckie had lots of ideas. The trouble was, most of them were bad!

Most of the family was watching *The Ed Sullivan Show* on a Sunday night when he had The Beatles on his program for the first time. They had just arrived in the U.S., and they were kind of sweeping the country even then. Girls were going nuts over them like they had been doing for Elvis Presley. You know the whole crying and swooning bit. Well, they came on that night, and we weren't overly impressed with them one way or the other. They were a pretty strange bunch of long-haired Englishmen. I will never forget grandma's remarks that night, though. She hissed, and said "they'll never amount to anything."

Another Sunday night later on, we were watching when the man landed on the moon and actually walked on its surface. It was pretty exciting to begin with but soon became drawn-out and boring. On later airings of moon landings, we barely watched or paid much attention to them. After a bit, the television networks reduced the coverage of the landings by a good bit. Most people were interested in the event, but after you watched the moonwalks and so on for a few minutes, it got pretty mundane.

Chuckie and I and some other guys about his age were hanging out in Bunning Park one day. All of a sudden, here came three brothers that we knew were about Chuckie's age, but they lived in another part of town. They were walking kind of funny. And when they got up to us, we could see why. They were all chained together with big heavy chains and padlocks. We knew these guys pretty well. We just did not ever have too much to do with them. Probably, mostly because they did not live nearby. You might say they were kind of a dysfunctional family. Anyway, the boys were known for getting into quite a bit of trouble, and their dad had taken to chaining them to the radiator in the basement when he had to leave for work or something. This apparently occurred quite a bit. These guys did not mind it too bad, I guess. They had got used to it. It saved their father a lot of trouble keeping tabs on them and having to look for them. On this particular day, they must have tired of each other's company and got bored with being chained to the radiator. They made a vigilant effort to escape, and in fact, it worked. Now they just needed help with getting loose from the chains and padlocks. Well, we helped them with that. Pretty soon, they were free birds. They decided they had better keep the chains and padlocks because their dad might want them back and have further use of them!

Like I said before, some of the people that we rented our downstairs to were real lulus. There was one family that was a mixture of whites and Indians. You might say they would really go on the warpath and get into big fights. One night there was a terrible commotion down there. Only the teenage daughter and the uncle were home. She was a pretty girl, probably about fifteen or sixteen; the uncle was a big, heavyset Indian guy. She made him mad about something, and he started beating her with a broom. She was screaming, and he was yelling. Dad was not home, and mom could not get him to answer the door. Somebody eventually called the police. Boy, did they, we had police cars everywhere. You would have thought somebody had been murdered. Well, the cops in those days did not like to referee family fights. They sorted the whole mess out and got it calmed down.

Another time dad, Chuckie, and I had come in from a deer hunt. One of them had shot a deer, and we had it in the yard, taking care of it. Chuckie had notions that he was a gunslinger, I guess. He was carrying a .22 pistol in a holster on his right hip. The people we were renting the downstairs to were a bunch of drunks. One of the guys came out onto the patio with a beer in his hand. He walked up to Chuckie and was talking to him about the deer. Before you knew it, the drunk had the pistol out of Chuckie's holster and fired it one time straight down into the cement patio. Well, the bullet ricocheted and splattered. Suddenly I felt like a bee had stung me on the, the, the buttocks! *Ouch!*

My dad was mad as anything at that drunk and chased him back into the house. Next thing I knew, I was upstairs with my mother. This involved tweezers, needles, iodine, and a lot of screaming, and it was not her doing the screaming. I guess you could say mom unleaded me that night!

45

There was a big brownstone house at the end of our block across the street from the Traveler's Lodge. I was never inside of it, but judging from the appearance, it was probably a very nice house at one time.

It was lived in for the first few years that we lived in the neighborhood, then for some reason, it became vacant. Once it was vacant, it seemed to take on kind of a spooky look. Then, little by little strange things seemed to start occurring around the place. Before long, we all knew it as the haunted house, and the rumors grew about ghosts and headless people being seen walking about in the house. Somebody was sure they had seen Dracula at the place!

All joking aside, though, there were some strange goings-on at the place. I and a group of buddies were going down the alley near the house one sunny day, and we heard some funny noise inside the fenced yard. It had a high wooden fence, so we could not see in the yard until we opened the gate. Once inside, there were old metal close lines strung across the backyard. To our shock, there was a cat hanging from one of the wire close lines by shoestring around its neck. The poor cat was still struggling, trying to breathe. So, this had just occurred. And whoever had done this terrible act had taken off and run out toward the front of Elias Avenue, or at least we hope that is what they had done.

We were all too afraid to try to help the cat. Within seconds, he was completely, graveyard dead. That was a pretty gruesome event, and it made no sense to us why somebody would do such a terrible thing. We looked quickly around the area, and here were more cat carcasses lying around in the yard. They were probably the victims of previous executions. Well, these kinds of things happen around a haunted house. We decided whoever did this could still be lurking about or might come back. Then it was a fight for the gate to get out of the yard, down the alley, and away from that mess.

After that, we would walk by and look at the place from the opposite side of the front street. None of us had the courage or desire to go on the property again. Well, after this, the rumors surely spread. Then finally, one day, I and some of my buddies were standing out in front of my house on the sidewalk.

A police car pulled up, and we began to look questioningly at one another, wondering who the poor slob was that was in trouble this time. The policeman got out and walked up to us. Happily, for us, it was one of the kinder-looking old policemen by the name of Officer Hansen. Even more of a relief was the fact that as he began to talk to us, we realized that none of us were going off to the big house today!

Officer Hansen was a little more than worried. Rumors were going around about the haunted house and strange things going on. Well, Officer Hansen was a nice enough guy, but we weren't going to spill our guts. Besides that, we did not want some cop prowling around our neighborhood and stirring up trouble. No, no, we laughed nervously. We did not know anything about a haunted house. It was all a big joke. We assured Officer Hansen. Well, okay, if we were sure of that, oh yes, Officer Hansen was certain of that. Just a bunch of bored kids looking for some excitement. We had probably just been watching too many horror movies of late. Well, he said, if we did see anything, be sure to let them know, and we assured him that we would, and he left.

This was just one more reason to stay clear of that haunted house. It stood vacant for a number of more years, and who knows what went on there. It was eventually torn down to make way for a gas station and some other buildings.

I saw another spooky site one day. Some kids said, "Let's go over to so-and-so's house in the old army barracks, there is something those guys have in and an old washing machine that is interesting to look at."

So, we did, and I did not have to look at it for very long. There was an old ramshackle garage by the house, and a bunch of kids was gathered inside the garage. Mostly it was older boys, teenagers. But they invited us in for a look. Inside the garage was one of those old wringer-type washing machines. We walked up to the machine then, the kid that lived there pulled the lid off it. That old washing machine was just full of great big old water snakes. I do not like snakes. There must have been several hundred that they had put inside of the machine. They were crawling all over each other, snapping and trying to climb out. It was terrible.

The older boys had been capturing water snakes for weeks along Bitter Creek and Killpecker Creek and putting them into the machine. That was a site that nightmares are kind of made out of! They really did not have any plan of what to do with the snakes. They just thought it was kind of neat to have them all collected inside of the old machine. We had seen enough, but the guys told us to be sure not to tell their mother about this as we left the place. I do not know what ever became of all those snakes.

I went to kindergarten through the sixth grade at Washington school. Chuckie completed school there and then was ready for junior high. My folks decided he needed some taming before he went on to further public school, though. So even though we weren't Catholics or even anything close to it, they put him into the Catholic school near our house for the seventh grade.

I went with him and my mom to enroll him in the Catholic school. Chuckie did not like this one little bit. The fact that he was not able to go to public school. Those old nuns were all business back in those days. They wore the black and white habits, and all you could see was her hands, fingers, and face. They did not smile much, and they certainly did not joke around. I was fascinated with the place. I thought, *Hey, this is right up my alley*. I did my best to convince my mother that I had to go to school here too. This was not to be. It was poor Chuckie that needed the help, she said.

Those nuns wore out lots of rulers on Chuckie, even though he only went to school there one year. I do not know if they did him a lot of good, but they sure did not hurt him at all. We had a funny thing happen that was associated with all of this, though. My dad's sister, my aunt Mary Lou, whom we called Baylou, why I do not know, was a Catholic or at least thought she was. So, when she heard that Chuckie was going to Catholic school, she told him that she would send him a missile. I thought, *just my luck; he gets to go to a really neat school, and he also gets a missile to shoot up into the sky*. He thought that is what he was getting to. Within a short time, the package came with the missile. It was sure a small and funny box to have a missile in it, we thought. Chuckie opened it up with trembling fingers, and I watched him excitedly too. Inside the box was a Catholic Bible, I guess what they call a missile.

It was a high-quality book, but Chuckie had no interest in that. To tell you the truth, I really did not either. What a disappointment! Years later, the book was still like brand-new.

Chuckie and a few other of the boys his age had a terrible reputation in the neighborhood. It was totally deserved, no argument about that. These boys were all in the same boat together, but Chuckie was the worst of them, and they were all buddies. The nice girls in the neighborhood wouldn't have anything to do with them. Parents had warned their daughters not to go near these guys, and, of course, the girls well knew that. None of these boys were to be trusted.

The Japanese family next door to us had two daughters, one of them was really very pretty. They were friendly with us, but they steered clear of Chuckie, and with good reason! They were the best neighbors anyone could ever hope for. They eventually built an addition onto their home, and the husband opened up a television repair shop. He did real good business there.

They invited me over several times for cookies and milk, and I would visit with them. One day, I innocently told them a mild Oriental joke. They laughed at it and were kind. When I got back home, I told my mother about the fun we had had. She was shocked that I had told the joke. She did not think it was one bit funny. She was not really mad about it, but she said, "Don't tell stories like that to people, Kenny."

The Japanese family were our neighbors for many, many years. One of the daughters became a professional librarian, and the really pretty one became a registered nurse. There were many good neighbors in this area, but none like the Haurice family.

Our neighborhood, like the town, was multicultural, multiracial and had some really rough and interesting characters. There was a new family that moved into the neighborhood from somewhere. They had two children. One was a teenage boy about Chuckie's age, and the other was a girl a couple of years older than me, and I was probably about ten at that time. She was a big tough girl, kind of pretty, but really built like a football player. She really liked boys, I guess. One day the neighborhood was pretty quiet, and she came over and wanted to go bike-riding with me. I had never been around her much, and I would avoid her like the plague after this day!

She wanted to ride my bike, which was really a much nicer bike than her bike that had a banana seat on it. So, we rode around for a while. Then she made it known to me that she wanted to get to know me much better. I tried a few excuses to get away from her, but nothing was doing. We first ended up in Bunning Park in broad daylight on a Saturday. To my horror, I watched her lie down in the flower bed behind some trees and take her clothes off. Now there were people all around this girl, it was unbelievable! She was urging me and telling me to get over here and get to know her really well, you might say. Cold sweat was pouring off my forehead and everywhere else. There was no use trying to run away. She would have caught me and pulverized me. Or if I did get away, she would have caught me the next day, so I had to wear this girl out somehow!

I acted all shocked and surprised, I said, "We'd better get out of here. I see the police car coming!" She grabbed her clothes and put them back on. We got out of the park. But she was not done. She knew another place she wanted to take me to. So, she had made me ride alongside her on the bicycle to an area a few blocks away. It was over by some railroad tracks. It was called the foxhole. We got over there, and it was a big hole dug down into the dirt about four feet deep with a big sheet of tin over the top of it for its cover. Obviously, a well-visited spot that she was very familiar with, quite comfortable around.

We had a repeat performance. She was laying down in the foxhole with her clothes off and telling me to get in. My mind was racing, *Ah, this should do nicely*. Suddenly, I told her, "I think I heard something. Somebody's coming, we'd better watch out," that type of thing.

She was like, "What, what," and trying to rise up and look out of the hole. I really put on an act now.

"I am sure that I spotted somebody trying to sneak up on us from the nearby buildings." She was suspicious and started to grill me, but nonetheless, I had her all worked up, and she began to put her clothes on. Whew, another close call!

She began to question me, "Well, you must have an idea where we could go that would be quiet and kind of private."

"No, no, I have no ideas like that." Fortunately, I had worn her down. She took her old bike back, and after we rode around for a little bit more, she went home.

So, we not only had some boys in the neighborhood like my brother, but we had some girls like this too. I do not remember too much about this girl or her brother. I do not even recall where they lived in the neighborhood, but they moved away after a year or two. Sometimes I have wondered whatever became of people like that and wouldn't it be interesting to run into them somewhere someday and see what they were like. Well, maybe yes, maybe no, she might still like to ride bikes!

One friend I had in the fifth grade was Brent. His family lived in a state house on the north side of Bitter Creek near Washington school. This house was their home and the local game warden station. Brent's dad, Max, had been a longtime game warden in the Rock Springs area. Max was a good warden and a hard drinker like a lot of men in town.

One afternoon Brent invited me over to their house. We went inside, and he showed me display cases and drawers full of Indian arrows and spear heads. Clay bowls and tools of the Plains people. His dad would take the family or at least Brent and his older brother Warren with him on patrols sometimes. They would use downtime to walk the prairies and plains and pick up the artifacts. I never had much luck finding arrowheads. I did happen to just spot one years later, probably a Sioux arrowhead, in very good shape when I was on Summit Ridge, on a turkey hunt in the Newcastle, Wyoming area. Brent's dad found a large jade deposit in his journeys, and when he retired from the state, he got rich with this find and a shop that he opened up on the north side of Rock Springs that made all kinds of jade handled knives and so on. He imported a good deal of jade to the oriental countries; they tell me too. I guess he eventually hit hard times, however, and lost most or all of the fortune, and the shop closed down.

My dad had a few friends or real lulus that were around the family. One of them was big Milt Harris. He was married to a cute little Indian woman that was an American native Indian. He was a huge guy that wore great big bib overalls. Milt loved to fish, and he loved to drink. We would go down to their house and visit, but they seldom came to our house. Of course, Milt loved to eat. Obviously.

We went on a couple of days on a fishing trip with them one time in the summer up in the Big Sandy openings. We had a car, and they had a pickup truck. Lots of people had cars in those days and no trucks that they would hunt and fish out of.

We had a pretty good time, but I remember the Milt would really put away the food, the booze, and he caught a lot of fish. I am sure he drove drunk most of the time, even though he seemed to get along pretty well. We were following them down the road in our car to go to another location when he approached the main highway. There was a stop sign, but Milt drove right through it onto the highway. A car was coming in the opposite direction on the highway, and they nearly had a huge collision. After a lot of cussing and yelling, Milt drove on, and we continued to camp and fish for another day or two.

Another time, on a trip that I did not go on with Milt, my dad and Chuckie went ice-fishing up in the Pinedale area with him. It was winter and cold weather, and they took tents and supplies and were going to stay for two or three days. They were supposed ice-fish on the lake. They had been gone for the day, and we were awakened early in the morning, it was dark and probably about 3 a.m. Dad and Chuckie were back home and pretty teed off. They said they were all set up to fish when Milt ran out of booze. He demanded that they load up the camp and head to town, so that is what they did because Milt had the only vehicle, and he was leaving.

Milt was a big red, beefy-faced man. They moved back to Oklahoma a few years later, and we heard that Milt had died. He was buried in his big bib overalls, but they could not find a coffin that would fit him. He had to be buried in a piano box.

Another time, we were coming home in our truck from a fishing trip. Yes, my dad had finally gotten us a pickup truck. It was mom, dad, Chuckie, and me. Grandma would never go with us. We were on the highway north Rock Springs, somewhere in the area of Farson, which was a little farming community along the highway. Traffic was light. It was a nice day and broad daylight. We were going down the straightaway, and there was a vehicle coming right at us in our lane of traffic. Dad began to slow down and blow the horn, but the car kept coming. It was moving pretty fast too. As a car got almost on top of us, we could see the driver had fallen asleep and was slumped over the steering wheel. Dad kept blowing the horn and was getting ready to steer off the highway. Suddenly, the guy looked up, careened into his lane of traffic, and came to an abrupt stop at the edge of the roadway. He jumped out of his car and began running around the car, shaking his pants. We can only imagine what he was shaking out of them! We came close to being able to shake something out of our pants too! My dad wanted to go back and work the guy over, but mom talked him out of it, and we went on home.

Chuckie had a bunch of goofy friends that thought he was in love with goldfish. Every birthday here would come a goldfish for him from one of his buddies. None of them survived very long. It is no wonder with Chuckie caring for them. He had a goldfish bowl that he would keep them in but usually only had one fish in there at a time. One day I and mom were watching him as he cleaned the bowl and put freshwater in it and put the fish back in. The fish was swimming around like crazy, and Chuckie said, "Oh look, he is so happy to have clean water." My mother thought something was suspicious. She went over and checked the bowl and found out the water was nearly scalding hot. Chuckie had, by mistake, I think, filled the bowl with hot water instead of cold.

Another friend of my dad was a guy by the name of Jimmy. He was a homely-looking character with big black-framed glasses. He, too, was married to a pretty little Native American woman, and they had at least three boys, all younger than me. Why this pretty lady would marry such a homely-looking guy was a mystery to me. Nonetheless, they would come over to our house to visit. Actually, more to drink beer, I think. They were the kind of people that did not know when to go home. I had a lot of toys. Not because my parents bought me a lot, but because I took care of them. I kept them in my room very orderly and clean. When this family came over, they would turn those three boys loose. I tried to play with them, but they were wild. It was mainly a job of damage control for me. The mother would pay no attention to them, and I would plead with my mother for help, but she would not be rude to company no matter how bad they were. So many hours after they left, it looked like a tornado had hit my room. Those three little hellions tore up more of my good toys, and I can imagine. I would have to clean all the next day to try to get my room back in some kind of order. I sure was glad when they moved away.

One of my friends was a Mexican kid by the name of Timmy. They lived in the old army barracks across the street from us. They were a large family. I think they had about ten or twelve kids. The mother was a Catholic, and I remember she really liked to chomp on her gum. The father would mostly stay in bed all day and sleep and gamble by night in the back rooms of the bars downtown. Timmy and I were friends for many years. He was a fellow crab apple thief. We ran around together all the time.

One time he got in a big argument with another kid, what it was about, I was never sure. Timmy was pretty laid-back and not one to get into fights. However, this ended up in the front yard of their home. His father had had enough of it, and these two boys were going to duke it out and get it over with today.

Timmy's large father hovered over the scene on the front porch. At least twenty kids ringed the fence around the yard to watch the big main event take place. Pretty soon, these two guys started fighting. It was punching and biting and kicking and gnashing of teeth. After a few minutes, a kid finally got Timmy down and was on top of him, pounding him with his fists. Timmy's dad had had enough of this. It was obvious that Timmy was losing and not going to recover. He bounded off the porch shirtless, cussing and growling. He pulled the kid off the Timmy and shoved him toward the gate, yelling some kind of vile things at him and Mexican. Then we figured he would pick

Timmy up and dust him off and comfort him, but no! He grabbed a big broom nearby and began beating Timmy with the broom and cussing at him and Mexican. Timmy came to life and bolted into the house with his dad following after him, all the while swinging the broom and cussing. Well, the show was over. Short but sweet, but I did feel bad for Timmy. I hated to see a friend lose the fight.

I did not do much fighting other than with my brother. I really did not need to. I was more the industrious type. If I was not slaving away for the Harvey family, I would be involved in one of my business ventures. We would get old wooden crates from the grocery store and build them into stands. Then we went down to the Bunning Park and sold juice and candy. I would buy the candy at the store, mark it up and sell it for profit. When business got slow, I would dig up worms out of Bunning Park and sell them to guys going fishing. Then I found a bunch of steel balls of all different sizes, and I would sell them to kids in the neighborhood. They were heavy, not much good for anything, really, but we all thought they were pretty neat. Finally, when business was really slow, I was a modern-day recycler, way ahead of my time. I would scour the neighborhood for pop bottles and aluminum cans. Pick up all I could, take the pop bottles to the store for the deposit refund and the cans to the junkyard, and sell them for aluminum. Sometimes my folks would give me an allowance, but you could not count on that. They would provide me with the necessities, but I had to buy the other things I wanted. It is kind of sad nowadays to see how parents cater to their kids' every whim. New vehicles, computers, cell phones, and fancy clothes. On and on the list goes while the kids learn nothing about being self-sufficient or about the economy or business. I am glad I grew up in the time period that I did. The only time preference I thought would have been to have of was with Custer in his glory days at the Little Bighorn. It is a good thing that there was no time machine available, I would have been off to Montana!

The old Washington school that I went to was quite an old monstrosity of a building, as I said before. The teachers were stern but efficient and seemed to do their job without two or three aids to help them. However, I did have one teacher in the fourth grade by the name of Mrs. Edwards. She was a little skinny woman that must have been on the maiden voyage to this country with Columbus. She did not like most boys, and she especially did not like me, though I never really knew why.

She really catered to all the girls and was a kind of teacher that really made it easy to dislike school. I was having some trouble with math. She had the habit of calling kids up to the board to stand by her and show off their math skills to the whole class. If you could not perform, then she loved to humiliate. Of course, this only happened if you were a boy. The girls would get a pass: "Oh, go sit down, my dear, and study a little bit more and will try it later."

One day to my great dread, I was a poor little urchin and called to the board. I had not a clue what she was asking me to do. I tried, but it was no use. Pretty soon, she got up and slapped me a good one right across the face. Oh, I could have taken her, but you didn't do such things then. Somehow, word got out to my mother that afternoon of what had happened with me and Mrs. Edwards. Otherwise, I would have never breathed a word to mom about it. Stuff like that was usually better forgotten. I could put up with the old hag for a year. Who knows, maybe we would be lucky, and she would kick the bucket before the school year was over.

When I got home, mom grilled me. Was I sure I had not done anything wrong to get slapped? Yes, I was certain of it. Mom was on the phone with Mrs. Edwards. She was hot. No, there would not be a meeting at school the next day. We would see her at her house that night. Mom just did not do things like this, but I had never been disciplined by a teacher for something I didn't deserve either.

Well, it was amazing, there is a God! The next day at school and on throughout the year, Mrs. Edward had taken a great liking to me for some mysterious reason. The change was stunning. I wasn't her pet or anything like that, I wouldn't have stood for it, but I was pretty close to it!

The old Washington school had a small playground on the north side of it and then a bigger playground across the street north of that playground. The larger playground only had a few tetherballs, basically, it was just a big open field otherwise. But this is where we had most of our recesses at. The playground was surrounded entirely by a low stone wall, except at the very front. Just north of the playground, there were pipe yards, and then there was Bitter Creek. If there were scores to be settled among the boys, it would happen over by the pipes after school. This was all a pretty historical area, however. It was in this area that the Chinese resided during the Chinese mining and uprising of Rock Springs, among other areas nearby. Much of the time on the playground, we spent scouring for old Chinese relics left behind from times past. With a little digging or stuff just naturally working itself up through the dirt, all kinds of interesting things could be found. We were constantly finding old Chinese buttons and sometimes coins. I found a handle to a teapot one day. It was white-colored with blue designs on it.

When the Chinese were attacked by the angry white miners, they had to flee from this area toward Bitter Creek and into the sagebrush and hills surrounding Rock Springs to try to hide out and avoid being murdered or injured. Many of their homes were destroyed, which were really only shacks, and much of their property was looted and destroyed.

Years later, this old playground was excavated, and many Chinese relics, antiques, and historical pieces were found by professionals. Then a new school was built on that playground area, and the old school was torn down and turned into the playground.

There was a bar on the north side of the downtown area of Rock Springs called Freddie's Bar. This was one of the milder bars in Rock Springs, and my dad spent a lot of time there. A good deal of Rock Springs was undermined with the old cold mines. Under Freddie's Bar, there was something more interesting than coal mines. My dad told me that there was an old Chinese opium den under that building. This was not uncommon either as the Chinese had opium dens they would go into and smoke opium in the old coal mining days.

My dad spent many hours at Freddie's Bar. Many times, we had to go looking for him to get him to come home from there. Things were really different back then. The county undersheriff (second-in-command) used to park his marked patrol car at the back of the bar. Then he'd go in and drink himself into a cloud in the bar with my dad and the other men. Nobody thought much of this, however, because this guy was tough and did a good job. He was an excellent boxer and helped many young men stay out of trouble by spending time with them at a local gym, teaching them how to box and use their excess energy in a good way. He was also known for showing up at troubled places and taking care of it, even though being outnumbered, he would do it with his fists and without the aid of other policemen or deputies.

He was the undersheriff for many years and then was eventually elected and served as the sheriff of Sweetwater County for a term or two. His only son joined the navy and was a medic, this was during the war, or, as some called it, the conflict in Vietnam. Medics apparently being in short supply at the time, he was assigned to ground infantry forces. The sad result of this was that his unit became involved in a firefight, and he was mortally wounded on the battlefield. There was a huge article in the local paper when this occurred about his death and the tragedy of it all. As you can imagine, it really devastated the undersheriff and his family, and it was a terrible loss of a young life that had much potential.

The big north side Catholic church was by our house. The priest at this church was an old foreign priest that had been in this country for many years. He was highly respected, no-nonsense and ruled with an iron fist. Nobody wanted to mess with him. He was a terrible driver, and he drove like a maniac. The police would avoid him at all costs. When you saw him coming, you got out of his way. Red light, yield the right-of-way, stop sign, mere child's play to him! Funny, though, he would caution other speeders that if they drove too fast, there would be no help for them. They would scare St. Christopher, and he would jump out of the car, and they would be at their own peril.

There was another Catholic church on the south side of town. The priest there was another tough older guy. But he was quite different from the other priest. He would show up at Freddie's Bar. Belly right up to the bar and drink and cuss, tell dirty jokes and smoke just like the rest of the men. I used to get a big kick out of him. He was a heavyset guy. You would see him standing out in front of his church on Sunday night on the sidewalk. It was before church began. He would stand in full view of everybody passing by, wearing all of his garb, including a tall priest hat. (Not sure what you call them). The funny thing about it was he would be leaning on the railing of the stairs, smoking a cigarette, and spitting on the sidewalk. You don't see them like that much anymore.

I used to like to read the kids' magazine called *Jack and Jill.* My mom would buy it for me on a subscription. She would read books to me and gave me an appreciation for reading. I became and always have been an avid reader. Mom was not big on reading, but she wanted her children to read. This did not take with Chuckie, but it did with me and one of my two sisters who were born later.

There was a story contest one time with this magazine. I concocted some tale and sent it in for the contest. I did not win the big prize, but I got an honorable mention, and they sent me a pretty neat certificate. I happened to mention this at the school one day, and the principal and teacher made a big deal of it. I still have the certificate, many years later. It is funny how you hang onto some things that really do not have much value, I guess.

I mentioned that we rented our downstairs to people, and one of the families had two boys that were Chuckie's age and kind of wild too but not really bad kids. One of the boys named Johnny liked to hunt, so I had a lot in common with him, even though I was younger. One day he got the bright idea of taking a bullet apart. Then he lit the powder with a match. He nearly cooked himself.

I ran around some with Chuckie and Johnny and Johnny's brother Tommy. Tommy and Chuckie were pretty close friends. But they were all older than me, so they were off in their own world most of the time. One time they were going to have a big all-night sleepover on the open porch at the downstairs of our house. For little privacy, they decided they would take a bunch of my dad's old tarps and nail them up over the openings on the porch. They made it pretty clear that I was not going to be involved in the sleepover. I was kind of hanging around watching them nail up the tarps and being a pest to them, I guess. They kept trying to run me off, and I wouldn't go. I just wanted to help. I just wanted to be involved with the guys.

Finally, I was on the inside of the porch, and they were all on the outside, nailing up the tarps with the sunlight behind them. They were all busy laughing and talking and nailing the tarps up. Being left to my own devices, I could see one of them silhouetted against the tarp. There was a hammer left lying on the floor. I decided to make my contribution to the little affair. I picked up the hammer, and with all my might, I connected with the head of whoever was on the other side of the tarp. Like a shot, the laughing and talking stopped. The poor victim screeched and fell. The silhouette immediately disappeared from my view. I dropped the hammer like a hot potato and fled. Like a shot, I ran into the house and tried to look innocent. Plus, I figured they could not get me in here. If I was outside once the guy recovered, I was fair game. I had no idea whom I had clobbered, but it did not really matter, there was great satisfaction in being able to help with that hammer.

In seconds Chuckie came charging into the house. He saw me and started bellowing to mom that I had hit poor Johnny in the head with a hammer and nearly killed him. Mom wanted to know if I had really done such a thing. I was not sure; I was just trying to help the guys. Well, not much happened, except I didn't get to go back down with them or spend the night. At least I had the satisfaction of knowing that one of them had a good splitting headache to camp out with.

We went sage-chicken-hunting one time and took Tommy with us. I was too young to shoot sage chickens then, so I just wandered around the prairie while everybody else hunted, and mom waited at the truck. Nobody would let me tag along with them. I had to entertain myself. It was September, and the mornings could be cool, but the days would get pretty hot. My dad would make me dress like we were going to the North Pole. I remember the hot itchy wool clothes that would drive me crazy. I still do not like wool to this day.

As I wandered around, it got hotter and hotter, and I kept taking off clothes. Somewhere in my journey, I dropped a good black sweatshirt. Now I liked that sweatshirt. It would have to be that that I lost instead of some piece of nasty wool long underwear. I had a general idea where I had dropped the sweatshirt. I searched and searched, but it was still sans the black sweatshirt. The prairie is able to swallow things and people up and there never seen again. Who knows what became of that garment? Probably made some birds a dandy nest. But you can never tell. There were several people that disappeared on the prairies when I was a kid, not too far from inhabited places. They were never seen or heard from again. Search and rescue parties were formed not for my shirt but for the people. But despite gallant efforts, their whereabouts are still unknown to this day.

I remember Chuckie and my dad volunteering and joining up for some of the search and rescue parties. This was in the early days before formal search and rescue groups and organizations were formed. It was almost like a sheriff's posse that had to be gathered. It was usually winter and bad weather, and the searches would go on for days. Some were rescued, some were found, for some, it was too late, and for some, never. It certainly made for a lot for a young boy to contemplate on. I loved to hear my dad and Chuckie talk about what had happened in the searches and the accounts of other searchers telling their stories. It was better than ghost stories by far.

There was a man that went to the church that we used to live by on A Street and go to occasionally. He was a really nice and dedicated man. He would talk us into going to Sunday school and church every so often. Then, to be sure we got there, he would come by and pick us up in his car and take us back home when everything was done. Mom and dad would stay home. Grandma would take me and Chuckie. But we did not go often at all. Sometimes on Easter, but never at Christmas.

This man's name was Mr. Comstock. He even drove us out one Easter Sunday after church so that I and Chuckie could attend an Easter egg hunt before he took us all home. His wife died a few years after that, and he became discouraged. But later, he remarried and picked back up where he left off. I knew him once again in later years, and he was really a genuine Christian man.

When I was about seven or eight, my poor mother tried to teach me to roller-skate. My folks had given me the skates for Christmas, and I saved them until spring and summer to learn how to use them. I thought this would be a cinch, and apparently, my mother did too. She would get behind me and try to hold me up while I tried to roller-skate down the sidewalk in front of our house. This went on for several attempts while I would lose my balance and kick back and skin, bloody, and bruise her shins with the skates. She did not say much about it but finally gave me some pointers and left me to my own devices to try to learn how to skate. Over the course of several days, I made different attempts, but it was not to be. The roller derbies were not going to happen for me, at least not as a participant!

Surprisingly, later, I was able to ice-skate a little but not too much better. It appeared that I would not be an Olympic ice-skating star or anything even close to it. I did not really mind the bruises and skins. It was just that I did not have the patience to keep on with this nonsense.

Another big deal for Chuckie and his cronies was skateboards. I got involved in this project too. Of course, you could not go buy a skateboard then, not in Wyoming anyway. We had seen kids on television using skateboards, and we thought that was pretty neat.

We got boards and crafted wooden pieces out of them that resembled skateboards. Then we would take a skate's part and attach it onto the bottom of the board in two separate pieces, with nails and screws. Voilà, a skateboard! After a while, we started painting them and really making them look like beauties.

The road on the east side of our house had just recently been paved, and it was a steep downhill. The road stopped abruptly at a large metal gate at the north end of Bunning Park. There were two options to go to the east or the west at that point. The road made a sharp curve to the east and went around the exterior of Bunning Park. To the west, it made an abrupt turn and went down the alleyway past our garage. This is where we rode our skateboards. There was not a lot of traffic, but you had to watch out for cars. Then as you went racing downhill, you had to be sure to make the curve to the east, or you were sure to have a terrific crash. Nobody had pads or helmets or much or anything like that. You just had to take your licks, bruises, and broken bones!

One day in particular, a bunch of us was out there riding skateboards when this really smart-aleck teenage girl came along on her bicycle. She was from a different part of town, enacting pretty uppity.

She just kept hanging around and being a nuisance. Finally, she rode off and her bike, but we figured she would be back to annoy us some more later. For what reason, I do not recall, but we had picked up a bucket of some really fine sand. We devised a plot against this chick, thinking she would come back soon. We sprinkled a good quantity of the sand on the road at the bottom of the hill and proceeding on around the curve.

We continued to ride skateboards when here came this girl again with a few of her friends on their bicycles. She had a really nice bicycle and was dressed in shorts and a T-shirt. The friends did not say much, but she started in right away again. So, we challenged her. If she was so smart, why didn't she ride her bike downhill as fast as she could and on around the curve. Old smarty-pants did not notice the sand on the street. There it was, the challenge was made. She could not lose face in front of her friends and all of us guys. She went to the top of the hill, and everybody moved off the street. She came barreling down the hill as fast as she could peddle. Her full concentration was on making the curve going on around the park. As soon as her bicycle touched the sand down, she went in a full slide. She was peeled like a banana. We were all whooping and hollering and laughing, and she was screaming and crying with blood flying all over the place. Her shocked friends rushed over and helped her onto her crumpled bicycle. Apparently, none of them noticed or gave thought to the sandy conditions that prevailed on the street. Off they went with old smarty-pants crying, bawling, and wiping away the blood. We never saw her again. We didn't see her obituary in the local paper, so apparently, she survived. We swept up all of the remaining sand that we could after this, but some of us fell victim to the remains of our plot with our skateboards anyway. Well, it was still all worth it regardless.

I had a small boy's bicycle that I had outgrown when for my ninth or tenth birthday, my parents bought me a really nice red bicycle. One thing that I recall about the small bicycle before I got my new bike was a day when I tipped the bike upside down in our yard. I set it on its handlebars and seat. Then I was seeing how fast I could make the back wheel go by turning the pedals with my hand.

Then I would apply the brake and start the whole process over again. Eventually, I got careless and got my left hand too close to the chain and rear wheel. My fingers went through the chain and caught up in the rear wheel as it spun around. Boy, there were some bloody mangled fingers and howling then. My curiosity was now satisfied with the workings of a bicycle.

I rode my new bicycle to death and had it for many years. Back then, if you wanted to go somewhere, you had to walk or ride a bike. Parents were more practical then. I guess they didn't want a bunch of fat slobs sitting around either. They wouldn't haul kids around like they do nowadays. School buses were for kids that lived out of town or a long distance off. If you could get somewhere and back in the days' time, well, then you had better get going and quit wasting time.

The first day I got this bicycle, I was riding it around the neighborhood. My mother had not been on a bicycle for no telling how many years. She got the idea that she would like to take it for a ride. So, I patiently waited while she rode it around Bunning Park. She was not gone very long, but when she came back, she had blood running all down her right hand. The bike was okay, but she sure wasn't. She was kind of embarrassed and acting a little sheepishly. She had not crashed, but she had run into something and skinned her hand up pretty good.

I kept that bike in really nice shape and only had one really bad crash on it out of all the years that I rode it that I recall. I was giving this kid a ride on the handlebars, and I told him to be sure to keep his feet away from the front wheel. He said, "Yeah, not to worry about it." We were going along at a pretty good clip, and we started yapping and looking around. Of course, he got his foot into the wheel, and over the handlebars we went. Fortunately, it was on a dirt road, but we still got banged up pretty good. He was whining about his foot, but I had no sympathy for him and told him so. Pretty soon, we got up, and he limped away while I pushed my bike on home, taking a survey of my own tragedy!

Dad would go off to work. Mom would take care of the house, and we would go to school, except for summer, of course, and holidays and what have you. Then very few ladies worked out of the home. She had friends that would come over in the daytime and have coffee and cigarettes and visit.

Helen was not really a friend. She sold various perfume products. She was an older heavyset woman that had a terrible chronic cough. She would get in coughing fits while she was explaining the wonders of her products. We would have to get her a glass of water that she tried to drink in between all of her fits. Then she would have a cigarette and go on. Mom was too kind to turn her away, and she would let her in and listen to her. She would offer her coffee and listen to her and usually buy a few products that she could not really afford, just to help poor Helen out.

Sometimes Helen would come, and we would not answer the door. She was persistent, though, so mom would caution us to be quiet and wait until she went away. She was not really a friendly person, but I used to like to sit and watch her while she sold her wares. Maybe I could pick up a few tips on how to sell a product. Otherwise, I thought most of the stuff that she sold was pretty smelly, not in a good way.

Like I said, we didn't watch a lot of TV. When dad was at work, I and mom would play a lot of board games. I liked to read a good deal too.

Dad had left the painting business and got a much better job when the mines went back into operation. He usually worked at night, what they would call a swing shift, which really was afternoons and evenings. He was an underground coal miner. It was hard work, but he made very good money. Up to that point, we had always only had a car or my grandpa's old pickup truck. But now, with dad making pretty good money, he was able to buy a nice used pickup truck. He had the truck for many, many years. It was only a two-wheel drive, but we took it everywhere, hunting, camping, fishing, and traveling.

Dad got vacations on this job, so we had two weeks, usually to use in the summer. Then sometimes, with the price of coal down, they would be laid off for a month, maybe two months, usually in the summer. This made money pretty tight, but it gave us time to go on long, extended camping and fishing trips. Those trips were some of my favorite family times.

Chuckie had been working for the city on street maintenance and garbage trucks. Those were good jobs, but he was able to get a job with my dad in the coal mines. They both worked there for quite a few years, actually, until the mines shut down again. In fact, it was expected when I got out of high school that I would go to work in the coal mines. Well, I like the outdoors too much to be underground. I had far different interests than being a coal miner. To my dad's dismay, I did not follow in his or Chuckie's footsteps.

My aunt Mary Lou, whom we called, as I said before, Baylou, was divorced from my uncle Wayne. She moved to California, never remarried, and became a sheriff's deputy for San Mateo County. When she retired, she moved back to Wyoming and lived in Rock Springs until her death. She would fly out and visit us every year or two, and we always had a great time with her. She was really a good aunt. She loved to drink scotch and some beer. She was fun to visit with and a very lively person. When she came back to visit, she would always comment on the blue skies and fresh air in Wyoming and really enjoyed that after living in California.

She did not make a big deal out of being a female deputy, which was unusual even in those days. But I did, whether she was female or not. I would brag to all the neighborhood kids about her, and I would talk her into showing me her wallet badge. Then I would talk her into showing a few of my friends her wallet badge. They were all too happy to see a real woman cop and her badge, she was good-natured about it, but she really did not want to make a big deal of it.

On one of her visits, I did not have a decent pair of dress shoes to go to church and other places. She walked me down to the Union Merc store, which was a nice grocery and department store downtown, and bought me a really nice expensive pair of black dress shoes. They were stiff and tight as new dress shoes could be, but I wore them on the way home anyway. I was always glad when she came to visit and sad to see her go back to California.

Once my dad had his new pickup truck, we would load it full of stuff and take off for the Big Sandy openings for several weeks of camping and fishing. This is a beautiful area in the Wind River Mountains. Some friends had told my dad about an area called Blucher Creek and Block and Tackle Hill. Well, we tried to get up Block and Tackle Hill. It was not named that for no particular reason. It was a steep, rocky, and narrow twisting road up a goat trail. It was really only suited for jeeps back then. My dad took runs at the bottom and made a vigilant try to get to the top. He would make it about halfway up and could go no further. Rocks and dirt would be flying from under the truck. It was bouncing around, tires spinning and whining on the rocks. Then dad would come backing down and looking kind of sheepish. The truck was a two-wheel drive, and it really required at least a four-wheel drive to ascend the area. There were not many four-wheel-drive trucks around in those days. He finally had everybody get out of the truck and tried it by himself. He made one final run at the steep hill. A little more distance was gained, but it was not to be. He hated to quit.

We left there and went a little further into Blucher Creek. This area was also not easily accessible, especially if it had been wet. You could easily get stuck in muddy spots or in meadows. Well, we had our share of that at times! But, if you are careful, you could drive clear into the head of the undeveloped camping spots where the road ended. Shucks, we didn't know what a developed camping spot was. Only tourists and city people camped in such things anyway. This is where we almost always camped out. We would see few other campers, fishermen, or otherwise our entire trip. Beautiful pine trees, aspens, fields of wildflowers, deer, moose, and all sorts of wildlife. A nice little creek with beaver ponds that was full of all sizes of brookies just begging to be caught. You could catch them on a bare hook without bait, lots of times.

On our first trip, we had my grandfather's old canvas wall tent. It was green-colored, old metal poles that had to be driven into the ground and tieback flaps for doors. It was an old heavy canvas tent, with the old smell that only old canvas has. We would stretch it out with ropes that were staked into the ground. It was in very good shape. We set it up with a canvas tarp on the floor and an old oil stove for chilly mornings or wet weather. Mom would cook most of the meals on a gas stove, but dad would cook anything else over the campfires, other than marshmallows and hot dogs, which we cooked ourselves.

We would catch brookies by the hundreds. Every morning, my mother would pan-fry the breaded fish. We had this with buttered bread and piles of fresh fried sliced potatoes. Powdered milk and hot coffee; it was a real feast. Mom loved to fry the fish, but she did not eat any. Chuckie and I ate our fill every day, but my dad would gorge himself on the fish. He loved eating those brookies.

We had great times hiking, fishing, and around the campfire in the evenings. A little beer would be consumed, but my father never got drunk and rowdy on these trips. We would dig worms for fishing from the meadows nearby, and I would pull wildflowers for my mother from these same meadows. They would go into an empty food can and adorn our table in the tent.

Most of the time, the weather was dry and pleasant. There would be some cold frosty mornings occasionally and every so often a good thunderstorm or day or two of rain. The tent always seemed so safe and secure, just a great place to be during bad weather. We had a big camping table we would set up inside the tent for keeping supplies and things off the floor. There were chairs to sit around inside the tent in the daytime if you needed or wanted to. At nighttime, we would fix our bedding all up on the floor underneath the table. What a cozy place to sleep!

One time in the early evening, mom and dad were in the tent. Chuckie and I were sitting around talking at the campfire. I had an old heavy glass olive bottle that was empty. I filled the bottle with water and put the lid on it. I asked my older and wiser brother what he thought would happen if I put this into the fire for a while. Well, he said he did not really know. I did not either, so I put it into the fire to see what would happen. The bottle sat in the fire for a while, and we lost interest in it and began to talk again. Pretty soon, there was a big loud *boom*, and big chunks of glass came flying past us out of the fire. This was a surer way to lose an eye than with a BB gun. Remember, the big thing about a BB gun was "Oh, you cannot have one, you will shoot your eye out," for lots of kids. Well, that was mere child's play compared to this exploding missile! Well, sometimes, in the advancement of science, you just have to try experiments.

Grandma always stayed at home and worked and took care of the house and the dogs when we went on these extended trips. It would have been nice to have our pets with us, but dad always preferred to leave them at home. So, they never went. Grandma had no interest in camping and fishing after grandpa was gone. We would stay usually for about two weeks, sometimes close to three if the mines were idle. My dad liked to get Chuckie out of town, too, because this helped to keep him out of trouble. I am sure the police enjoyed the break in action with old Chuckie, or maybe it made for boredom for them, who knows! Chuckie was always grandma's favorite, and she always babied and catered to him. She was convinced that the police had nothing to do but follow him around and try to nab him. It required very little following or watching of Chuckie to catch him at some devilment, he could be one guy on a regular crime spree. A bonanza for the ticket book without the police even trying. On these family trips, he was a different person, though, well, mostly anyway.

We usually were only able to make one trip a year. I would have rather taken a beating than had left there when the trip was over. On days when I was bored with school, I would sit and daydream about this wondrous place called Blucher Creek and the Big Sandy openings. Fantasize about pulling the wonderful brookies out of the water and the good times to be there. Peaceful and quiet and just a laid-back time for the whole family.

On our camping trips, we would usually make a stop at Dill's store at Eden Valley, Wyoming. Eden Valley was another small community just south of Farson, Wyoming. Dill, his wife, and his son ran the store, which was also the local post office. Dill was probably in his 60s or older at that time, and unbeknown to us, he was on the fish and game commission.

They were very friendly people and were easy to visit with. We would usually buy some ice cream, canned beer, little treats, and maybe some gasoline. One time we left camp, set up, and drove into the store for a few supplies and such. We had more fish than dad thought that we had to keep at the time. Dad always talked about a game warden showing up, but we never saw one. There was always plenty of fish, and it really helped the ecosystem to catch more fish than you were legally allowed. That was because there were really far more fish in the waterways than they could support. There was very little fishing or other predation that took place, and the fish would become stunted in their growth due to overpopulation. Anyway, dad took a big bag of the fish with us and asked Dill to freeze them for him until we came back. Dad explained that we were going back to camp and fish for about another week and he did not want to get in trouble with the game warden. Dill took the fish and did not say much. True to our plan. We showed back up in about a week and added the frozen fish to our catch and went home. Nothing was ever said, and Dill was always friendly and helpful. Dad was surprised when he found out shortly after that Dill was on the game and fish commission. We sure did not want to put Dill in a bad position, though, so there was never a request like that again. Times have sure changed!

We made trips to a ranch near Boulder, Wyoming, where there was an old indoor swimming facility that had hot mineral springs. The family would go there and swim for the day and usually have a picnic. We made a number of trips there over the years. It was pretty inexpensive, and it was operated by a friendly ranch family that owned the property. It wasn't advertised or well-marked from the highway. You had to drive off the highway and several miles of gravel-dirt road to get to the place. It was open to the public but was never overly crowded. There was a children's pool and a very large adult pool. It had old indoor dressing rooms with showers, and they provided inner tubes for folks and kids to swim and float with. They had a little concession booth at the front entrance where you paid admission. They would rent towels and bathing suits as well as sell some pop and candy bars.

Sometimes no one was at the swimming hole when you would arrive there. No problem, there was an old phone that had a crank on it that you would wind to make the phone ring at the other connection. This, of course, went to their house some miles away. They would answer, and within a short time, someone from the family would show up and open up.

We made our last trip there when I was probably around ten, just before Jan was born. We arrived at the swimming facility, and no one was there. Dad cranked the phone several times, but no one ever answered. That had never happened before. We waited a bit, but no one was around. Then to my great shock and disappointment, but true to dad's character flaw (I am being generous), he tried the door. It, of course, was not locked. So, he went in, and everybody followed but me. They, at dad's direction, started hauling stuff out of the front area. A small tan-colored electric radio, candy, pop, towels, and just used stuff like that. I stood back by the truck while dad said, "Come get some stuff."

I said, "Don't take these people's stuff," but he paid no attention. After the haul was made, we loaded up and left and never went back. The name of the place was Steel's. Called that, I am sure, because the Steel family owned the ranch. They were just common ranchers of the era. Certainly not rich. They had always been nice to us, and they were good people. I was so hurt by the family doing this. My dad just had sticky fingers if given too much opportunity. He would take stuff and even hoard it. Stuff we didn't even need. He just had the need to get the better of somebody, even someone like the Steels that had been good people.

Usually, our family trips were good, though. I am told that the ranch has since been bought by rich out-of-state people and nothing is open to the public anymore.

Regressing to when I was about four, my mother had a terrible goiter. This was caused due to lack of iodine in her system. She did not seek treatment for quite some time, and the goiter grew to be huge. Eventually, she had to be taken to Salt Lake City for surgery. This turned into quite a serious case, and she had to remain in Salt Lake City for some time. On dad's days off, we would make trips down to see her. Grandma would remain at home, and, of course, only my dad was allowed in the hospital to actually see my mother. We sure missed her.

During this time, I had a green fuzzy stuffed monkey that I became very attached to. I called the monkey Snooky. I loved that monkey and had him for many years. Much of the fuzz was worn off him from all the years of packing him around. No teddy bear for me. I loved the monkey.

On one of the trips down to visit my mother, we made the typical roadside stop. There were no rest areas in those days. So, with no one around, dad and us boys relieved ourselves. Me being a little tyke, I had trouble getting my zipper back up. After a bit, dad came to my aid. The trouble was, he was not gentle about it and caught me in the zipper, *ouch!* I was not happy about this, but what really got me was that dad could not help but laugh about it. He wasn't being mean; he just could not help himself. I guess I can understand that now, but at the time, I thought he was not very nice, and I sure missed mom and her gentle ways.

Oftentimes my dad was an example. Unfortunately, a bad one a lot of the time. He would take us to the carnivals when they came to town in the summer. One evening we were at a carnival when something came off the ride and struck dad over the left eye. He had a small cut and some bleeding, but he immediately saw dollar signs. He began making a big deal out of it, but he would not stop there. We went home, and he forced mom to take a razor blade and enlarge the cut. Then we went back to the carnival. He ended up at the manager's trailer, and after a lot of bickering and conniving, they gave him one hundred dollars. That was quite a bit of money, but I am sure he had visions of much more. That sure took the fun out of that trip to the carnival for us.

Dad was always what he would call "wheeling and dealing" and had to "make a buck." Many of his ventures were good, but a lot of them were not. We were always going to people's houses that had cars and bartering for cars or parts. We would have to wait for long periods in the car while dad would be visiting and bartering, buying, or selling.

I wore high-top tennis shoes quite a bit. Field boots were also quite popular. They were black rounded toe leather boots. They were durable and inexpensive, and we wore those quite a bit too. When boots were worn out, they were taken to a boot shop for replacement. This was quite inexpensive and saved discarding the boots. Now we are a throwaway society. Nothing seems to last very long, and when it quits working, we simply throw it away. Seems that we even do this with people now that just need a little help or fixing. People now are just too self-centered and far too busy, or so we say. We have little or no time to give a hand to a friend or neighbor, let alone a stranger. Sad to say, lots of "Christian" or "church people" are the worst about this.

Anyway, I have never forgotten as a young boy going with my brother Chuckie to one of these shoe repair shops. We took in his field boots and asked the man if he could fix them. His reply was, "I can fix anything but a broken heart." He said it in such a no-nonsense way too. Undoubtedly a lot of truth to what the man said for himself and each one of us. Years later, when I was buying a vehicle in Anchorage, Alaska, a used car salesman made a quote that I have never forgotten. His name was Joe. He was a big, heavyset guy. We were discussing vehicles when he said, "If a man makes it, it will break." You can say, what you want about a used car salesman, but Big Joe was right about that.

When I was probably about six or seven, my dad had suffered some kind of injury and was in the hospital for several days. So, we made lots of hospital visits where I had to wait in the waiting room while mom and Chuckie got to go in and see dad. It was pretty peaceful and quiet around the house with dad gone for several days, but we missed him.

During that time, mom took us out for one of our infrequent visits to the five-star drive-in and restaurant. This was back in the days where you drove up to the place and a carhop came out and waited on you. You could also go inside and sit around the lunch counter or small tables, and that is what we did. Sitting at the lunch counter. We all had hamburgers with fries and drinks. I was just a little guy, and I was eating regularly, but I was starved on this particular day. I finished my hamburger and fries and asked mom if I could have another hamburger. "Of course, as long as you do not waste it," she said. When we finally finished, I had consumed six hamburgers, including my first original order. They were great homemade type hamburgers, but I still have no idea how I could possibly have eaten so many of them. People in the restaurant were amazed that a little kid had eaten so many hamburgers. Some of them probably thought my mother had been starving me, and a few of them even gave her funny looks. Poor mom, she seemed a little embarrassed but said nothing. She didn't like the attention we were receiving from my feasting. I was well-nourished, though, and healthy. This was a family-run business, and the cook, who was the mother in the family, was a big, heavyset friendly lady. She was amazed that I had eaten so many of her hamburgers. She said I was her customer of the day, her best customer. She awarded me a pack of double mint gum!

Mom tried hard to keep the home together. She had a difficult job but was pretty good at it. One time when Chuckie was in his early teens and dad was not at home, Chuckie got pretty big for his britches. He objected to something mom had told him to do and started to raise his hand at her. She didn't back up an inch. She told him right to his young face that he might be bigger and stronger than she but added in no uncertain terms, "Sometime you will go to sleep, buddy boy, and when you do, I'll use the frying pan on you." He knew she wasn't joking. That was a cast-iron frying pan, too, not a wimpy aluminum pan. He never raised his hand at mom again.

In the early '60s, one of the biggest murder cases probably took place in the county, maybe even the state. Right across the street from our house at the pink apartments. The family that I had mentioned earlier that operated the Rogan mortuary and were friends of my aunt Mary Lou were the main actors in this case. That is to say, mainly their son and his wife were. They were a very well-to-do family with plenty of money and property. The father of the family, who went by the name of J. Warden and the last name of Opie, operated the mortuary. They had a huge fancy home near the top of A Street, and he had a collection of old antique cars among their many riches. In fact, one day before we had moved from A Street, Mr. Opie came by and took me and Chuckie for a ride in one of the old early 1900s cars. I do not remember a lot about it, but I do remember it was quite an interesting old car. He kept the cars in prime shape.

Anyway, their only son had been spoiled rotten by the mother and was kind of what you would consider the poor little rich boy. He had married, and he and his wife lived in the pink apartments near us. As I understand, he was kind of prone to be wild and crazy at times. He was probably in his early 20s at this time. There are several versions about what had happened and allegations that his family had tried to help hide the crime from the authorities, but basically, he came home intoxicated one early morning. At some point, as his young wife sat in an easy chair in the living room, he shot and killed her.

This created a lot of excitement around the pink apartments for several days. This kind of stuff just did not happen at these ritzy apartments, but in fact, it did. When all the dust cleared, a handsome young man named Jerry was charged with murder. This case resulted in one of the biggest murder trials in Sweetwater County up to that time. Young Jerry Opie was tried by the local county attorney at the Green River courthouse, which was the county seat for Sweetwater County. The family would have nothing to do with local attorneys. They hired a big-city attorney by the name of F. Lee Bailey. This all made for sensational news coverage and stories. Bailey came to town and was going to roll over the little-time prosecutors and local cops. He evidently intended to dazzle the local cowboy hick jury. When it was all over, young Opie was convicted of murder and sentenced to the state penitentiary for a long term. Bailey apparently cost the family a fortune. J. Warden no longer had the old antique cars, and their riches had been depleted a great deal by Bailey, who was never seen in Sweetwater County again. Years later, Mr. Bailey was involved in many high-profile cases around the country and often seen in the national news.

There was an army surplus store, not too far from our house downtown. I spent plenty of my hard-earned money in this place. It was a regular treasure trove of real army stuff from World War II and Korea, very much unlike the army surplus stores of nowadays that carry pretty much generic outdoor equipment and very little of actual army surplus. We could equip ourselves with all kinds of genuine, honest to Pete war goods, and we did in large quantities.

My dad also had two heavy World War I English helmets that he would let me play with. With these helmets and all my other goods, I spent many days playing war with the other guys in Bunning Park.

Bunning Park was especially inspirational for playing war in. Besides having all kinds of neat places to run and hide and shoot from, there was a large war memorial in the middle of the park. The memorial was a large stone block with a metal sheet on its front. The sheet had the names of soldiers killed in World War I and other conflicts; I think too from the local area. We would carefully examine the names and the dates of death on this big plaque. But of far more interest was what was on top of the memorial, which was a lifelike figure of a World War I doughboy, complete with a rifle. He appeared to be in combat, walking along with his left hand raised that, I think, had a grenade in it. We would marvel at this memorial, and we spent lots of time around it and playing on and near it.

Every Veterans Day, the local VFW and National Guard would hold a ceremony at this memorial as well as others around town. We would not miss the one at Bunning Park. Among the small crowds it would gather was an honor guard fully dressed in their uniforms. There would be the blowing of taps, speeches, and prayers, and then the twenty-one-gun salute. Flags and banners, and then they were gone and on to the next memorial site. When it was all over, they raced to the local VFW, Archie Hay Post, to belly up to the bar and suck down beer.

That memorial still stands to this day in Bunning Park minus the rifle. One late night several years later, some local idiots worked feverishly and removed the doughboy from the memorial. Then they realized it was too heavy to pack very far and had to ditch it in a nearby alley. They covered it with bushes, but it was eventually found and placed back on top of the memorial. The rifle was never recovered. This was a senseless and stupid crime, and there was a lot of public outrage over it. The culprits were known, but no arrests were ever made, unfortunately.

In the winter, besides having to help dad keep snow cleaned away from around the house, I would canvas the area after school for folks willing to pay to have their sidewalks cleaned. In this way,

I would pick up a little extra money to buy Christmas presents for the family.

Chuckie and I always had to share a bedroom room in our house. In fact, we shared a bed until I was about twelve and my dad finally broke down and bought us a used bunk bed set. Chuckie could be quite a nuisance to have to share a bedroom with or anything else for that matter! My mom not only expected us to keep our bedroom clean and orderly, but she also expected us to help with household chores. So, we would have to help most times. Vacuum and sweep, wash or dry dishes, dust, take out garbage, and all that fun stuff. This stuff was to be done usually after breakfast, and there was no going out to play until it was completed. That was during the summer, of course, we still had to help some during school, but it was not as rigorous.

We had no furnace in the house for heat. Our large upstairs was heated with a natural gas stove in the living room, and in the kitchen was a natural gas cookstove used for heat and cooking on that side of the house. Doors had to be left ajar inside so rooms wouldn't become completely cold. We would gather around the kitchen cookstove during the cold winter mornings. Mom would usually make us hot oatmeal or hot cream of wheat. Then it was off to school with a brown paper bag containing your lunch. The grade schools would provide you with a little pint carton of milk for lunch if you paid the weekly milk fee. If not, there was no free milk!

Another odd thing that happened in schools back then was that the teachers would come by and look in your throat with a little light. If they did not like the look of your throat, you were sent down to the lunchroom. Not for lunch, but to have your throat swabbed. This was always a worrisome and torturous process. Then your swab would be cultured, and if the results were not good, it was off for a wonderful adventure to the doctor for the penicillin shots. If that was to be my fate, I could only hope that Mabel would be the nurse giving the shots, or the fight would be on! Fortunately, my cultures were usually negative, so that was the end of it, at least after I was in the second or third grade.

Grandma Frances lived with us, as I have said before. My family were pretty much night owls and never in too much of a hurry to go to bed. Except if we had to get up early for some event. Grandma Frances was the opposite of this and usually went to bed much earlier than the rest of us. She had a habit that would raise the dead and sure got the attention of visitors after she had gone to sleep. Out of the blue, she would have a reoccurring nightmare. It was always about the same; she would start off with a low yell, and then her volume would increase substantially. She would be yelling at some intruder, and this kept on until she was awakened by somebody in the family, having to go in and shake her. There was never an explanation, just the same loud nightmare every so often.

Every once in a while, as a young boy, I would sleep with her. Not very often, but the first time or two that I did, and she had this nightmare, it was pretty frightening. Then I got used to it, and it wouldn't even awaken me. I would peacefully sleep while somebody had to come to wake her up. It was pretty funny to see the faces of visitors sometimes when she started this howl! Sometimes, my dad had some of his friends over, and they be drinking and having a loud party. Then good old granny would have one of her nightmares. It *sure* would throw cold water on the party and quiet things down for a bit!

Grandma had a number of her old ways that she brought with her to Wyoming and kept. She was superstitious about stuff like if someone gave you a sharp object like a knife, you had better give them a penny in return to avoid a future terrible incident with it. Or like if you spilled the salt shaker on the table, you had better put some in your hand and throw it over your shoulder, or there would be a big fight or argument in the family. Some really odd stuff like that and plenty more. Before I go on, I should also note that grandma and dad would really get into some loud and protracted verbal arguments sometimes. I don't know if this salt thing had anything to do with it (kind of doubt it), but one of them would start picking at the other, and before you knew it, there would be long nasty arguments that probably the whole neighborhood could hear without any trouble. This only occurred after grandpa was gone.

Grandma was a worrywart and just had to have something to be afraid about or to worry about. I don't think she was happy otherwise. She especially liked to sit up into the night and worry about Chuckie when he was out on a big toot and never came home till daybreak or later. I don't believe she ever lost much sleep over me for any reason, valid or imagined!

Granny had some two or three old worn paperback books that we called dream books. Which they were. If you had a dream, you could look up the subject, and it would tell what the dream was about and what it meant and give advice or warnings in regard to the dream. Grandma would consult these books often for herself or others if told of their dream. They were about as helpful as fortune cookies, astrology, and the like. In later years I would laugh at granny for consulting these books, and she would get kind of mad about it and say that you just didn't know what you were talking about. She would defend their authenticity. They seemed to me to just be something to make one worry and dread about the future, which was right up her alley, maybe that is why she liked them so well.

Our little family of four plus grandma and the dog began to grow in 1965. Without any warning, mom was going to have a baby, and I was almost ten years old. My brother was nearly six years older than me. It appeared that things were going to change. I had mixed feelings about this, of course, and really did not know what to expect. I guess none of us really did.

Anyway, we had not been consulted about any of this by my parents, so it was time to start taking bets around the neighborhood. A boy or girl. I was pretty sure mom would have another boy. So, I placed my bets on the sure thing. The only bet I can remember now is the one that I lost big-time. I had bet one of the teenage brothers living downstairs, named Johnny, a full coffee can of earthworms dug out of Bunning Park. He had such a can of worms that he showed me that he had recently dug up. This was to be our wager. It was a beautiful sight to behold! A coffee can, full of worms, no dirt, just worms. Just imagine all the fish to be cut from this treasure, it was more precious than gold!

Mom and dad went off to the hospital on the night of May 8th. I and Chuckie were staying at home under the watchful eye of grandma. This was one of the few times that grandma actually had to "babysit" us. I can just recall one other time that she watched us while mom and dad went out for dinner one night. On that particular evening, Chuckie was standing in front of the mirror in the main bathroom with the door open. He had an old razor and some soap and was trying to shave his lightly haired face. This was too good of a chance to pass up, and I began to torment him. I would appear near the door and harangue him. He would yell and threaten me, and I would back away for a few seconds. Then it would all start over again. He continued his shaving and would call out complaining to grandma about the little nuisance. All of this only enticed me to make him whine more. Grandma always babied Chuckie and would take his side whether I was right or wrong. So, of course, in this case, she would be telling me to leave poor little Chuckie alone too. Then, of course, there were threats that she was going to tell my dad when he got home, and I would get it. This phased to me not a bit.

Finally, I guess Chuckie got a little irritated, he turned and threw the metal razor at me. As usual, he was a poor shot, and I was a good ducker! The heavy metal razor went flying past my head, *whoosh!* Then there was a loud crash. The razor went through several rooms and struck a big window by our kitchen table. This was a double pane window, and the razor had come to rest with one neat hole in the inside pane of glass. Now there was a lot of yelling and excitement!

This was not good, and it would never do. So, we rounded out the hole in the glass to the size of a hard rubber ball and began concocting a story about how the ball had been thrown and broke the window. Just playing—these things happen, you know. There would be heck to pay, but maybe at least not as bad as the real account would bring our way. We worked and connived and tried to get grandma to go along with us, but, of course, she would not. Curses, foiled again! This all seemed a good argument to me as to why people should grow beards and not shave!

We awoke to a gray wet morning on May 9th. It had been unusually wet and rainy. There was no news of any addition to the family as of yet. We had breakfast and then went out and rode our bikes with Tommy, who lived downstairs. Tommy was Johnny's younger brother and Chuckie's good friend.

The nearby Catholic school was paving the big dirt lot in front of the school. It hadn't been paved yet; it was all just dirt work being done at this point. So, there were all kinds of neat holes and hills and courses to ride bikes around on. It was a bit muddy, but it made for some pretty good bike riding.

It was still pretty early when we saw grandma summoning us from the front of the house. We rode over to find out that we had a sister born. We were pretty excited about this. It was happy news, except for the loss of my worm bet. It was a few days later that dad brought mom home with our new sister. Charla Janette Weimer. She was named Charla as a feminine version of Charles after my dad. She was called Jan. It was pretty neat having a sister, but it did create quite a bit of work. I was expected to help with her care quite a bit if I was not at school or something.

Then for some reason, my dad really got in gear. Not many months later, another child was expected in the Weimer household. Oh boy. This was getting crowded now. We were not consulted once again. And once again, mom and dad took off for the hospital in the dark of early morning on May 14th. Not too long afterwards, the joyous news came that we had another sister!

So here came another little bundle of joy home with mom and dad. Tamara Joyce Weimer. I am not sure how her name was picked. Chuckie, of course, after my father, Charles, or Chuck. My middle name, as I said, after my grandpa Joe, and my first name, Kenneth, was supposed to mean "handsome." Mom probably thought this was true in my case, but another name would have probably been more appropriate for me in my estimation. That is if you go by what names are supposed to mean. So anyway, we called her Tammy. Once again, we were proud of her and happy to have her, but it was a lot more work. Let me tell you! I was sure hoping at this point that my dad would slow down.

One of the dogs we had for quite a few years was a little dog named Sandy. We never had dogs fixed or taken to the vet. That was for rich people. Sandy was a good little dog, never wandered far from home. And was usually inside the house. One day she disappeared for several days. She came home looking pretty worn out. The next thing you knew—it was puppies. Now Sandy had never been one to run around. But once she started, it was a chore trying to keep her at home. Every time she came in heat, we had another batch of puppies, and she was already pretty old by this time. Well, my dad was not that old, but it sure gave me cause to ponder the situation.

I was not musically inclined, but I had an interest in learning to play the piano. I kept pestering dad about this, and finally, through his old painting employer, the Mormon bishop, he was able to buy a used piano from the Mormon church. It was a nice piano, but one of those big heavy things. We moved it into my playroom, it took lots of manpower. It was an upright piano and in very good condition. Dad did not have to pay much for it, but I appreciated it.

Nobody in the family played instruments. Chuckie had tried to play the trombone when he was in the Catholic school. He was cleaning it one day and got a rag stuck in it and could not get it out. The trombone had to go to a music shop to have the rag removed, my dad was really mad about that. Chuckie never learned to play the thing. He just made a lot of terrible noise and drove us all crazy with this practice, which was pretty limited. He really did not want to play the thing. Shortly after his colorful short career at the Catholic school, the instrument was put away and seldom seen again.

Chuckie did try his hand at an electric guitar as well. Dad found some good deal on a used electric guitar and a small amplifier. Chuckie and a few other wannabes messed around with the guitars for a while, but they never really learned to play either. They even had some instructional books and learned to cord a little bit, but that was about the extent of the musical career for them.

Grandma could play a few tunes on the piano, but not much either. She taught me to play chopsticks. She would play and sing a song called "Life's Setting Sun." I would request her to play this song every so often. I liked to hear her sing and play the melody. It was a song about your life coming to an end and you going on to your reward with the Lord. Usually, before she played it, she would always tell me about her aunt Mattie, who was a missionary to China. I had heard the story many times, and there were not a lot of details to it, but I liked to hear the story again and again. Grandma would tell it, whether you ask or not. This tune was beyond me, and I never picked it up, however, as far as playing it on the piano. Still, many years later, I remember the tune and the words to the song, I guess you could say it made a lasting impression on me. She always liked to tell another story about a boy not paying attention to what his father told him, and consequently, he was bitten by a snake. She would carefully caution how important it was to listen to your parents. I always felt a little sorry for the boy in the story. Grandma always told it with a great deal of seriousness and made it a drawn-out tale. The story was pretty mysterious as it was not a Wyoming incident. It was something that seemed to have happened far away in a foreign land.

I plunked around and tried to learn to play a little on the piano by myself but was not very successful at that endeavor. Dad kept promising that he would have some music lessons provided to me so I could learn to play the thing, but this never happened. I finally grew frustrated and bored with trying to play the piano. It eventually became just the dust and junk collector in the room. Dad would criticize me every so often for not learning to play the piano and using it, but he would become eerily silent when questioned about the forthcoming music lessons promised. Several years later, the piano was sold to make room for a large deep chest freezer to be put in its place. We mustered another poor crew together and moved the thing out, and off it went to another hopefully "happy home." Fortunately, the deep chest freezer proved to be much more useful.

Jan had been born in May and probably a month later in June. We went on a big camping trip to Blucher Creek. Jan was certainly a newborn at this point, and we were all trying to adjust to the addition to the family. But none of this delayed our camping trip. We arrived at our old campsite and began setting up camp. Something was wrong with Jan's breathing, however. Mom kept holding her all wrapped up in her blankets and really keeping a watchful eye on her.

Dad said we had to go ahead and unpack things, but he seemed worried. He cautioned us that we might have to load things right back up and head for town. So slowly, we unloaded the pickup and set camp up. As the afternoon went on, Jan seemed to be feeling better and doing better, and it looked like we could stay.

The next day we had camp all set up and were ready to stay for a couple of weeks. Mom and Jan were in the tent most of the time. Dad was too. Chuckie and I were outside, enjoying the nice day, digging worms and just messing around. Dad came out and told us Jan was feeling better but that we needed to be quiet and not disturb her. She was not out of the woods yet with whatever had been bothering her. There was still a possibility that we would have to head for town.

Finally, our minds wandered onto some fireworks that dad bought us to shoot off around the Fourth of July. There was a big meadow in front of our camp. We would go out there and shoot them off at the appropriate time. We decided we had to shoot off one of the fireworks. So carefully, we examined them and came to the conclusion that a big silver-colored tube thing that set on a small wooden base appeared to be something that would be quiet to shoot off. We took the fireworks out into the meadow. Chuckie had some matches. He gave me the matches, and I lit the firework. We backed off, expecting to watch sparks and smoke in a beautiful display. Instead, it sounded like a cannon went off—*kaboom!* And it echoed all around the mountains, just making it worse. My dad came out of the tent like a shot. Boy, was he hot. There were sparks flying, but not from the fireworks.

Jan steadily improved, and we were able to stay the entire planned length of our trip. The next year we took another newborn. Tammy, on the same trip. Tammy did not seem to suffer any consequences from going off into the mountains. And year after year, we had many wonderful times at this remote site in the Wyoming mountains. Both of my sisters learned to love the mountains and outdoor activities as most of us did. This was especially true with Jan; she became even more outdoorsy than Tammy.

Jan was always a big hardy girl. Tammy was always short and slender. They were like Mutt and Jeff if you know what I mean.

When not in school, I was always required to help care for both of them quite a bit. I liked doing stuff with my sisters, but sometimes it did cut into my playtime and so on.

As Jan got bigger, probably around two or three, I found an old small mattress like out of a baby bed. This was just large enough to put over the bar on my boys' bicycle in front of my seat. Jan was able to sit on this pad or mattress and hold on to the handlebars. It was pretty cozy for her, and she loved it. We spent hours and put-on untold miles riding my old red bicycle around like this in the neighborhood and around town.

Then I would take Jan by the hand, and we would walk downtown. With our limited resources, we would go into the dime stores and buy a few little items. Then, for a special treat, we would stop on the way home at the New Grand Cafe. I would treat us to a hamburger deluxe.

Then, as Tammy got bigger, I would take both girls by the hand, and we would walk a few blocks downtown. We would go to a little store that had a lunch counter in it. It was called Paul's. The wife Jenny and some of her help ran the place, but it was named after her husband, Paul, who was a coal miner. We would go there every so often and buy a few little doodads. Mostly we went there to have vanilla malt at the lunch counter. We would each usually get our own little malt. They were twenty-five cents. More than a fountain soft drink, like a cherry soft drink, which cost a dime. They were delicious and well worth it. I would save our pennies for this, and every so often, mom would kick in a few coins too.

One particular summer day, Jan was not able to go with us for some reason. Tammy and I walked the short distance down to Paul's. Some of the old sidewalks were cracked and not level. On the way there, Tammy tripped. I had her by the hand, but I could not keep her from falling onto her face. She hit pretty hard. She knocked out and broke some of her front baby teeth. She was pretty tough. She did not really cry or complain. There was blood all around her mouth and her teeth, but she was determined to make it on to Paul's and have the wonderful vanilla malt. That would make anything feel better, even broken, missing teeth! We walked on. On the way there, a lady passed us. In passing, she wanted to stop and see my pretty little sister. We thought nothing of it. We stopped, and the lady began to admire Tammy. Tammy smiled really big at the lady. For all the world to see, were all these broken, jagged, missing front teeth and the bloody mouth. Tammy just kept smiling really big. I remember the lady gasped. She said something but hurried on past us then. I guess she had seen enough for one day, or maybe she had some pressing appointment. Well, it was not that big of a deal. We went on and enjoyed our vanilla malt, and not much more was said about any of it at Paul's or at home.

Tammy was always quiet and kind of reserved. Jan was just the opposite. Very friendly and outgoing, of course, and very curious. She was into everything in the house. Loved to prowl and mess with things. I had an old desk in the house that I would do my homework on along with my other big financial projects. I had bought a little bottle of gold-colored ink with a special pin you dipped into it and wrote with. It was nearly new; I had barely used it. The ink of this color had to be used sparingly, and so I did. One evening I opened the drawer to find the bottle of ink nearly empty and the contents of the drawer covered with the ink. I immediately knew who the culprit was in this case. Later that week, I bought a hasp and padlock for the drawer. I would be safe until Jan learned how to pick locks! I don't guess that she ever learned this trade, but it would not have surprised me to learn that she was a master at it.

I read quite a bit, but otherwise, if I was not having to help with Jan and Tammy, I would be outside running with my buddies. We mostly terrorized the neighborhood and spent our time in Bunning Park. Sometimes we would go on day hikes up north of town into the foothills or over toward the RS Mountain, which is now called College Hill. It was called the RS Mountain because it had the big RS standing for Rock Springs painted on the hill. Most of the towns in Wyoming would do this on nearby hills around town. Then they would hold ceremonies in that area during high school football games. Kind of like pep rallies, I guess it would be called nowadays. Back then, there was nothing up on top of the RS Mountain. We would go hiking or rabbit-hunting up there. There were some pretty interesting rock formations that are probably gone now. One of the formations was like a big room with thick walls, without a roof on it. There were even ledges inside to set on. Now there is a junior college, hospital, and all kinds of homes and offices on the hill. Near the bottom of the RS Mountain, there were Killpecker and Bitter Creeks. They were mostly muddy creeks, at least until you went a little further north. Then Killpecker Creek turned into pretty nice clear water. Bitter Creek was always muddy, as I recall. We would make little campfires and open cans of pork and beans and warm them over the fire for lunch. Spent lots of time looking for lizards at horny toes. Some of the guys liked to shoot at gophers with their BB guns. We were within a mile or two of Rock Springs, but you would never know it. It seemed like we were out far into the wilderness. Nothing or nobody was around. Any moment you almost expected some wild Indians to come riding over a ridge and all of us having to fight for our lives with our pocketknives and BB guns.

We were really just a typical bunch of boys in that time period. Not bad guys, but lots of room for improvement. Some of the families came and went. But mostly, the neighborhood remained the same. The Hobert family moved on to Elias Avenue, further up the street from our home, when I was probably around twelve. They were a large family that had moved from Utah and were sort of Mormons. By that, I mean they were really not strict Mormons, some people called them Jack Mormons. They had kids younger than me to clear up to Chuckie's age and older. Billy was just a bit younger than me, and we became friends. The father ran a gas station, and in later years, the family really suffered lots of tragedies and trouble. One of the boys that was Chuckie's age died prowling around in an abandoned coal mine north of Rock Springs, several of them ended up unwed mothers in the state penitentiary, and Billy died of a drug overdose when we were about seventeen or so, as I understand. I had lost touch with him as we went on separate paths in life, and I had not seen him for several years.

Marijuana was starting to show up, but mostly it was alcohol and tobacco. Guys in Chuckie's age group were into this stuff and chasing girls and fast cars. I and my buddies were just into being kind of little wild explorers and adventures.

The family was doing pretty good with dad and Chuckie both working steady in the coal mines. We still had our wild family times, however. Holidays like Christmas and Thanksgiving were usually a mix of peace and festivities as well as knock-down-drag-out fights and drunken rowdiness. The holidays were something to look forward to as well as to dread.

Chuckie was spending most of his money buying really nice cars. He drove like a madman and wrecked them all. He had lots of traffic tickets, expensive insurance, nearly killed himself, and was in the hospital several times with injuries from the collisions. I would not ride with him if I didn't have to. He drank a lot, and my dad would lecture him at the kitchen table for hours about his wayward ways. Chuckie would get bored with it all and begin to fall asleep. This would make dad really mad, and he would be talking louder and even yelling. Then he would even reach over to swat Chuckie once in a while on the head. This would go on and on but never really did any good at all. In fact, I am pretty sure that my dad was just jealous of Chuckie, going out and being wilder than he was.

One time during one of these lectures, dad even had a .22 pistol out. Dad got really mad at Chuckie, and Chuckie jumped out of the chair and bolted from the house. He ran out the door into the dark of night. He took off down the street, running like a banshee around Bunning Park. Dad stood at the open backdoor and emptied the pistol on him. He never touched him or apparently anything else of importance, for there were no complaints of property damage, dead bodies, or that sort of thing. Chuckie came back home, and the next day everything was all back to normal.

By the sixth grade, I was getting pretty bored with school. The teachers were all women and catered to their favorites, usually girls. Some of the subjects were pretty uninteresting. A lot of time was wasted, you were made to do a lot of silly things that most guys did not like at all. I just quit going to school lots of the time. Oh, I went enough to keep my grades up and pass on to higher grades, but I was probably only there about half the time. This went on through my junior and senior high years. I liked school better after the sixth grade. Loved civics and history, hated PE—they spent most of the time trying to make you into a gymnast. The school would be after you all right, but as long as you made up your work and weren't a troublemaker, they pretty much ignored you. Mom and dad would get after me some, but as long as I helped out around the house and kept out of major trouble otherwise and wasn't being held back in my grades, they did not bother me too much either.

You could say that from the sixth grade through high school graduation that I completed school in half the time over the course of those years. I did my work, read a lot, helped out around the house with my younger sisters, and stayed busy. During high school years, among other things, I would spend a lot of time out rabbit- and coyote-hunting. Spent a lot of time fishing at the Flaming Gorge. I used to joke with people that if they needed me, they could contact me at my office at the Flaming Gorge. I had a good friend about a year or so younger than me in high school, Steve, that would get really mad when I said that to him. His parents made him go to school all the time. And he did not like it that I did not have to go. He would get really irritated and ask me how I could miss so much school and why didn't I go, and on and on he would try to grill me. I would just make him angrier by laughing at him and joking about it. Besides the crack about my office, I would tell him that I did not need to go because my grades were so good, that I had important fishing to do, and on and on until he would become furious. Then he would go off to school, and I would head out with a rifle or fishing pole. The truth was, he loved to hunt and fish. He didn't give a lick about school either and was just mad because he could not go with me. In truth, my grades were generally pretty good and certainly all passing (except for some gym classes). I would go back to school for a few days, take whatever tests I needed to take, and score higher grades than kids that were there all the time. This would upset some of those kids and make them none too happy about the whole matter. I would just make it worse by saying stuff to them like, "I can't help it if I'm smart and you're dumb." I would never make class president doing that to them, oh well, who would want a dumb job like that anyway. Not me!

One day when I was about eleven, I found grandma sitting at the kitchen table with some church literature. She was looking through it, and it drew my attention. Out of curiosity, I asked her where she got it. She began to tell me that a man had just come to the door. A man by the name of Pastor Swink. He was from the little Assemblies of God church on A Street that we went to years ago. He was by himself and just happened to be going door to door in the neighborhood, talking to folks, passing out literature, and inviting them to church if they didn't go somewhere already. She thumbed through the literature and put it aside. I picked it up and began to look at it. For reasons I could not explain, then I was drawn to this literature and really curious about this man that came to the door. I guess I was amazed that a preacher, a complete stranger, would go out of his way and spend his time to stop at our house and show any concern for us or people in the neighborhood. To my knowledge, not many people in the neighborhood went to church except for the Catholics, and most of them went to the big church nearby quite regularly.

I quizzed grandma some more about the visit, but she could add few other details. Said he was an older man, dressed in a suit like a preacher would be and that he was very nice. Not much more was said about it, but it weighed heavy on my mind through the week.

I determined that I was going to go to this man's church and see what was going on. If he went out of his way and came to our neighborhood to invite us to his church and to inquire how we were, then I was going to go see why he cared enough to do this. Now, I fully realize that it was the drawing power of the Holy Spirit, using this pastor's efforts and the prayers of Christians, to win the spiritually lost. I had not even seen the man at our home, had very little other information, but I was inexplicably drawn to that little church.

I got out my old gray-colored wool suit, thin tie, and dress shoes that I seldom wore. Nobody else in the family had any interest in going with me, even though they were a little curious why I was doing this. I was determined to get cleaned up on a Saturday night and show up that next Sunday morning for church.

That Sunday morning, while everybody slept in, I was up and made breakfast for myself. Got dressed and left the house on foot. It was late fall or early winter, I think, and kind of cool. It was several miles' walk from our house to the church. Up to the A Street over-pass, over it, and then a way further to what then seemed like a very large two-story brick building with a white wooden cross high above the double front doors. A large black and white sign hung on the side of the building. It named the services and the times to be held. Near the bottom of the sign, it named the pastor. I walked up the flight of concrete steps to the front doors of the building. Then I recalled one summer day when we lived on A Street, having snuck out of the yard by myself. It was to this very place that I came. Just a little boy sitting on the steps of the church. It was a weekday, but there was some special meeting going on inside in the middle of the day. I remember tugging at the heavy door and pulling it ajar. Curious as to what was going on inside. I could hear lots of people singing. They sounded pretty happy. I couldn't see much peeking through the slight gap in the door. The door became too heavy, and I let it close. I sat on the steps a while longer and then went home before I was found AWOL by mom. Yes, I remember being on these steps before. But now I was going inside, walked into the vestibule where there was another set of doors in front of me. Opened these doors and was welcomed in by men in suits. There were quite a few people seated inside, and the service seemed to have just started. I was seated some-where near the back. I don't remember a lot about what happened that Sunday morning, but at least I saw this man Pastor Swink. He was on a stage at the front of the sanctuary with some other men in suits. He was standing behind a big wooden pulpit at the time while the other men were seated. He was a dignified-looking older man, probably in his late 40s or early 50s. Tall and kind of balding. He had a wife and two teenage daughters, both older than me and very pretty. Most people paid no attention to me, not that I expected them to. Others were kindly and friendly. I was invited back, and so I returned. They explained to me that I had to come a bit earlier, however, so that I could attend Sunday school. The classes were held prior to the church service, and they were held in the basement of the building for young folks and children.

I returned the next Sunday, and I arrived in time for Sunday school. The classes as described were held in the basement of the building. Since I was eleven and nearing twelve, I was placed into a youth group class of teenagers. I was younger than most of the kids in that class, and we were seated on metal chairs in the open area of the basement. There were other rooms all around us that contained the parsonage and other classrooms.

The class was taught by a young, recently married man that was probably in his early 20s that wore thick dark-rimmed glasses. He was nice enough, I guess, but seemed to cater to the older boys in the class and seemed to me that he wanted to be viewed as cool and accepted by all of them. The pastor's daughters and some other girls were in the class. It seemed to be a big flirt session where the guys were all trying to get the attention of the pastor's daughters. The teacher worked to keep everybody on track, and soon everybody had Bibles and books and was attempting to study and discuss these materials.

I was given a spare loner black-colored King James Version Bible. Pretty soon, the teacher began calling out Scripture verses to be looked up and read, and most of the kids were thumbing through the Bibles and finding and reading the verses. I had not a clue how to find the scriptures. I didn't know the Book of Job or Revelation. If only somebody would give me a page number! I didn't understand it. There were page numbers, but nobody used them. They just kept calling out books of the Bible and chapters and verses. It seemed that most of the kids were finding these without much difficulty. I felt somewhat embarrassed as I thumbed through the Bible, trying to find some clue to what was going on. We were sitting in a large circle in clear view of one another, and I am sure people must have noticed my confusion. But no one came to my aid. I was mostly ignored by the group and treated as the odd man out, I guess it would be a pretty accurate description at that point. Things didn't change much even later with that group either in regards to my relationship with them.

Most of the class was pretty much a big clique. The main endeavor of the boys and girls was to be neat and cool. It seemed to me. No one showed much interest in me or gave me the time of day in that class, including the teacher. I was not one to seek or expect attention from people, but this group, well, I could not remember meeting or being around people this detached or cold since viewing a body at a mortuary a few years back. And I do not mean other people that were there to view the body. I mean, the deceased!

I was more than relieved when the class came to a conclusion. I was happy to return then to the vaguely familiar upstairs sanctuary and be seated among people that were mostly friendly and welcoming. I was determined to get a Bible and learn how to use the thing. Obviously, there had to be some secret code or way unknown to me at the time to find your way around in this sacred book. Wow. Who would have thought! The church offered inexpensive King James Version Bibles for fifty cents. I made sure I had fifty cents and bought my own Bible either that Sunday or the next. I was determined to learn how to find my way around the book in that, for some strange reason, nobody used the page numbers! I still have that Bible, these many years later, though it is quite worn and tattered. The Bible came with a goldish brown colored paper cover. It had an inexpensive black hardcover underneath this. The paper cover to this Bible disappeared many years ago. The Bible was from the American Bible Society of New York. My mother had very beautiful cursive handwriting. Inside of my Bible, front and back, she had written in blue ink my full name, address, and our telephone number. She had written the date that is still clearly visible, "February 12, 1967."

I continued to attend the youth class. It continued to be mostly unwelcoming, but I found it interesting and helpful to attend. I now had my own Bible and was getting some idea of how to find scriptures in it. But I really enjoyed the services upstairs after Sunday school. Much of the service was still a mystery to me, but I liked the singing and the preaching, and some of the older people were really nice and friendly.

I clearly had my own Bible now and had been packing it with me for several weeks. This I thought was obvious to anyone. But one Sunday morning in the main service, the youth Sunday school teacher got up to the pulpit and began telling the congregation that someone had lost their sword. "Sword" was a word that some Christians would use for their Bible, based on some scripture. He was giving his little spiel and then waved one of these Bibles around, similar to the one that I had just purchased a few weeks ago. Then to my surprise and horror, he called out my name as being the one that had lost my sword. I hadn't lost my sword, I had it right here in my hands. I felt a little indignant about this oversight. I sort of started to object about it, to explain, no, I had my Bible. Kind of wished that they would have just noticed that I had a Bible, but their intentions were good. So, I placed my Bible on the pew. I left the pew and walked up to the pulpit, and gratefully received the Bible that they presented to me. I was a little more than embarrassed to get called out in front of everybody like that. But I did not want to hurt their feelings, and I said no more about it. I made sure that no one noticed that I now had two Bibles, or at least I did my best to accomplish this. I still have this Bible many years later too. I used it some, but it was basically a spare Bible. It still has the goldish brown paper cover on it. Inside they had inscribed in red-colored ink, "To: Kenneth Weimer. Presented to you with love that you may use it to glorify God. Your Sunday school teacher Donnie. Presented by: First Assembly of God Sunday School." At some time, I cut out a picture from a calendar that I liked of a boy with his big dog. That picture is still inside of that Bible

I continued to attend church and Sunday school regularly. Every Sunday, unless we were going somewhere. I would follow the same routine. Dress in my old suit after breakfast and take off on foot for church with my Bible. One Sunday a few weeks later, however, I was shocked when Pastor Swink was preaching about how a person had to hate their parents and family in order to follow Jesus. I could not believe what I was hearing. I thought Jesus wanted you to love everybody. And why should I hate my parents? My dad could be a real jerk and problem, but I would never hate him. Mom I loved dearly and surely could never hate her, no matter what. I looked about, expecting other people to be shocked and getting up to leave the congregation. But there was no surprise or shock, no protests at all on the part of anyone. I could not understand this. I thought Pastor Swink had to be confused. He was not a hateful man. I was having a really hard time with this information. I was wanting to get up and walk out and stay away from such a place, but I was riveted to my seat, fortunately. Had I got up and left, who knows what would have happened. What path my life might have taken, not good. I am sure of that. The scripture the pastor was speaking on that morning was found in Luke, chapter 14, verse 26. "If any man come to me, and hate not his father, and mother, and wife, and children, and brethren, and sisters, yea, and his own life also, he cannot be my disciple."

As I said, fortunately, I stayed for the service and came to learn that Jesus does not want us to hate anyone. But that he does require for us to lay everything down and put God first and foremost in everything. As the scripture clearly says, "seek ye first the kingdom of God and His righteousness, and all these things will be added unto you." Matthew 6:33, or for those who might be confused as I was about finding scriptures in the Bible, that can be found on page 6 of the New Testament!

You don't find perfect people at a church, at least not if they are honest about it and true Christians. Oh, to be sure, you will find young people and others like I encountered in that youth Sunday school class. But I am sure that if you attend a Bible-preaching, Bible-believing church and give them a chance, don't get up and walk out like I was tempted to do that Sunday morning when I was confused and didn't understand, whatever the denomination may or may not be, you will find people that love God and love other people as well. People that are helpful, kind, and loving. You'll find some good friends there—of all ages. People that have been through it all, that can understand trouble and be a real help and support. Folks that are fighting similar battles as you may be, or they have been there before. Folks with plenty of trouble of their own sometimes but still willing to lend a hand and get involved. Still willing to rejoice with those that rejoice and mourn with those that mourn. Give it a try if you are not a Christian—living the Christian life. Don't be timid, and don't throw in the towel like I nearly did. Come on back. If you have got discouraged, for whatever reason, and left a good church. Or maybe not even so good of a church. Go on back somewhere where they really believe the Word of God—the Bible. Where they teach it, preach it, practice, and live it.

Pick up that Bible and begin to read and study it again, or maybe for the first time. Start with the Book of John in the New Testament if it has been a while or never before. Pray and talk to God. He loves us, and He cares. He cares so much that He did not even spare His own son, Jesus. John chapter 3 verse 16 tells us so. God does not want any of us to perish. He tells us further in His Word that if we will draw nigh or near to Him, He will draw near to us. If you've never made Jesus your Lord and Master, you should. Your life will become blessed and good beyond your hopes or dreams. You'll be saved from terrible hell, which is a real place. Ask Jesus to come into your life and change you. Tell Him you are sorry for all your sin and shame. Proclaim with your voice that Jesus is your Lord. That you believe that He is God's son and that God raised Him from the dead. That there is no other way into heaven than through the provision of Jesus. Receive Him and let Him help you to live like never before. You will be glad of it in this life and even more so for your eternity.

I still had lots to learn and did not understand much of what went on. After only a few weeks, Pastor Swink told me about a group of boys that met on Saturday nights at the church. They wore uniforms or parts of uniforms if they had them. If not, it was okay. The group was called the Royal Rangers, and there was a big emphasis on spiritual matters. There was marching and drilling, lessons from a book, prayer and Scripture reading, sometimes basketball and games to be played, even baseball sometimes. There would be hikes and camping trips with boys my own age. That all sounded good, that was for me!

So, in addition to Sunday school and church. I began attending the Royal Rangers Saturday nights and other activities held with that group too. Most of the men that were leaders wore full uniforms or most parts of the uniform. Pastor Swink was the main commander of the group. It was great fun, and I made lots of friends. Boys were my own age. Some younger, some older, primarily between the ages of about ten and maybe thirteen. The uniforms had to be purchased by yourself. You could buy them in parts, and they were not overly expensive, but still, I didn't have money for that, or at least it was going to take me some time to buy the uniform and parts and pieces. First, I paid for my Royal Rangers Pioneer Handbook. It may have been a dollar; it was used but in very good shape. It had belonged to some other boy. So they placed a sticker over the part of the book inside that said, "This book belongs to," and they wrote on the sticker in blue pen, "This book belongs to Kenneth Weimer." Ken or Kenny would have been okay with me, but that is what they put just as they had in my Bible.

I still have that handbook today. It is more worn than it was when I bought it, of course, but still in good shape. It was a great book and highly interesting. It taught you how to advance and get pins and awards for your uniform. Full of good information about Jesus and God in spiritual matters. It covered ranks, first aid, your church, marching in uniforms, personal care, physical fitness, camping, and nature. I mean, this book to an eleven- or twelve-year-old boy was a treasure trove of ninety-six pages. The cover itself was mesmerizing. The front with a young boy in pioneer dress and an old musket rifle. Mountain scenes and an eagle soaring. The back cover with an old fort with an old pioneer wagon and forest scene. Not to mention a bear cub underneath the hollow of a tree. What a great book! I can still look at it and read it today and enjoy. This book was for boys, ages nine, ten, and eleven, and they had more advanced books for the older boys. I next bought a necktie, and that is about as far as I got with the uniform. We had some great times in the Royal Rangers. True to Rock Springs, the group was full of all kinds of guys and different races. It was mostly white guys, but there were the Collins brothers and some other black kids, the Mora brothers that were Spanish, and some other Spanish kids. We mostly got along great, and I had some great friends out of this group.

During the summer, we went on an overnight camping trip. Tents, campfires, hot dogs and marshmallows, ghost stories around the campfire from one of the adult leaders. Prayer and Bible study. Good talks and visits with the leaders and other guys. There were nature studies in the field and then the requirement that each boy build a campfire with two matches at the most. Most of us, not having had much practice with campfires or matches, did not succeed at this effort on this trip.

We had gone down into northern Utah, around the Sheep Creek area. I had never been there before. It was a beautiful area. Forested with mountains, lakes, and beautiful scenery. I was riding along in the car with Pastor Swink and some of the other boys, there were several carloads of us, and I remember Pastor Swink kept marveling at how you could see the layers in the mountains from the ancient flood in Noah's day. He kept pointing this out to us and all the other beauties of God's creation. It was beautiful weather and a great time. It sure ended too soon.

Before the trip was over, we took a day to hike. It was not that long of a hike, but the funny part about it was that the pastor, who was quite fair-complexioned, couldn't take much sun. Here he was in his uniform with this terrible-looking white greasy stuff all over his face. I never saw anybody with that stuff on their face to go out in the sun. He was pretty serious about it then, and, being the nice guy that he was, none of us wanted to laugh out loud about it, but it was hard to keep from laughing. Quite a sight, it was. He led us on our hike, greasy face and all.

It was some months later when Pastor Swink announced he would be leaving and a new pastor would be coming. I hated to see him go. That was pretty much the end of the Royal Rangers group. The new pastor came, and some people came and went from the church. The new pastor was younger, a Southerner. He had a wife and a young child. Pastor Phillips. He was a great guy, there were no more Royal Rangers, as I said, but he was big on youth group (Christ Ambassadors) aside from Sunday school and did a lot of stuff with the young people. Like in the winter, he would load us up in his old battered green station wagon and drive south of town onto Aspen Mountain in an area known as Three Patches. There were lots of snow, and we would spend the day sledding and playing in the snow.

I had to become pretty good friends with the Sonny and Tommy brothers of about one year apart in age. We had met in the Royal

Rangers, and our friendship continued on after its demise. They were a poor Spanish family that lived on the southeast side of Rock Springs. Their mother was a heavyset overbearing woman, friendly, but could be awful annoying. There were six boys in this family, with Tommy being the oldest and about my age. Tommy was a fat kid and the only one like that in his family except for his mother. They lived in an old white house that they rented. The father was seldom seen. He worked and drank. Their mother and the children came to church, but not their father. She wouldn't let Tommy and Sonny come to my house, but she was glad to have me come visit them. I would ride my bike down to their house, and we would enjoy each other's company for the afternoon.

I would like to say, with all of this light, learning, and good and godly influence, that I had a conversion experience early on like Paul had or something like that. Of course, he was struck blind, and I wouldn't want that. But while I had good friends like Sonny and Tommy that were good Christian kids and I was becoming more acquainted and friends with kids in the youth group my age and older, I still could not say that I had made a commitment to Christ for sure. I was close, but yet far away, spiritually speaking.

I attended Sunday school and church almost without fail. If I was in town. The youth group met usually on Sunday nights, and I usually went to that too, but I was still running with kids in the neighborhood, and without exception, most of them were a rough bunch—now teenage boys with raging hormones and curiosity. So, I tried to be friends with them and take part in their activities. I was also trying to live in the other world as well. Something had to go. Something had to change. Surely if I kept on this way at some point, I felt sure I would head off in the wrong direction and end up more like Chuckie, my older brother, and/or my dad, or the guys I was friends with than I would ever want to be.

I was probably about twelve or thirteen, and I cannot tell you the specific date, but I came to realize that a decision had to be made. Jesus said you cannot serve two masters, and that was true for sure in my life. I couldn't ride the fence and try to walk two separate lifestyles. Not that I expected that I would be perfect, not make mistakes, or not have troubles. I was either going to try to be a disciple for Christ and live a life that would please Him and would be right or give up on that because there is no halfway. I realized that at my young age. I felt the conviction of the Holy Spirit for sin in my life. I sensed the danger ahead of not doing something about it, and that pretty quickly. The Bible says that today is the day of salvation. There is no guarantee that we will be around to take care of it tomorrow. Or that the Holy Spirit can woo us to make the right decision at another time. There are stories in the Bible as well as plenty of present-day examples of people that ignore God speaking to them. Their hearts become hard, and pretty soon, the opportunity is gone and never to be had again. This was not for me.

Here I was really with a pretty good life in many aspects, living in Wyoming. But here I was, lost in Wyoming. Spiritually lost with no hope. Even at this young age, things were sure not to get better if I ignored my present condition and plight.

It did not have to occur in the church building, but it did. Without further delay. I knelt down at an altar during a service. I cried out to the Lord, confessed my sin as best I knew, confessed that Jesus is God's son, and I believed it. Asked Him to forgive me and cleanse me of all sin. To change me and help me to walk and live in a way pleasing to Him. A huge burden was lifted from me. I had peace and a change of heart. I was no longer lost in Wyoming but found! I had been spiritually blind, but now I saw. It was amazing—undeserved grace.

I had a greater longing to pray and seek the Lord, to read the Bible, to be at church. Time spent with my old neighborhood buddies grew less and less, not because we didn't like one another, but it was like driving down a highway. Pretty soon, you see a sign that says, "Routes divide ahead." A bit down the road, the roads separate in different directions. That is how it was. I and my old buddies now had different interests. They were going off in one direction, and I, the other I, definitely now enjoyed the company of Christian teenagers from the church and could be found with them. I loved the smell of beer still, especially on a hot day. But there was no more of that for me. It was not perfection, and still isn't in old Kenny Weimer, but what happened that day brought about a radical change that I never could have made on my own. It took me from a path, which would have eventually led to trouble, failure, darkness, and death.

To a life and a path completely opposite of that. I could have tried to be good, it made improvements, but this was something completely different. Jesus told Nicodemus in the Bible that he had to be born again. Nicodemus was a very religious man when he was told that by Jesus. But Nicodemus still had to be spiritually born again—radically changed and not just on his own. Like trying to be good or improve some bad habits. It would never work. That is not what Jesus was talking about. But being born again is what happened to me and must happen to each and every one of us if we want to live that abundant worthwhile life and make heaven our home someday. Certainly, I wanted heaven someday. For certain, I did not want to end up in hell. Read the Bible and see what it says about hell and the lake of fire. You will not want to go there either. It is a terrible place of torment, loneliness, and suffering forever! I did not want that. But that was not the main reason I became born-again. At the time, the main reason seemed to me to be that I didn't want to throw my life away and I was seeing plenty of examples of that all around me. Then there were plenty of good examples of Christian people of all ages living a great life, an abundant life. That was for me! That is what Jesus promised. Life, not death, life, and more abundantly. Not to be lost in Wyoming or any other location but found—spiritually found and saved because you and I choose to be. It can only happen if we choose to and accept it. *The great gift of salvation that is to whosoever will... I was whosoever, and you are too! No longer Lost in Wyoming was I but found!*

1. Kenny and Dad at home on A St. about 1959.

2. Kenny and Grandpa Joe in front yard on A St. about 1956.
The Rock Springs Junior High buliding appears in the back ground. The
rod iron fence was installed by Grandpa and is still in fine shape today.

3. Dad, Mom, Chuckie and Kenny on an Easter
Sunday after church on A St. about 1958

4. Grandpa Joe with his bull moose and Dad,
Chuckie and Kenny on A St. about 1957

5. Ken as a young Rock Springs patrolman,
ending a graveyard shift in 1977.

6. Grandpa Hamilton and Ken at Reliance, WY, north of Rock Springs
with the coverted bear skin hide-robe given to him by Grandpa.

7. Ken and Steve Reichel at elk-deer camp in
the Wasatch Forest, WY about 1978

8. Grandma Frances cooking at home on Elias Ave. about 1980.

9. Wedding Day. July 17, 1982.

BOOK 2

My good friends, Tommy and Sonny, had moved with their family to Green River after our first year in junior high, where their father was employed in the trona mines. I didn't get to see them very often after that because they didn't come to Rock Springs much and I was too young to drive. But I was making good friends with Leonard and Joe, brothers in a large Spanish family of probably about ten kids at least. Their father was a coal miner. He worked in the same mines that my dad and brother worked in. The mines were called Rainbow Coal, or otherwise known as The Quealy mines as they were located in the old mining camp at Quealy, Wyoming.

The large family of Leonard and Joe lived in a very old green-colored stucco house located on the south side of town. There were kids that were older than Chuckie and as young as Jan and Tammy, my younger sisters. Leonard and Joe were two or three years older than me and attended the church and the Christ Ambassadors youth group known as CA. Once in a while, their younger sister and her younger brother would come to church too, but usually, it was Leonard known as Lenny and Joe that were at church or youth group. So as a little time went on, we began to know each other and became better buddies. They were both athletic and in high school, and I was still in junior high and did not really take part in sports. I had played some flag football in grade school, but that was about it. Didn't really want to invest the time in school sports. I had too many other irons in the fire, places to go, and people to see!

I was still about fourteen years old, and the pastor at the church, Pastor Phillips, impressed upon me and Joe how we both needed to be baptized in water. This seemed like a good idea and was in keeping with the Scripture as I came to understand. One afternoon on the weekend, the baptistery at the front of the church behind the pulpit was filled with cold water from a garden hose, and we gathered in a small ceremony to be baptized by the pastor. My mom felt that it was very important that she and dad be there, so they showed up with my sisters, who were still quite young. Nobody showed up from Joe's family. I am not sure how much effort he made to have them there, but they were kind of a rough bunch of people, and even though the family had attended the church earlier, they didn't have too much interest in it now. Joe was baptized first, and then I was next. Then the pastor led us in a song that I had never sung before. It was, "I have decided to follow Jesus, no turning back, no turning back." It was a good service, but pretty quiet and unassuming.

One Sunday evening service, there was this middle-aged couple that came to church, that had come from Texas. She was to sing a special before the pastor spoke, and so up on the platform she went at the appropriate time, and she sang a very nice song. She had a good voice, and the song was a blessing to the service. She was wearing a big fluffy dress, and her husband was seated on one of the front seats in the church. There was a step off the platform that was not stationary and would often move a bit when used much. This poor lady came off the platform and stepped on the outer edge of the step, which caused it to roll over and forward. This threw her head over tea kettle onto the floor in front of everyone. The big fluffy dress went up over her head, and she rolled around on the floor, trying to get control of herself. Everyone was so shocked that we just sat fixated for long seconds watching the poor singer in her despair.

Finally, her husband gained his thoughts and jumped up, going to her aid. After a few seconds, he was able to get her dress back down and get her on her feet. She was red-faced and terribly humiliated. She was clearly not happy or taking lightly this revolting development. Well, that's part of taking up your cross, I suppose. It was funny all in all, but you didn't dare laugh at the time. The pastor finally fixed the step later that week.

Then, being Pentecostal, the pastor impressed on us the importance of being baptized by the Holy Spirit, so this was to be next in our spiritual lives. However, it was actually later when I was baptized in the Holy Spirit. I was sixteen or maybe seventeen. The exact time I couldn't say but the experience I could not forget. It was in an evening service at the Rock Springs church. I was seeking the infilling of the spirit at the front altar platform on the east side of the pulpit. As I was kneeling and praying with upraised arms, the spirit fell after only a short time. I was baptized in the Holy Spirit that night with the physical evidence of speaking in tongues that were certainly unknown to me. I could certainly tell the difference. More joy and peace. More power and boldness to preach and testify. No one was praying with me when this occurred, but people were gathered around the altars praying at the conclusion of the service. I think I was the only one filled that night, as far as I know.

Not only I could not play instruments, but I was not any great singer either. Lenny and Joe could both sing quite well and were in choir at high school as well as sports activities. But unfortunately, it was not too long after this that Pastor Phillips left, and the youth group kind of faded away. A little time passed, and a new pastor and his spouse showed up. They were a young couple from California and just out of Bible school. Pastor Mackenzie and his wife. We commonly called the pastor brother rather than reverend or pastor. This used the less formal title but showed respect for the position and/or age. Back then, you would also use "brother" or "sister" in front of adults' names at church and usually in conjunction with their last name—not their first name. No way did you just go address an adult by their first name.

This young couple had a tough job ahead of them. For some reason, quite a few people had quit coming to church, and the youth group continued to fade. The young pastors had to live in the basement parsonage, which was somewhat dreary and isolated. The young pastor even had to take up a job working at a grocery store, which was not all that uncommon for a pastor of a small church in those days. The downstairs had been the parsonage area for pastors since the church was built. But still, it was not much of a good situation for a young couple from an upbeat area in California. I never once heard them complain. They worked hard to accomplish a lot of good for the church. Our small group of teens, mostly I and brothers Leonard and Joe, would keep them up late on Sunday nights after services, playing table tennis in the basement. The pastor had a little blue foreign-made car, and he would drive many of the kids and older people to and from the church as well every week. Often multiple trips were needed to accomplish this feat.

The Mackenzie's and as many young people as we could stuff into the little Volkswagen would take off on Friday nights once a month for a church within what we called the section. This was usually somewhere within one hundred miles or so of Rock Springs. Other churches in that section would show up also, and we would have what was called a fellowship meeting for the night. There would be singing, special songs or music presented, preaching and visiting, and a big dinner. These were fun times and times of good spiritual growth for people. Good social-fellowship times that people seemed to be just too busy for once the 1980s arrived.

On occasion, we would go to the Indian reservation near Lander, Wyoming, and have the fellowship meeting at the little church there. The Indian folks were very friendly, and some of the young girls were too friendly. Our group of teen boys from Rock Springs was like fresh meat at a barbecue! We had to hang together and fight them off. One time we had to climb some trees to get away from them. Fortunately, by about 10 p.m. or so, we would leave and head home. On some of the drives back home, we would encounter terrible blizzards or storms. It would be a long, slow drive to get home, sometimes not arriving till 2, 3, or 4 a.m. There were some white knuckles driving and riding along on some of those trips.

Despite the Mackenzie's' efforts, the church continued to dwindle, and pretty soon, we were having no more youth group meetings, and there were just handfuls of people in the services. About this same time, the Pacheco brothers began straying away from church. I guess Joe was like a lot of other people and soon forgot about not turning back on Jesus, like we had just sung about some months before, during our baptism. I would ride my bike up to Leonard and Joe's little green-colored house to see them often, and we still did some stuff together. But clearly, we were growing apart as they headed off in different directions, and a good deal of their directions were not good ones. I tried to encourage them to come to church, and they would show up some. But increasingly, they were seen less and less at church. This is not to brag on myself that I stuck with it. There were times early on that I could have easily walked away too.

One time when I was at Leonard and Joe's house, Joe and I were playing rock baseball in the field near his home. We could only come up with a wooden bat. He and I would take turns pitching rocks while the other would bat. On one of my turns at pitching, Joe made a great hit. I turned to watch the rock go sailing by, and it is a good thing that I did. Instead of the rock sailing by, it hit me right in the back of the head. I saw black for a few minutes but never passed out. I was a little woozy and had blood all over the back of my old green army jacket. We went into Joe's house and worked for a few minutes on my wound until we got the bleeding stopped. I wasn't too worried about it, but Joe was pretty rattled. He hadn't been in church for a while, and he promised me he would be there on Sunday. I guess he felt pretty bad about it, though it was only an accident—a dumb one, though there aren't too many really intelligent accidents that probably occur, come to think about it!

After a while, I went home, and I was going to be really nonchalant about my injury. I didn't want mom to see it or make a big deal of it. I figured I would wash up and put some iodine on it and be okay. I forgot about the blood on the back of my jacket, apparently, there was a good amount of. I got home and was telling mom about visiting at Leonard and Joe's house, and she was asking me about what we had done. I started to walk into my room, and mom spotted the blood. Then there was the devil to pay. She wanted some information and explanations. I tried to be low-key, but there was none of that to be had. I had a pretty good gash in the back of my head. It was off to the emergency room, where I had to see Doctor Preach. He thought it was kind of funny. Mom did not! I was aggravated to be put through this and was mad at myself for forgetting about the bloody jacket. It was shaving of the wound, stitches, and a tetanus shot. A lot of work and torment that just a little iodine would have cured!

Well, good to his word, Joe showed up that Sunday at church. I guess he thought that would make me feel better about it, I was glad to see him at church, otherwise, I did not need any placating or apologies. Maybe he just wanted to make sure that I was still all in one piece, and maybe he just felt a little guilty, which he shouldn't have over the injury but maybe should have about the way he was living at the time.

Pastor Mackenzie asked me if I would like to be the church janitor, of course, he would pay me out of his own pocket for this work because the church had no budget for it. I agreed to do it. I think I worked for a dollar and a fifty an hour, which was not too bad. I would usually show up every Saturday afternoon and clean the church and all of the Sunday school rooms. It was quite a bit of work and would take me at least three or four hours of steady-going.

I was not working too much for the Harveys anymore. I had started doing weekly yard work in the summer for my aunt's friends that owned the Rogan mortuary, the Opie family. The family really consisted of only Mr. and Mrs. Opie at this time. Their son, Jerry, was now in the state penitentiary for the murder I described earlier. They lived in a big white house in a nice neighborhood on the south side of town. They had a very nice home. It was full of expensive furnishings, including a grand piano. Mrs. Opie was a difficult person. She was very unhappy and lived to complain. She obviously had been very hurt with the tragedy of her son, and no doubt she had much to complain about. She smoked a lot and had dentures that were ill-fitting. My dad and aunt swore that she took the dentures from a cadaver at the funeral home. Probably not true, but it sure made me wonder about it. She was pale as a ghost with jet, black-colored hair. She was thin as a rail. She would interrupt me a lot and take up a good deal of my time while I was trying to take care of their yard. She would always have something she wanted me to give attention to, and then she would chat and visit for a while before I could get back to my original task. I think she was pretty lonesome and just wanted to talk to someone. I would visit with her some, but she was not an easy person to visit with. As far as talking about religion or the Lord, she only wanted to talk about her Catholic religion and would hear nothing else. Mr. Opie was not a religious man and constantly chewed or smoked on a big cigar. He was usually in a suit and tie and wore a dress hat. He was not one to visit, and he and his wife seemed miles apart from one another. Once in a while, they would have me come down and clean up around the grounds of the mortuary too. Then I would have to go to the mortuary office and see him every week to get my check for the work I performed for them.

Usually, I would just cut the grass and do some general yard work at their home. On one occasion, she wanted me to trim all of the shrubs and bushes around the house. I just had a general sense of what needed to be done with pruning, though I never had any training or education about it. I cut most of the greenery down to the stems and the major branches. Mrs. Opie went crazy when she saw this. She was none too happy about it and called me a tree butcher. I figured that would be the end of my employment with the Opie family. But within a few weeks, she was asking me to come back and work in the yard. And what a changed and taken place, what had been a bunch of dead overgrown bushes and shrubs was now beautiful, healthy, growing greenery. Mrs. Opie could not say enough about what a great worker I was. An absolute wizard she proclaimed to all who would listen!

Another time was I working away in the yard, and she came rushing out onto the back porch yelling at the top of her voice. Over the noise of the lawnmower, I had no idea what was going on. She was packing a big white plastic garbage can with smoke rolling out of it. Once I got the mower shut down, I could hear her squawking about having thrown a lit cigarette in the garbage can, and now it was on fire. I quickly grabbed the hose and went to her aid, putting out the growing blaze in the burning, melting garbage can. Aw, you would have thought I saved the world.

There was an older retired couple that lived near the Opie's that apparently had heard of what a good worker I was, and they had me work for them for several years too. I was chopping weeds and doing general yard work around their house and some rentals they had nearby. They were really nice people. It was hard work, and I worked hard for them, but they paid me well and would always have me come in at lunchtime, no matter how dirty my clothes were. They gave me a place at their kitchen table to eat a sandwich and milk or juice she had prepared for me. Then they would let me have my privacy to enjoy lunch while they remained in the living room. Their name was Jamieson's. They were old-time Rock Springs people and were just very sweet and nice.

I was going to junior high school, the seventh and eighth grade, which was located near the Assemblies of God church and our old house on A Street. I liked having a mix of male and female teachers and having different classes and schedules. But still, I was bored with a lot of school and found it to be a great waste of time. Especially all the social stuff like dances and assemblies, and then there was a lot of goofing around with teachers and kids just doing stupid and lazy stuff. Some stuff was repeated until I was sick of it, but some of the kids needed that. I really liked history, social studies, government, health, and biology, but that was about it. I continued to miss a lot of school but always stayed pretty busy doing other stuff. It just seemed to me that the stuff they were teaching us could be done in about half the time of what it was taking.

I went to the old junior high school that had been the high school that was located on A and B streets. Just over from where I lived as a child before moving to Elias Ave. It was an old three-story stone building. It has since been torn down.

Rock Springs was beginning to experience the boom, and the town was beginning to gather more people in it than it was equipped to handle. There was an annex building that was a shop and music room over from the main building, and then the school put in a couple of modular buildings, too, to accommodate the increase.

We were required to take shop class. The teacher was an old guy from Reliance, Wyoming. He was nice enough and tried to keep us dummies from losing a finger on lathe machines, power drills, and band saws. We were required to make some wood product like a letter holder or something like that. Also, to make a metal tray out of sheet metal. I did not enjoy any of this. Probably drove the poor teacher nuts. I completed my projects, but they were mostly junk.

I think I pulled Cs in that class mostly because the teacher was a patient, kindly-type man.

The school was a tough place. Most of the teachers were a tough bunch of people, especially the men. Rough old veterans, hard drinkers, and former miners or sons of miners. They took no one under their wing, and most of them would have made good trainees for the marine corp. Back when the military was much tougher than now.

About half of the kids were criminals or from tough sordid families. Fights were common, mostly after school and off the grounds. Kids and teachers heckled one another, and the teachers would pile on a poor kid too. There were a few really nice and concerned teachers, but we knew who they were, and they were few. The principal was a big older man, Mr. Johnson. You didn't mess with him. He had been there since Columbus came over. He was usually in his office, but that was a place you did not want to be called or sent to. It was like a dark hole. Kids went there and were never heard from again—ha-ha.

This was the only junior high school, and now we were all thrown in together with kids from all over town and those bused in from local communities. There were some real examples of the human race put on display there. Teachers' pets, thieves, fighters, hecklers, good students, athletes—jocks, losers, and perverts.

There was one kid a year older than most of us that was wild. He loved to talk about sexual stuff in front of all that would listen when the teacher was out of the room. He loved to heckle the girls with sexual comments, and anytime only boys were in the room and the teacher out, he felt the need to quickly expose himself to all the guys and then laugh like mad about it. He liked to stand up and mimic that he was playing the guitar and jamming to Norman Greenbaum's song "Spirit in the Sky."

We would have these dumb assemblies where everybody had to go and sing this stupid song about white and blue, white and blue, the school colors. There were a head boy and a head girl who were pets of the teachers. The girl I don't recall, but the guy was a chubby, baby-faced kid. He thought he was hot stuff. Got to be up on the stage in the auditorium with the flag and all that stuff.

There were two assemblies that were worthwhile. A relative of Buffalo Bill, or Bill Cody, was there all decked out in full fancy cowboy attire. He told stories about himself and his family that were interesting. Then there was a man and his wife that came all decked out like cowboys. They both did tricks and speed pistol shooting up on the stage in the auditorium. Shooting balloons and small targets. They were good. Boy, have things at schools changed now?

The kid I mentioned above that was all lit up by sexual stuff, Larry, was not a bad-looking kid. In fact, he was liked by lots of the kids and teachers. The girls hated him. He saw himself as a rocker and an easy rider type of guy. He was even funny lots of times. About half of the classes I had were with him. One of the classes was gym.

For whatever reason, one day in the gym, the teacher was up in his office, which was usually where he was other than when he came down for gymnastics equipment "teaching" or when he wanted to kick kids around. Larry decided that he and I needed to have a race around the gym track. This was unusual as I hardly ever talked to him or had anything to do with him. Besides that, he was a good deal taller than me and, as I said before, older too. Neither one of us was involved in track, but we could both run.

The track was a wood track suspended above the gym floor and made an oval around the entire second story of the gym. Probably about one hundred yards in length. Apparently, Larry decided he needed to humiliate somebody that day, and he had about half the gym class gathered around to watch him run over the top of me and leave me in the dust. The guys were all laughing and snickering and really enjoying this show. I really didn't want to race the guy, but he wouldn't drop it, so we lined up for the one lap and took off when one of his minions yelled, "Go." I immediately took the lead and kept it. You should have seen all of the shocked and humiliated faces when I came in ahead of Larry. Boy, he was burned. He later tried to challenge me to a fight after school, which never materialized, but otherwise, I never had any more trouble with him.

I really didn't have trouble with other kids in school as a rule. Always thought the little pecking orders were stupid, and I avoided having "peeing" contests with them. Not many of them were open to hearing about the gospel either.

I hung out in junior high with old friend Tommy until he moved to Green River and a Chinese kid named Louie that came to Rock Springs from China via Salt Lake City. Poor Tommy was chubby and was picked on a terrible lot in junior high. He especially was targeted in the locker room in the gym.

One time the art teacher who was an Indian or Spanish-Indian mix decided that all of his classes needed to learn how to do Indian dance. He was alright as an art teacher, and Tommy and I both had class at the same time with him. When we found out that we were supposed to show up in the gym for art class in the next period and Indian dance, neither one of us intended to subject ourselves to that nonsense. We weren't dancers and sure didn't want to hop around acting like Indians at this age. Not wanting to have the art teacher be able to zing us for skipping school and thus opening up the likely possibility of getting paddled or knocked around by the principal, we made a risky decision.

Instead of going to the gym, we went to the dreaded principal's office and told them that we were not going to do Indian dance. That our church frowned on it, and we had no intention of doing it. I was nervous but poor Tommy, he was dark-skinned, being Spanish, but now he looked white as a ghost. I never saw Mr. Johnson so surprised, but we were too when he didn't start belering like usual and throw us out. He told us to sit down, and he left. A short time later, the art teacher came in, and he was hot. I don't remember all of the threats and nasty stuff he said to us, but we did not relent. He left, Mr. Johnson never appeared again, we didn't dance, and when the bell rang, we went to our next classes. I never heard another word about it and didn't suffer any retaliation from the art teacher. So, you can fight city hall and *win!* You just have to be willing to risk it and not let them move you.

On the second floor of this school, some years before, a kid had become really upset with a large female teacher. The windows were open on a warm day, and he picked her up and threw her out the window. There was a tree immediately below this window, and she fell into the tree and was not injured. I never heard what became of this kid. He probably became the mayor or something. However, there was a cement plaque at the base of the tree that displayed the name given the tree after this incident. It read, "Hero Tree." Sometimes you just have to be in the right place at the right time to win!

I hated gym. Most of the time, it involved tumbling on mats, parallel bars, uneven bars, trampolines, and the like of torture equipment. The teacher would appear for a short time to tell everybody what to do, and then you never saw him again until he would come through the locker room yelling at kids for not showering and making them strip and get a shower before putting street clothes on again. It wouldn't have been so bad if we could have played some basketball, track, baseball, and stuff, but no, it was far easier to just set up gymnastics stuff and use it most of the year.

Junior high was the seventh and eighth grade at that time, and I spent two years at the school. During this time, a new high school was built, and the junior high was moved to the now larger former high school building located on the east side of town. Junior high now included the ninth grade, so I had to go to that school for one year. This building has now been torn down too, and a new school was built on the grounds in addition to another junior high being built on the west side of town.

Lots of kids that I had gone to school with and knew were now absent from the ninth grade and later high school. They just dropped out. Unless parents made you, you could quit school after the eighth grade. Some of them left town, some got in trouble, some did nothing, and some went to work.

I didn't like school the way it was operated, but I did not intend to quit. I planned to be the first one in my family to graduate from high school. More people were moving into the area with the energy boom and the building of the Jim Bridger Power Plant east of Rock Springs. There were all kinds of people and strange faces added to town and, of course, school.

I did okay in the ninth grade. Missed as much as I could— about ⅓ to half the time. Kept grades up and got through it and onto high school. I had a speech class in the ninth grade. I was not a public speaker. I was only used to teaching small groups of kids in Sunday school, not making formal timed and graded speeches. I hated it, but it was good for me, and I did okay. I learned about having eye contact with your audience and the importance of notes—being prepared, voice control, timing, and how trying to make a presentation last ten minutes seemed like an hour.

The school swimming pool was located in the junior high building. None was being built at the new high school. In addition to the gym, I now had to go to swimming classes. I went to the first few and learned some basic swimming because I really didn't know how to swim. But then, as it got more detailed and annoying, I had had enough. I went to class but wouldn't suit up. I went into the pool area and sat there reading so I couldn't be counted as skipping class.

The swimming teacher was a little short Mormon guy that had been there for years. He constantly blinked due to the light reflecting off the pool from the large glass windows in the pool area. He was not about to let me not swim. This became an interesting battle of who could hold out between the two of us. I was respectful to him, but I just told him I had had enough, and I had no intention of suiting up or swimming, not even one more stroke in this class or any other.

Oh, he was hot. Told me that he was going to flunk me if I didn't swim. "Well," said I, "then you will just have to flunk me. I will show up and watch and be here, but that's it." We never spoke again during the year. He would just mark me present and give me looks like he wanted to drown me. But when it was all said and done, he gave me a D grade. I completed the requirement and got the credit for the class. Maybe he was just counting his lucky stars that it was calm little me in his presence instead of my big brother, with whom all of the teachers were well acquainted. In junior high and especially in high school, the teachers would really look me over when classes began that year. They would then ask as they cautiously eyed me with an inquisitive look, "Is Chuckie Weimer your brother?" Nothing more would be said about it after that. I never really had any trouble with the teachers other than I describe in some cases, such as swimming class. I just did what they required and didn't mess around or cause trouble. I generally carried A and B grades. Cs in gym and shop. I was busy and had not been to school in several weeks. The day I showed, I had a test in a civics class. Took the test, and the next day the grades were announced. One kid in the whole class had an A on the test, which was quite lengthy. All the kids shouted out, "Who is it?"

The teacher sheepishly said, "It's Weimer." Everybody looked at me in amazement. Shocked and some not too happy about it. Most of them had been there every day, and here was the goofy kid racking up an A grade on a difficult test that only showed up every blue moon.

The church had dwindled down and was now without a pastor. Albert Morris was about to take over as an acting pastor. He worked in the trona mines and was in his 60s. He had taught Sunday school and been at the church for years, but he was not a preacher. Well, it was either closing the doors or him to assume the position as a pastor for the time being. He couldn't do this alone. He asked me to be his assistant and mostly take care of midweek service as well as other duties. I was fifteen years old. Never had preached. I knew I was called to ministry but not necessarily pastoring, but I knew this was the thing to do, and I agreed. So, in November 1970, I climbed into the pulpit and began to preach to and conduct the service for the small but faithful group of those gathered there on that wintry Wednesday night. Occasionally I would preach on Sundays as well. The people had great confidence in this young kid and supported me and Brother Morris in every way.

It was a cold stormy winter night. There was a small crowd at the Sunday night service. It seldom mattered how bad the weather was, the older people would be there. We had one lady in a wheel-chair, but otherwise, none of them used canes or walkers as is so common now.

As the service began, a stranger came in and sat toward the rear of the sanctuary. It was a blond-haired woman in her early to mid-30s. Once the service was over, she approached Pastor Morris and me. She explained that she was very low on money. She was traveling through in this bad weather, trying to get to some location that I don't recall now. She had eaten but had no money for a motel. We discussed this situation along with the pastor's wife. We didn't especially like this situation but decided to offer the women the use of the empty parsonage downstairs for the night. She was happy to have this offer and readily took it up. She was to just leave early that morning. All seemed to work out well with this situation until the next month when the church received the phone bill. The women had apparently spent the night on long distance and ran up a terrible charge. As you might assume, dear reader, we never heard from her again.

Junior high completion was not that big of a deal like nowadays. There was no graduation and all that luggage. You simply were done and went on to high school. The new high school was a really nice brick building that opened in '71, I believe. It had no swimming pool, so that was most welcome to me. It was located on the far east side of town.

I started there in the tenth grade. Finally, a "tiger" and not a "kitten" (school mascots). Lots more people were moving in, and Rock Springs was becoming wilder and crowded. There were lots of fights, shootings, knifings, all kinds of assaults and disturbances. Murders and sexual assaults were now common, and there were lots of thefts, burglaries, robberies, and prostitutes all over downtown. Drunks and drugs were ever-present. CB radios in vehicles were big then. They were stolen out of vehicles, locked or not, by the score. The bars and stores were full of people from all over the place. There were suicides—often. People moving in and out. Lots of illegal immigrants that only spoke Mexican Spanish. The small police force was overwhelmed. Money was flowing from the boom, but Rock Springs was not prepared at all for this invasion. People were living in tents and camping trailers. Staying in cars. There was nowhere left to rent, and the rent was high. Schools were crowded, even with the new high school. Traffic was badly congested. Stores were doing jackpot business but oh, so crowded. This country was rough and foreign to many of the people coming here. They were not used to the isolation, lack of services, and cold wind and weather. One dear older lady in our church told me that she came to Rock Springs in the '40s with her husband and children. They came from the east to work in the mines. Everything was so bleak and barren, she said that when she saw it, she just cried. She lived here for the rest of her life. There were several years about this same time (the '70s) of really bad winters. Very cold, windy, and lots of snow. Many antelope perished along with deer and other critters. One year it was so bad that for days the whole town was shut down. Snow drifts blocking the main streets, and no one out. Oxygen and medicine had to be taken by snowmobile to older people in town by the search and rescue squad. Howling winds and thirty to forty below temps without the wind. I and Leonard would be out walking around town. Cars wouldn't start, and roads were impassable. It was eerie. Like a deserted town. Nothing was open for days. We had to wade and fight through big snowdrifts to walk around except where the wind had swept the snow clear.

New people began coming to the church, including the Reichel family with which I became longtime friends. They had a son and two daughters just a bit younger than me. The youngest daughter was badly disabled from birth. They came from Denver, where he ran a finance office and was going to do likewise in Rock Springs. They had been the Foursquare church people and planned to now come to the Assemblies of God church.

It was good to get growth in the church, we needed it badly. The congregation was small and mostly older ladies and a few men. Except we did run a pretty good Sunday school and had quite a few kids come. I taught Sunday school and conducted children's church during the adult morning service, in addition to ministering as an assistant pastor. I would spend some time each Sunday morning traveling about town to pick up kids for Sunday school and church. Then back home afterwards, while parents were occupied with other interests. I had the car stuffed full on each trip or two. This was all before seat belts and airbags. How we survived is a mystery.

The Wyoming District was not really thrilled to have Pastor Morris and me in place, but there was no one else that would come, and they did not want to close the doors either. The District finally recognized us but called me an assistant to the pastor, not an assistant pastor. They didn't recognize that position. It didn't matter; it was all just semantics. But the church said, "We don't care what the District

calls you, you are *our* assistant pastor." The people were supportive and would stand up and fight for us if needed. Most old Rock
Springs people were a determined, tough bunch of people, and the
church was no different for the most part—a good thing. It would
have been easy to shut the doors and call it off.

I had learned a lot from being in Sunday school and church
over the past few years. I built on sermons and ways of preaching that
I had observed from past pastors, evangelists, and preachers. I would
never miss Billy Graham's crusade on television. All of these things
were huge helps to me in being able to preach and conduct services.
Of course, the anointing of the Holy Spirit was most important. But
I knew that I needed to learn much more. The Assemblies of God
had the correspondence school called the Berean School of the Bible.
Certain courses were required for a person to be considered for min-
isterial credentials, which neither I nor Pastor Morris had.

I began paying for and taking these courses through the mail
from the Assemblies of God headquarters in Springfield, Missouri.
This was in addition to still doing yard work and odd jobs for pay,
helping around the folks' house, hunting, fishing, and camping. Being
a kid, going to high school and assistant pastoring and preaching in
some other nearby Assemblies of God churches on the invitation.

I completed the standard course of study and received my
diploma from the Berean Bible School before high school graduation on May 16th, 1973. This took a lot of reading and study. Each
course involved from one to several books, and then there were tests
to take and pass. All of this was a great help to me, even though the
course of study was far less than going to Bible college.

My dad felt an infrequent tinge of kindness and gave me an
old 1961 two-door hardtop car that he had dealt and connived for.
This was my first vehicle. He would come up with old wrecks and
sell them for a big profit to the drunken Indians that came to Rock
Springs for several days while working for the railroad. They had been
paid and spent it all in the bars and on buying cars mostly. Maybe a
new cowboy hat or boots. Our yard and all around our house were
like a used cars' lot. Dad made a good deal of money selling cars, but
most of it went back to his habits of gambling and drinking.

My first car was a faded red. I liked it. It had positive traction, and if it wasn't high-centered, it would get around for hunting and fishing in the rough country like a tank. The tires I ran I found mostly at open unmonitored dumps around the county. You could run over a dime with most of them and tell whether it was heads or tails! I had lots of flats and could usually only purchase a few dollars' worth of gas at a time. However, gas was about thirty cents a gallon to begin with. I would pull up to the station where the attendant pumped the gas, this was just prior to self-serve stations coming into existence in Wyoming. The man would take my dollar or two and put the gas in. He never complained about the small purchase, not that I could have done anything differently. Anything beyond two dollars was big money to me at the time!

Dad gave me the car but told me it was my responsibility to pay for the license, insurance, and upkeep. He was in no way going to help with that. I repainted the hood with a brush as it was faded worse than the rest of the car. A nice bright red. I think it had been in an accident and had the front end replaced or parts of it anyway. The car was pretty good except that every so often, the starter would jam up, and unless you could roll down a hill or get a push or a pull, the car would not start. It was a manual transmission. Every so often, I would have to get under the car and pull off the starter to get it to work again. This was a nasty chore, and usually, it was nasty weather when this occurred. I put on new rebuilt starters, but it did not matter. The car would do fine for some time, and then, without warning, there you sat. I always tried to park on a downhill incline. Especially if I was out in the sticks somewhere or the weather was especially nasty.

Of course, before I could drive the car, to begin with, I had to get my learner's permit. This was easy enough. Just go to the driver's license office. Fill out some paperwork and pay a small fee, and I was given a permit to drive. It looked like a photocopied piece of paper. No picture, of course. I was fifteen.

With this in hand, I bought liability insurance and began to drive. To start with, I drove mom around as she instructed me. I then would take the family for a ride out on some old county road on the weekend. Finally, I turned sixteen. Old enough to go take my test and get a driver's license.

Now I had to take the written test, vision test and then drive the examiner around town for a few miles. No problem, except that that examiner sure made me nervous. He was a skinny old guy in a blue uniform with a police-type hat. Not one bit cordial. He was an old alcoholic and did not want to even make small talk. I tried to out of nervousness, but that didn't help matters.

He curtly gave me orders on what to do and where to go. I had driven only a short way when he snapped at me, "What's that other hand for?" I was so nervous I didn't have a clue what he meant. I had inadvertently been driving with one hand on the steering wheel, and this was no good. I looked at him like he had snot all over his face. Then he snapped, "Get that other hand on the steering wheel."

"Yes, yes, I will," and I did.

Without further incident, we made it back to the office in the old civic center. The fee was paid, and I was now licensed. I was a careful driver. My brother had so many tickets and wrecked so many nice cars that I had no intention of doing likewise. Certainly, did not want to damage my car. I took good care of it, and I did not want any trouble with the police.

The officials of the Wyoming District of the Assemblies of God gave Pastor Morris a minister's license. I met with them when I was sixteen. They were kindly but very stern and business-like. I was asking for a less credential than that of Pastor Morris. It was then called an exhorter's permit. It is now called a minister's certificate. They were appreciative of my ministry and support to the church and felt sure that I would be eligible for credentials later, but not now. That was a bit discouraging but really didn't affect much in the current situation. The next year I met with them again and was given the permit and now had the title of reverend but could only do limited service (not authorized to solemnize a wedding and legal matters as such).

When I was twenty-two years old, I met with the district officials again in Casper, Wyoming. I was now seeking a minister's license, which was just below ordination but provided all authority to perform all aspects of gospel ministry. This I needed in order to serve or lead a police chaplaincy. It is interesting how unkind some religious people can be. Jesus faced this often with the Pharisees and crowd. The pastor from Texas that I describe in a few pages ahead was still in Rock Springs. (Also, there is more on Pastor Griffin ahead.) He came to the meeting, the former Texan, and he had it in for me. He did his best to talk them out of not credentialing me. Some of the district officials were of the mind too that you should only be credentialed if you are going to pastor. A chaplaincy in a police department and jail was not what some had in mind. Now, as I write this story, there are many varied ministries that involve very little pulpit ministry. Despite the opposition, Reverend Beard, the district superintendent at the time was a big man with a big heart, he fully supported me and would have none of this nay-saying. Along with that was Pastor Griffin from Green River, who had been my mentor and friend. He would describe himself when someone accused him of being stubborn as no, not that at all, he was simply a determined individual. He was the sectional leader for southwest Wyoming for the district as well. I was approved for the credential. The pastor from Rock Springs was soon to leave the area, and a good thing too.

Regressing back now to Pastor Morris and my time with him. We would have terrific services many times. Especially on Sunday and Wednesday nights. Times when the Holy Spirit would move powerfully. Many times, people were filled with the Holy Spirit, gave messages in tongues, and were in prayer and worship for long periods of time. No one wanting to leave the building and just waiting on the Lord and receiving from him. The presence of the Lord would be heavy and powerful. Many times, whoever was to preach, never got to. The Spirit fell, and that was the end of the normal course of the service. We just worshiped and let God do His work. People dancing in the Spirit, healings, people called into ministry and delivered from all kinds of problems. Many people came to salvation experience during these times.

Lots of young people started coming to church, especially of high school age, and some of the local Jesus People were in the congregation. We were having home Bible studies, Sunday morning and evening services as well as Sunday school and children's church. Wednesday night service was still my purview. Church had very little to do with being just a social activity. Most of the people that came did it because they were hungry for more of God and His work in their life. Not to say that there wasn't good fellowship among the church, though, because there certainly was. Many lifetime bonds were made, and several people met their mates and were married.

During this time, there was one young man about my age that started coming to church. His name was Bill, and he was not a Christian. He just came with somebody one time to see what it was all about. Speech and English were his interests, not really religion or church. His church experience was at a formal mainline church. His family was upper class and would not normally come to an Assemblies of God church.

For about three weeks, I preached at the services he came to. He kept coming and could not pull himself away. I, to his amazement and mine as well, spoke each time in perfect English. This was the power of the anointing of the Holy Spirit. He became a Christian and kept coming to the church. I did not and do not speak in perfect English, and I have not since those times. Not many Westerners speak in good or perfect English.

We had a man, Hank, and his son Pepe come to the church. Good guys. Hank moved to the area to work at the Bridger Power Plant construction. Pepe was my age, and Hank was probably in his 50s. They were Cajuns from Louisiana. For several weeks I could hardly understand a word he spoke as we were trying to get acquainted. I tried as I did not want him to feel unwelcome or strange. It was funny. I tried to follow him and carry on a sensible conversation and answer his questions. Finally, the light kicked on, and I could understand him perfectly. He sure didn't speak perfect English or like a Westerner.

It was an experience, meeting and getting to know all of the different types of people from all over. There was a Brother Good. He was a higher-up with the company having the Bridger Power Plant built. He was an Easterner. Very formal and civilized, proper. A distinguished and serious type of person. He was telling me about being at his home church during a Christmas program, and something went wrong as he was crawling across an open baptistery to quietly go correct some problem. He fell into the empty tank and was injured. I couldn't keep from laughing. He told the story so seriously that it really made it hard not to laugh as I observed his antics and pictured the event in my mind.

The Jesus People were different. People from all over that came to Wyoming to work and live. Hippie-like in actions and dress. Mostly in their 20s and 30s. Most were good additions to the church body. There was one Puerto Rican young single guy, Louie. He really attracted the attention of the young people. He was outgoing and was out about town, witnessing and passing out gospel tracts. He did this alone and had only been in town a few weeks. He was always at church service, but I noticed that he never spent much time at the altars in prayer like most others. He seemed to avoid me and Pastor Morris.

After a few weeks, we came to Sunday morning service, and all of the buzz was that Louie had been arrested Saturday night and was in the local jail. The story went that this was because he had been out witnessing and passing out tracts. This seemed not too credible. Later that day, the truth came out that he had been arrested for being drunk and disorderly. Never saw Louie again after that. There were a few other ringers among the folks that came through, but most were genuine.

Pastor Griffin and his wife had considered the Rock Springs church when Pastor Morris and I were beginning, but they decided to take the open church in Green River, Wyoming, instead. They were a middle-aged Indian couple. Very sweet people, and we became long-term friends until his wife passed many years later and he eventually passed in 2017.

He and I kind of became like a Paul and Timothy relationship. He asked me to preach for their New Year's Eve watch night service when I was fifteen. Only been preaching for a few months. The service was late in the night, and I couldn't drive there by myself. He drove over to my home and got me. He brought me back home the next morning when we were done at around 2 a.m.

It was a well-attended and powerful service. I preached on Noah and how God had shut the door to the ark when the time came and how that applied to today. God has a timetable in which the door of His mercy—this present church age—will end. We will either be in right standing with God as the shout is made and the trumpet sounds, or we will be like those left outside of the ark as the waters rose and they perished.

I preached many times at the Green River church after this and also was asked to preach for the Big Piney-Marbleton church many times. Pastor Griffin became a leader of our section of the state for the Assemblies of God churches, and he was always supportive of me and my ministry. Even years later, as I ministered in even more unconventional ministries.

The Assemblies of God churches would have fellowship meetings of the sections in those times. Churches would meet on a Friday night within a one-hundred-mile or so radius at one of the local churches. The meetings were well attended by all age groups. We would load our cars full and take off after school in order to get there by 6 p.m. or so. There would be a fellowship pot bless dinner and a great service with special music and one of the ministers preaching. They were usually powerful and welcome times. These really created a strong bond among the scattered congregations.

Pastor Griffin got a kick out of ribbing me about my old hack car and the fact that I had actually not had to push it all the way to get to the event. It was all in good humor, and we had a lot of laughs about stuff like that.

They had their own horses and were big on riding. We would take horses from all over the state to the youth camp meetings at the state fairgrounds in Douglas, Wyoming. Steve Reichel and I became the wranglers for these events. I had done some riding and dealing with horses, but the first year was more of a learning experience for me. Each year got better. We had to feed, water, and care for the horses. Get them all saddled up in the mornings and reverse that in the late afternoon. We took campers of all ages on guided trail rides out through the prairie near the fairgrounds.

Pastor Griffin was in charge of these activities. Steve Reichel and I went for several years and helped with this until jobs and other activities in life changed our availability to go. We would stay in the stables at night with the horses and equipment and keep an eye on everything. I learned a lot about horses during these years, and Pastor Griffin was a great teacher and easy to work with. We would begin the morning with all or anything we wanted to eat in the camp dining hall. Pastor Griffin cracked us up. All he wanted for breakfast was fried baloney. The camps were five days long, and the rides cost the riders twenty-five cents for about a forty-five-minute ride.

Every night we were required to be in the nightly chapel services, which were very good. Otherwise, we spent all of our time wrangling. Well, I did anyway. Steve always fell in love with some lovely at camp and would wander some until Pastor Griffin noticed him being AWOL and got him back on target.

It was a lot of fun, and I really enjoyed it. We generally had about twenty horses or so to take care of, and lots of the riders were inexperienced. The pastor from Gillette always brought a bunch of his horses. He was kind of a loud, overbearing Texas guy. Several of the horses were pretty green. Pastor Griffin was upset with him because he would try to interfere with the supervision of the program, and Griffin was tired of us having to break in his "young, green" animals.

Most of the time, the trail rides went without incident. We did have one time when my horse laid down on me on its side. I was not injured at all and made the lazy critter get right back up. Mounted it, and off we went again. Another time there was a young group of singers from the Washington Bible College that wanted to take a morning trail ride. For some reason, the horse that one of the girls was riding bolted and took off at a full gallop. She hung on but could not get the animal stopped, and it was headed for a deep ravine. Steve and I took off at faster gallops on our horses out through the prairie as Griffin and the other riders watched in shock. We were able to front the rider and get ahead of the charging horse and stop the excited mount and its frightened passenger just a short distance before it got to the ravine, where disaster would have ensued.

Another time a teenage girl did get injured by one of the horses she rode, that was a Gillette horse. We were climbing out of a wide creek bed and going over the top in single file when for some reason, she slipped off the rear of her saddle, and as she slid over the horse's flank, the horse became frightened and began kicking up its rear legs. As the girl slid off the horse, it kicked her in the ribs and broke several ribs. Otherwise, the rides were generally well supervised by us and went well. They were a highly enjoyable activity offered to the campers and staff and always one of the activity highlights. I am told that nowadays, they have discontinued this sought-after activity at the camps due to liability. Sad.

After digressing from the fellowship meeting tales, I will now continue on that vein. There were winter trips to these meetings, however, that turned into real dangerous trips on the way home. The weather would be pleasant that day, and by the time we headed home late that night, it would be a raging blizzard. Hardly any traffic out, a white-knuckle drive, and a chore just to keep from running off the road into the deep snow. Visibility was horrible, and it was cold. A car full of people. But we always made the best of it and really didn't worry or fret about getting home. The Lord always got us all home safely and without incident. Very few ever chose not to go the next time.

The Nicky Cruz organization was to put on a two-day crusade in Rock Springs one spring during this time. It took a great deal of preparation and planning to put this together with the minister's organization of which I was a member, from Rock Springs and Green River. I was in charge of the offerings for the event. Getting a means of collecting the funds during a service with receptacles donated by a local fast-food place, having ushers, and securing the funds until the treasurer received them.

The meetings were all put together. They were well advertised and promoted for weeks as well as the book that was well known about Cruz and David Wilkerson, *Run Baby Run*. We had the large new high school gym in Rock Springs for the two evening services. Everything was in place and ready when Cruz arrived. This is not to throw mud at the man, but I was not at all impressed with him. He obviously was not too excited about Wyoming or anybody involved in this effort. He only met with the minister's group twice. He kept his part in the meeting very brief and was not friendly or outgoing at all. Then he would leave as quickly as he came. He was a small-built man. His English was still pretty broken and hard to follow, especially for public speaking, at this stage in his ministry. He was quite cold and complained about situations. He would appear to speak at the meetings and then go immediately to his hotel room and not be seen again. The meetings were poorly attended. Several people came forward for salvation each night, and I did altar work with some of the younger people that came forward. This was good, but the results were not at all what was hoped for. Wyoming is not an easy area to minister in. The population then and still is not religious or interested in spiritual things by and large. They certainly were not too interested in Nicky Cruz, no matter if he was a nationally recognized figure, and they didn't show up. This is not to demean the Cruz ministry. Wyoming just wasn't ready for Cruz, and maybe he wasn't up for this way different place either.

I was now spending most of my limited "kid time" with new friends that had moved to Rock Springs. Steve Reichel and his family and then the Littlefield family. They moved from Kansas for the father to find good work. He soon became employed at the Bridger Power Plant. They appeared to not have been overly prospering in Kansas. The Littlefield family consisted of three teenage daughters and Brother and Sister Littlefield who were probably in their late 40s.

I began to go around with the two oldest daughters that were my age, Debbie and Lottie. Debbie, the oldest daughter, drove the family car and always wanted to take us after church or other times to a drive-in for a root beer and then drive around town. They were fun girls, and all three of them were very attractive. Debbie was the most dedicated Christian, while the other two girls were far less. In fact, Lottie even had a noticeable wild streak in her.

Our relationship was that of friends only. I was too busy to mess with dating. Debbie became infatuated with Leonard, who still came to church some. Steve Reichel and I both tried very desperately to convince her that she was making a big mistake getting involved with him. But that was like trying to plug the leaking dike with our fingers.

Leonard was getting wild about this time, too, and would run around some with Debbie, but mostly, he just strung her along. She would just cry over him, and it was hard not to laugh at her because it was so ridiculous. Strangely, though, she later ended up marrying him, and they moved back to Kansas. They had a boy, and then he left her and returned to Rock Springs. The last time I saw Debbie was when she came to my wedding by invitation. She was apart from Leonard then and doing well, I hope she still is.

One Saturday afternoon, Debbie, Lottie, and I went for a root beer. Debbie then wanted to drive into the south side of town and go by Leonard's home to see if she could spot him. He was on the high school football team and just used her for a quick date, rides someplace, and that type of thing.

I advised against looking for him, but she drove there anyway. On the way back home, we were passing through old neighborhoods in the south part of town when at a blind intersection, another vehicle failed to yield and came roaring through and hit us hard on the passenger front and side. The two sisters were in the front, and I was in the back of the small two-door compact car.

Everything came to a deafening halt. Their vehicle began to erupt in steam, and we all sat there stunned in the middle of the intersection with the other vehicle sitting beside us all battered up. Lottie began to scream and would not stop. Nobody was hurt, but the damage was extensive. In fact, the cars were both total losses. Debbie began telling screaming Lottie to shut up. In her Kansas drawl, she would forcefully tell Lottie, "Oh forevermore, would you quit screaming." This was repeated several times, and finally, the wild-eyed Lottie regained her composure and stopped the high-pitched screaming.

Lottie started giving her parents fits and sure had a rebellious side to her. She tried once to get me interested in her, but I was not. The family stayed in Rock Springs for several years and then decided they would return to Kansas. Brother Littlefield was a big man, as was Sister Littlefield a large woman. He had made good money working at the power plant, and they had a nice trailer home, vehicles, and horses. He had really gotten into hunting with all of us, especially for elk. They were in the process of selling out and ready to move in late December when he decided that he and another man that he knew from work would make one final elk hunt to the Kemmerer area before he moved. They left in the other man's truck early that cold winter morning.

Steve Reichel and I were in the basement of the church making a large Christmas card out of cardboard for a high school teacher that he wanted to impress or suck up to! It was the afternoon of Christmas Eve. The phone rang at the church, and it was Steve's father calling for him. I stayed at the project while Steve was on the phone. In a short time, he returned and looked stunned. He began to relate that Brother Littlefield had been killed early that morning on the highway while en route to the hunt. In fact, both men in the truck had been killed in a freak accident. They were on a two-lane highway when a semi-hauling metal pipe passed them. At that time, the chains holding the cargo broke, and the pipes fell onto the truck and knocked it off the highway. The truck overturned and began to burn. Both men perished in the fire. This was an awful thing to happen and especially at Christmas. The family then moved several months afterwards to Kansas as planned.

After several years of me and Pastor Morris ministering at the church, it was decided that he would retire, and I was ready to move on too. The church had grown and now had a good, active congregation. It had been badly in debt and unable to pay its mortgage when Pastor Morris took over. He was very good with money, and he saw to it that things were managed so well that before we left, the church was debt-free, could pay its bills, and had some funds in the bank.

A pastor that had come from Texas and had been pastoring in Big Piney for a short time now applied to become the full-time pastor of the Rock Springs church. I knew him only from a few briefs talks I had with him and his wife, and we liked each other okay at that point. He and his family moved in, and things were good to start. They were like a good deal of people that had come to Wyoming. Like fish out of water. His wife was kind of prissy and uppity. He was heavyset and slow. They had two little boys, and he was not easy to joke with. He was really touchy.

A bunch of us had gone in the late summer to a fellowship meeting in Jackson Hole, Wyoming. It was the plan for me and Steve Reichel and the pastor to stop on the way home that night in Pinedale, Wyoming. The purpose of this was to try to get antelope permits that were being issued at a sporting goods shop for the areas around Pinedale and Big Piney in the fall.

Steve and I were in my old battleship-sized car, and the pastor was in a big luxury he had bought that was a real lemon. No wonder, it was a newer car, but he had bought it used from another out-of-state pastor by the last name of Fink. Everybody else went home from the meeting in other vehicles. The speedometer didn't work in my old car, and not being absolute at judging speed as I said before, we arrived in Pinedale well ahead of the pastor, even though we all left together. He didn't like it because we had "run off and left him." We thought it was funny. Things were getting rocky between the pastor and lots of us at this point, so we didn't have too much regard for him now anyway.

Steve and I had never hunted antelope before, so we were pretty excited about trying to get a permit. This was the last year Wyoming issued permits in this fashion. Really too bad. It was a way of life that was already disappearing even then. You had to wait outside the store all night in line if you wanted to have a chance to get the limited licenses on a first-come-first-served basis. People would camp out all night. Laying and sitting on the sidewalk in lawn chairs, sleeping bags, and some just standing—like me and Steve. The store would open at about 8 a.m., so there we were beginning at about 11 p.m. the night before. Some people slept, lots of people visited, played cards, read, and the like. It really was fun. It was like a bunch of hunters just enjoying time together. We just visited with guys and listened to the telling of interesting tales, stories, and jokes. It got chilly, but actually, the night was pretty entertaining and went by quick.

Steve and I stayed in line all night, and we were pretty far back. The pastor, against our advice, decided he would sleep in his car and get in line later. He liked his comfort. More people came into line as the night progressed, and Steve or I went over once or twice and woke up the pastor and told him he had better get in line. He ignored us.

About 7:30 that morning, the pastor finally got into line far behind us. He looked like he had been hit by a truck. The store opened, and we were issued our antelope permits for the Big Piney Area 89. We paid our fee and went outside to wait on the pastor. Only a few more licenses were available after ours. The pastor finally got in the store and came out in a few minutes. He was only able to get an archery permit. All of the regular licenses were gone. Hunting that fall, Steve and I both got our bucks and had a great hunt. The pastor had no archery equipment. He borrowed an old crossbow from Bruce Hamilton and went out once or twice and flung arrows at some critters but never even came close. When he told us how he hunted, we knew why. He was not one to crawl and sneak around or to sit in a blind or anything like that. He went out and just took long arching shots at the bucks and would scare them off. Had he practiced much with the weapon, we asked. Didn't have time. He kind of blamed us for his troubles with the license and the hunt itself. Go figure.

One night after church, all the young people were to go up to the Brince's trailer home on the southwest side of town. The Brince's were folks that had moved to Wyoming for the jobs too. The parents were in the late 40s, and they had three teenagers. One son and daughter about my age and then a younger boy. They were nice Christian people but really not in their element in Rock Springs. The father tried to be rather stiff and formal. He had sort of an English accent as well. Like many others, they would have never moved there except for the work. The father worked at the Bridger Plant being constructed. He was a bit stern. He especially gave me and Steve Reichel the eye of question and warning, you might say. I think he thought we were kind of wild church kids, and he was not too fond of us getting any ideas about his daughter, Marcia. Well, some of his thinking was probably correct, but neither one of us had any designs on Marcia. She was a tall pretty bespeckled girl and liked us but tried to act like we repulsed her. She was prissy and overdressed, especially for Wyoming standards at the time.

Anyway, the night we were going to their new trailer home, I had a carload, and Steve had his dad's old gray four-wheel drive following me. In with Steve were several passengers, and Marcia happened to be one of them. She was seated in the front passenger seat next to the door, it was a cold dark winter night. I parked at the Brince's home, and a few minutes later, Steve showed up. Marcia got out of his old heap, she was wearing heels and a long fur coat. She was limping, looked disheveled, and her glasses were lopsided on her face. She was not one bit happy. I stood at the trailer home front, and as she passed me, she made some comment about me and my crazy friend trying to kill her.

It was hard not to snicker. Steve came up to me laughing. He related that they were coming up the hill into the trailer court, and as he came around the curve, the passenger door came open, and out went Marcia. He was kind enough to stop and wait for her to get up when she quit rolling around and hobble back into the vehicle, but boy, she was upset at him and his old junk four-wheel drive. This did not endear Mr. Brince to us, and I think he urged his boys to avoid us too. But the boy our age, Alan, was okay and was still friendly. In fact, Marcia still tried to put on her front to us. Really liking both of us but trying to act like we disgusted her, even though she made it a point to be around us and try to exchange barbs and so on. She was okay. Probably, made some guy a nice Christian wife.

We were active guys and liked to fun around, and I suppose some of the older stuck-in-the-mud folks didn't think that was to swell. I think Sister Reichel, Steve's mother, was that gave me a bumper sticker for my old red car that said "God Squad." I really liked that. If we had spare time, usually Steve and I, we would cruise the town a few times after getting a big quart of root beer at the drive-in.

We both got really good at making ourselves sound like a siren out the car windows, especially while going through the M Street Underpass. One time we were behind a large passenger bus there and let go with the siren. That bus pulled over so fast that we couldn't believe it. I don't know what the occupants of the bus thought they had for police cars in that town when we went past them in the old car.

I was a big fan of *Adam-12* and *The Blue Knight* television programs. Reed and Malloy in the rolling black and white and Bumper Morgan (George Kennedy), the walking beat cop, were just what I would be if I was an officer. Bumper Morgan seldom even had to chase anybody. He threw his nightstick at the feet of a fleeing criminal, and down they went...wow.

I still attended and was involved in the youth group. I would preach for the pastor on occasion on a Sunday night and lead song and worship services. He asked me to be the church treasurer, and I was elected by the church membership to this position. Things continued to sour over time between me and him. I finally quit as a treasurer after about a year, and this pastor was now running off more people than he was able to keep or replace. The Reichel's began going to a Baptist church and asked me to go as well. I did some, but I had started working security at the Bridger Power Plant and was preaching some at the Green River and Big Piney churches.

I still would go once in a while to the church as I did not want to go more than a couple of times to the First Baptist Church on C Street, and with filling in preaching for absent pastors or invitations to preach at churches out of town and working and with the deteriorating conditions with the pastor at the Rock Springs church, I was showing up there very little now. But one Sunday morning that I was able to go, one of the dear little ladies came up to me when I came into the building. It was Sister Mime. She was round and about four feet tall. In her late 70s or 80s. She, Sister Bucho, and Sister Simmons had been some of my most faithful and steady supporters over the years. Very godly saints. She reached up and got me by the shirt collar. She looked me straight in the eyes and said, "Young man, give an account of yourself." I had to laugh, but she was not joking around. The folks like her were having a hard time with all of this disruption in the church.

I digress here a bit now back a couple of years. Bruce Hamilton went to the Assemblies of God church. He had mental disabilities from a childhood illness. He was probably in his 30s. Lived in

Reliance, Wyoming, with his mother and father. His mother went to the Nazarene church, and the father, actually his stepfather, had nothing to do with any of it.

I knew the Hamilton family from years before. They lived in mining towns surrounding Rock Springs and had been coal miners among other things. Bruce loved to sing and yodel western songs. He was kind of loud and avoided by most people.

We began to visit some at church, and I got a kick out of him. He was different but funny and good-hearted. I was still having flats by the score, and he had a manual tire repair machine in his old garage in Reliance, Wyoming, where the family lived. He invited me out to have tires fixed whenever I needed. He would do it for free, whereas I was now paying a buck fifty of two bucks for each repair.

Then we also began talking about fishing and hunting. Bruce was working at Little America, west of Green River, Wyoming, and he didn't hunt much anymore, but he liked to fish. He said I had to come out and meet Pop, his father. He had just retired, and other than prowling the old open dumps around the county, about all he did was hunt, fish, and trap. He was sure I would like Pop.

Not long afterwards, I went out to the house. This began a long-term friendship with the family that lasted even till today with Bruce in his 80s.

Pop was a salty old, sometimes bearded, outdoors-looking guy that held me spellbound. He was short and stocky and wore glasses. Mom, or mommy, as Bruce called his mother, was a sweet lady who knew how to pray and cook. She kept such a clean house that you could have eaten off the floor. She was a character too. A product of the great depression era, there was no wasting of anything. They had ridden a motorcycle all over the country in their younger days. They thought it was a crime for anyone to own anything but a manual-transmission vehicle. She still washed on Mondays using an old wringer washing machine and drying the clothes on a clothesline. They had a small garden, and Pop would spend time in that too. In fact, several years later, he was showing me his garden. This was a requirement of almost any visit to the home. He took great pride in the vegetables he grew. As he was giving me the weekly or so tour,

I noticed one plant in particular that was growing profusely. I mentioned that to him. He said, yes, he didn't know what it was but that the large leafy plant was small to start with and just appeared in the garden after one night. I looked even closer at the plant. Then I told him the bad news. Bad because he had been caring for it for someone, unbeknownst to him. He expected something edible to appear anytime on the pretty plant. "No," said I, "it is a marijuana plant." He was shocked. I told him that it would have to go, and he planned to pull it out that week, but he had to bring himself to it. Several days later, before he pulled the plant, he said that it suddenly disappeared. Somebody enjoyed the old fellow's efforts at gardening.

I seldom left their home without garden goods, repaired tires, good clothing, and other items of value that I needed that Pop would find discarded in the dumps. They always wanted to send you away with plenty. He would say, "Everybody wants to cut your throat, here we try to put something in it." He was a character. I called him Mr. Hamilton, but this he did not like. I had no grandpa on either side of my parents, they had both passed away. The Hamilton's knew our family. They wanted me to call them Grandpa and Grandma. They thought I was just alright. They had grandkids that lived nearby, but I had grown closer to them and saw more of them than actual family. So ever after that, it was Bruce, Grandpa, and Grandma.

On one summer day visit after I had been going out to see them for several months, Grandpa had something he found in a dump that he was sure I would like. It was an old bear-rug Indian headdress that had probably been made at one time by a boy's troop or some such group. I liked it but wondered if it was flea-bitten, not that I said so. I had to try it on. It was out in the truck bed, so Grandpa and I got it, and I put it on in their yard. Grandpa was all smiles. He was sure he had found what I always had wanted. Bruce or Grandma got their camera and took a picture of Grandpa and me together with me in the Indian regalia. I was seventeen. I still have that 8×10 framed picture on my office wall, as I have for many years. The headdress, which I wore on occasion, has since gone the way of the carrier pigeon.

It was amazing, those open dumps had all kinds of nearly new and good stuff in them for the taking. So many people were coming and going from the area, and with money all over the place, people would just throw truckloads of furniture, clothes, good canned food, and stuff away rather than fool with it.

Another thing that occurred on the visits to the Hamilton's was that Pop would have to show me detailed finds of his from the dumps. This got me interested too, and I began to go out when I had free time and prowl the places. I would also, like Pop, scavenge all kinds of pop and beer bottles to redeem. Aluminum cans and aluminum off old campers and stuff to sell at the junkyards. I also began to walk along busy roads on the edge of town and pick up cans and bottles to redeem. It wasn't really like work, and I was picking up pretty good money doing this stuff. Plus, it was nice to be out in the fresh air, even when cold, and work independently.

One time I found a pretty good dirty bike—motorcycle at one of the dumps. It started up with one kick of the kick starter and ran quite well. It still had gas in the tank and everything. I loaded it up and hauled it home. I didn't want it, but I put it up for sale and immediately had interested parties. A kid around my age and his dad bought it from me when I assured them, I had not stolen it but found it in my dump rounds. It netted me one hundred dollars, which was a nice chunk of change.

I had sold my red car and had this big white battleship-sized car that I previously described a little. Well, it was a gas hog, but fortunately, gas was still only around forty-fifty cents a gallon, so I was able to keep it running. The car was a rocket. It still made a pretty good hunting and fishing vehicle, but it did not have the traction on the poor ground like my old red car, so I had to be more careful where I went with it.

I had started going fishing some with Bruce and Grandpa Hamilton. Now it was fall, and Grandpa invited me to join him for a few days at a hunting camp that he and his son-in-law, John, would have set up north of Pinedale in the area of Sour Moose Creek, just south of the Jackson Hole area. They were in a camping trailer and were to hunt deer and elk. I only had a Friday and a weekend to hunt, so I drove up with a deer license in hand and found their camp.

We had a great time. John was a big tall guy in his late 40s. He tended to be a Jack Mormon and wasn't thrilled to have me in camp but made do and was friendly enough. Grandpa wanted me there, and that was good enough.

I hunted with them for a day and then alone for a day and then with John on the last day. I got a doe deer and had to leave late that Sunday afternoon. The weather had been really pleasant fall stuff. Just beautiful. A few deer around, but hunting was slow. They had lots of time to hunt and were holding out for elk and deer that suited them.

One night while sleeping on a cot in the middle of the trailer, John and Grandpa each had the bunks at opposite ends of the little contraption, the head end of my cot fell down. I was a hard sleeper as a young person. Still kind of am. I wore glasses and later contacts too from the age of eight till I was forty-four. I would sleep with my glasses on most of the time. People couldn't figure out how I did that and kept from messing them up, but I never had a problem.

At any rate, I awoke early and saw John and Grandpa getting up to hunt too. They were both having a good chuckle. They said they heard the cot fall—crash early in the night. I didn't budge, so they left me alone. I had slept just fine all night with my glasses on and my head almost on the floor. The rest of my body prone on the cheap little cot. It must have been a sight. Ever after that, Grandpa would joke me about being the kid that slept on his head. He even found a cartoon in *The Born Loser* comic strip that was applicable and cut it out and gave it to me. The Hamilton's had chuckles about it, and I did too. They would call me, "Our Kenny, the kid who sleeps on his head."

Years later, I could be sleeping by one of the loud ringer telephones and never hear it. But once I awoke, I was wide awake and ready to go. There was another time while I was still living at home with my folks that illustrates what a peaceful sleeper I was. It was summer, and not having air conditioning, we had the windows open in the house on this warm summer night.

Some guy came out of Bunning Park and went from the north gate there, up the sidewalk past our house, while firing off a loud big-game rifle a number of times. He passed right under my bedroom window, which was over the sidewalk, while firing. I never heard a thing. I got up the next morning, and all the buzz in the house was that the whole neighborhood had been up with police all over the place and nobody sleeping but me.

There was one other time that was funny as well. Chuckie came home half-plunked one early morning and saw me peacefully sleeping in the bunk bed above his. He decided it would be hilarious to get mom's fingernail polish and paint my toenails. This he did without disturbing Sleeping Beauty. After being up a short time that morning, I noticed my nice nail work. Oh, he did laugh. Not for long, though.

He would sleep pretty sound, too, not as bad as me, but if he had a little to drink, it helped. I waited about a week till he had been out and came home and went into a coma. He had to go to work early in the morning in the coal mines, where they all dressed in a bathhouse in their miners' garb. I found the brightest color mom had and put a heavy coat on his finger and toenails. He got up that morning and went to work, not having time to remedy his beauty treatment from his brother.

That was in a time period, especially in the West, when men didn't wear polish, earrings, and such "garb" as many males do now. He had plenty of strange looks and lots of laughs and jabs from the miners in the bathhouse that morning. Seems that I broke him from sucking eggs if you know what I mean. I never awoke with painted anything after that!

I learned some good hunting methods and ways while with Grandpa and John. My dad and Chuckie were not great hunters and did not put much effort into real hunting, so other than a few basic things, I really did not know what I needed to from hunting with them. This was now changing.

We said goodbyes and loaded the deer in the trunk of my car, and off I went. The drive into Rock Springs was well over a hundred miles, and, of course, you had to go through Pinedale too and many miles of curvy road where speed was supposed to be reduced. All in all, I made it into town in less than an hour and a half. That car would fly, nearly bald tires and all. I must have kept the angels hoping with that heap.

I had been out at the Hamilton's visiting, and finally, the time got to be around 8 p.m. It was dark now, and I headed home. I was just about a mile out of Reliance and had picked up to around probably sixty when—*boom*—my front passenger tire blew. The car tried to take off on the right side of the road. I held it and was able to slow down and get stopped at the road edge. Made a quick tire change and off again. Of all the miles I drove on horrible tires, that was the only blowout I ever had.

I kept the big white car for some time and then found a 1966 four-wheel drive for sale in Green River. Dad went with me to check it out. We test-drove it and ended up buying it. Bought it from the private party and took it home. I then sold the car and had my first four-wheel drive. I didn't own many cars after that. I stayed mostly with trucks and four-wheel drives. The four-wheel drive actually had decent tires on it, and I pretty much quit running dangerous tires after that.

I was fishing now more with Grandpa and Bruce. Usually at the Flaming Gorge but sometimes on the Green River or the Fontenelle Reservoir. I was learning a lot about camping and fishing from Grandpa. I copied as close as possible the gear and methods he used to fish as he knew what he was doing. He almost always caught fish, even when we and others didn't. He used to chuckle and shout out to us and anyone else as he reeled in fish, "I catch 'em where there aint none."

The big problem I found with Grandpa was then and later, too, he drove old heavy two-wheel-drive pickup trucks. He wouldn't even entertain the thought of getting a four-wheel drive. For some reason, he had the idea that his pickup was unstoppable and that he could take them where four-wheel-drive outfits couldn't go.

We got stuck several times. Once all night at the Flaming Gorge near the lake. It was an old muddy road with no bottom to it. Bruce, I, and Grandpa spent the night and wee hours of the morning jacking the truck up with a heavy-duty truck jack. Hauling slabs of rock from nearby and putting them under the tires. Then putting the truck back down on the rock and driving as far as we could. This procedure was repeated numerous times until we made it back to the good road. It was a lot of work, and we were worn out but made fun out of it anyway. Grandpa was quite a jokester and didn't worry over things like being out in the prairie with his truck completely buried to the frame in mud and no easy way to remedy the situation. He took it all in stride, that was just part of hunting and fishing. Anyone with him had better not worry about it either. It wouldn't do a bit of good.

I found that the worst thing to do with him when he came up to some area that was obviously impassable and looked like the wagons on the Oregon Trail had been the last to come through there was not to indicate at all that we did not have to drive in there. That was like a red flag to a bull.

Bruce didn't hunt with us, and he started staying at home more with his mother when we went. He also had to work some, but I think he was just growing weary of the trivial trials of getting stuck all night. He had injured himself at work and had a bad back, so hauling rock all night was probably not the best activity for him.

The last time I recall being stuck with Grandpa, I was probably about twenty. We had gone fishing without Bruce in Grandpa's truck. We had been fishing most of the day at the Gorge, and it was getting late on this cool April afternoon. We had fish, but he was wanting to try another spot. We drove down on this big flat that appeared dry but had water in it earlier when the water level was higher.

I knew that was a bad area to drive into. He had to have too but wanted to drive out toward the water to see if we could fish out there. I made the tragic mistake of saying we did not have to do this. We might get stuck. He laughed like a fiend and drove on. We had gone probably 150 yards onto the flat from the road when we started sinking in. Too late. A few more turns of the wheels, and we were buried. All four tires—to the frame. No bottom to this stuff. I started whining some about what a horrible idea this was and that I said we did not have to do this. It was like water off a duck's back.

This was going to be a long night. It was not long till dark, and we had seen no one in the area for hours. He merely laughed and said not to take on, that he had his jack in the bed of the truck, and that it would involve a little labor, but we would get straightened out.

I followed him around to the bed of the truck. He lowered the heavy metal tailgate and began looking for the jack. Suddenly, a cold look of disappointment came on his face. No jack. Oh no, his last dump run involved him taking the jack out and leaving it in the garage so it wouldn't be in his way for the short distance and the great haul he was to make.

The trouble was, he forgot to return the jack when he was done. This would have been a big problem even so. It was a long way to any rock from the flat. This was just a mudflat with a little dry dirt on its top. But with no jack, there was no way to get out.

"Well," he said, "why don't you walk up to the road and see if somebody comes along or if you walk a way and find somebody to come give us a hand."

"Oh no. I told you not to drive down here, but oh no, you did it anyway. We are in this mess together. We will walk till we run into somebody." He didn't like it. He was in good shape for an eighty-year-old, but he would have preferred that I went for help.

I would not relent. "*We* are going." So, we got an old flashlight that he had and a few items and took off. Onto the road just as it was getting quite dim light. No one around. We started up the dirt roads that led toward Big Firehole. We had not seen anyone most of the day on the route we had been, so we figured we go the other route and hopefully find somebody. Of course, we knew that the only place around with someone would be the Currant Creek Ranch, about twenty miles away.

It got dark, and the wind started blowing, and then it started to spit snow off and on. It was uphill most of the way out of the Gorge area. No one came along. We walked and walked and walked. He tried to stop, and I would let him take a short break, but then I told him we had to keep going.

Finally, at about 2 a.m., we stopped. He laid on the cold ground and said he couldn't go on. I would just have to go onto the ranch and get help. "Nope, we are both going to walk every mile until we get somewhere." He got up and kept going. It wasn't really too bad for walking a ways on a cold dark night. Coyotes entertained with their nearby howls, and the stars were pretty to look at.

Finally, that morning around 9 or 10 a.m., we made it to the ranch. There were two young couples there. They seemed glad to have our company. They were amazed at our story. Oh yes, the rancher would go over there with his truck. He had long metal cables, and we could hook onto the truck and pull it out. First, they insisted that we rested and ate. They fed us a fine meal, including a fresh-backed berry pie that his young wife had just made. We visited while we ate. They were super people.

About an hour later, the rancher drove us back to the scene of the crime, and with not too much trouble, he pulled us out. How do you really thank people like that? "Thanks" and little gifts seem small. He would take nothing. I think I may have finally taught my old mentor to be more careful in the future of what he drove off into with his unstoppable tank.

We had all kinds of adventures. One time fishing on a hot summer day on the Green River, Grandpa went further downriver to fish. Bruce and I sat on the bank and fished with worms. We were having laughs and enjoying the day. We started catching nothing but whitefish, "Mormon trout." They ran about one to one and a half pounds. Fun to catch but not what we wanted to eat. I cut one open. They were black inside. We must have caught forty or fifty of them and had the bank behind us covered with the stinky things. The birds probably loved it.

Another spring day Grandpa and I had gone to the Gorge. We parked up high on a ridge and walked down to this steep bay. It was late afternoon, and the weather had been pretty unsettled. We usually fished the Firehole side of the reservoir. I was fishing the north side of the bay, and he decided he liked the looks of a spot on the south side of the bay—a little further over, so he went over there.

We had been fishing for about an hour when suddenly, from Utah—the west side of the lake, I saw a huge black cloud coming our way. The wind started howling, and it began to rain and snow, mostly rain. In a matter of minutes, it turned into a howling storm.

I grabbed my stuff and took off for the truck on the high hill, about a mile away. I saw Grandpa doing likewise.

I made it to the truck in about fifteen minutes, the rain was blowing sideways. I felt frozen, and I was sopping wet—hat, jacket, and all. I had been driving his truck, so I got in the driver's seat. About fifteen minutes later, Grandpa appeared. He looked frozen. Like a wet, cold rat. He threw his stuff in the bed of the truck and climbed into the passenger seat with a loud sigh. We sat there talking about this revolting development and trying to wipe faces and glasses off. Warm up the truck and get going. Then I noticed. He had no glasses on. I asked him where his glasses were. He said he was walking along as fast as he could when a big tumbleweed hit him and nearly knocked him down. It grabbed his glasses off his face and went on its merry way with the glasses in tow and never to be seen again.

Steve Reichel would go with us once in a while to fish or hunt if he could escape school and his mother's wrath. Grandpa was tough. He would keep up with us young guys all day. Never complained. Steve use to drive Grandpa nuts, though, and he would do it on purpose just to get him worked up. He would say when we were hunting, "Oh, if I get them in my sights, they're mine." This would really get him for some reason. It was funny. Grandpa started calling Steve "Dead Shot Dick," and he didn't mean it to be a term of endearment. However, this was a common term applied to a guy that claimed to be a crack shot. It came from years earlier when a guy named Richard-Dick made such claims to the disgust of his listeners.

Another time fishing with Grandpa Hamilton at the Gorge, we went there in an old brown station wagon that he had got somewhere. It was piled full of junk in most of the car, good stuff but still junk, and this was so in every vehicle he had. He kept the floorboards full of loose hand tools, chains, and so on. So, when the passenger rode, there you rested your feet on the tools instead of the floorboard.

The clutch was bad in the car. We drove down a steep dirt road to a bay we liked to fish at. It was a cool spring day. We caught fish alright. Nice German browns and a few rainbows too, while we were there, another car came down the mountain goat trail and parked at the bottom. It was a little foreign-made bug car. The occupants were fishing further over, and we never saw them. We had all the fish we needed, and it was getting late in the afternoon. We loaded up and started the car up the hill. We could only get about a ⅓ of the way up before the slipping clutch got hot and would go no further. Not to worry. We parked, so the other car could get by if it needed to, and put a big rock under the back wheel to prevent any possible roll-down disasters. Unloaded fishing equipment and went back to fishing.

Then we heard the little car start up, and we were sure that it would not get up this steep hill without trouble. We dashed over the bank to watch the show. Disappointed, we saw that the car not only went up without spinning a tire on the rocky, rough dirt road, but it was gone. We had to repeat the procedure with the station wagon twice more before it finally went over this hill, and we headed home with a load of nice-size fish.

In this same car, we went fishing on a summer day and were going to stay for several days, which we did. Bruce went with us, and we went north to Willow Lake. The fishing was slow, but we had a great time. Beautiful country up in the Wind River-Pinedale area.

We headed home late that day. Grandpa Hamilton always drove fast, and this was no exception. After we left Pinedale headed south, he throttled the car up to ninety-ninety-five, and we were sailing down the highway in dim light.

We passed through Farson and Eden Valley in the dark, and the engine light came on, on the old heap. Due to the high-speed antics and the warm night, the car had overheated. We stopped and opened the hood. It looked like Old Faithful. The car was hot as a firecracker.

Never too big of a problem, Grandpa said, there were some irrigation ditches with flowing water in them off to the west in the prairie. He and I got a big white plastic five-gallon bucket out of the car and were to go get water. We had the big flashlight with us, told Bruce to remain in the car. When we got the water and returned further down the road, we would shine the light in his direction, and then he was to come slowly ahead and meet us. No problem.

We started off down the road. We were to go a few hundred yards and then out into the prairie. We had only gone about half the distance when the car started up, and here came Bruce. Grandpa was aggravated. "That lum head." Bruce drove up to us, and Grandpa chewed him out as the car began boiling more again.

Repeat this plan again. Bruce was sure he understood now. We went further down and were about where we thought we had to climb the fence and go out into the prairie to the ditch. Grandpa shined the light out toward the prairie—opposite to Bruce, and here he came. "That lum head," he said again. Bruce drove up to us and received another mild tongue-lashing.

We finally got out to the water and back to the highway, just a short way from Bruce. We shined the light at him, and voilà, here he came. The dry car took all of the contents of the bucket. Home we went at high speed.

Grandpa Hamilton and I had been fishing at some lakes up in the Pinedale area in the summer and were headed back home with his old pickup. It had wood sideboards on it but was open in the back otherwise. We had it packed with stuff from camping and fishing.

As he roared down the highway in the Farson area, my old green army surplus sleeping bag that I had used for many years somehow was caught by the wind and flew out onto the highway. By the time we were able to stop and get turned around and back to it, lying on the highway, another guy had stopped and was getting ready to pick it up. I yelled at him as we lurched to a stop that it was our sleeping bag. He looked puzzled but never said a word and just got back in his truck and left.

While the bag had lain on the roadway, another vehicle had run over it and put several holes in it. The inside was filled with chunks of white fiber cotton. I poked them back in and patched the bag with several pieces of duct tape when I got home.

Several years later, while on a spring bear hunt with Butch (described further on), we were in the Big Sandy area. It was cold, and lots of snow still around. We slept that night in a two-man tent that belonged to him. I slept just fine in that bag, but when we awoke, I sat up, and he looked at me, shocked and in wonder. During the night, some of the duct tape had come loose, and big chunks of white cotton filler had come out of the bag and were stuck to my head and face.

I took Bruce antelope-hunting a couple of times. On the first trip, we went to the Big Piney area, where we had permits for any antelope. On the way there, just as we entered our area, we were still on the highway when I spotted a herd of antelope just yards away from the highway fence. We stopped. They paid no attention to us. Two nice bucks had their heads together and were pushing each other around while the does stood watching the show.

The dirt flew, and the fight went on for a couple of minutes. Quite a show at close range. Finally, the smaller of the two bucks won. He chased the bigger buck off. Bruce said, "Let's shoot him." No, after that, I was not about to shoot either one of them. That was too grand of a performance.

We went on and spent two- or three-days hunting. I had a big old stretch four-wheel-drive outfit, and we just stayed in it at night. The weather was pleasant, and there were plenty of antelope. I took Bruce all around to start with and kept getting him into nice setups to shoot his animal. He had an old open sight .300 rifle that he assured me he could shoot pretty good.

He threw lead at the critters most of our hunt until he finally gave up and said, "Here," handing me the rifle, "you shoot my antelope for me." Obviously, I was going to have to do this, or he would soon be out of ammo. I used my .270 and readily shot an antelope for him. He was pleased.

There were lots of antelope back then, far more than there are now. I found a very nice buck, quite a way out in the prairie. Not being a big fan of terrific long shots, I found more satisfaction in getting a close stock in to the animal. I was able to cover the considerable distance on foot, down a dry ravine. The buck was a nice one all by himself feeding.

Then I began to bell-crawl. I crawled for a long distance. Inching along and stopping each time the lone animal raised its head to look around and chew. The ground was now open, but I crawled within just yards of him and finally shot. He knew something was up before I shot and was getting noticeably nervous, but he never knew I was there. Even though I was in an open view of him.

The weather had been typically warm in the daytime, so after getting Bruce's antelope, we went to a bar in Big Piney called The Watering Hole. We asked them if we could hang his animal in there outside the cooler. They were very accommodating. It was the next day that I got my animal.

The next time I took Bruce, we had a good trip into the same area, but I had to shoot his animal again. On that trip, he came down with diarrhea before I got my antelope. I was having to stop every few minutes for him to get behind sagebrush and relieve himself. I was getting a big laugh out of it. I got my antelope, and then it hit me. Same thing. Now we were both becoming good friends with the sage.

We had picked up some kind of flu. Felt sick and weak, and it was all we could do to get my antelope taken care of and head home. I helped Bruce get his antelope hung in their open bay garage and took off. A day later, I felt fine and called Bruce to see what his condition was.

He was better but down in the dumps. During the night, a pack of dogs in the little place had come into the garage and pulled his antelope down and had a fine meal at his expense. That was the last hunt with Bruce. Grandpa did not like to hunt antelope and wouldn't. He called them goats. I was the only one in my family that hunted them too until I got Jan and Tammy, my sisters, involved with them. My brother Chuckie and his wife went out one year at my urging, and he shot an antelope, but only that one time.

My Grandpa had gotten into trouble over an antelope when before he was killed. A warden came along and took the antelope away and took him to see a justice of the peace. After a big turmoil over it, he paid a fine and was released. After that, no one in my family hunted antelope until I started. I loved hunting them and usually had several licenses. They are fine animals to hunt in usually delightful fall weather, and if taken proper care of, they make very good table fare.

I hunted and fished with Grandpa Hamilton until he suffered some kind of dementia and was placed in the veteran's home in Sheridan, Wyoming, not too long after I married. He had told me, Bruce, and Grandma on a visit we made to see him, in which he was lucid for a few moments, that if he ever found a way out the front door, he would escape. He did not like being kept inside. Then the light went off, and he was gone into some past memory.

It was sad to see him decline like that. One time he would recognize us, and then another he would not. I was seeing him at the hospital in Rock Springs before he was taken to the veteran's home. He was in the room alone and confined to the bed. He knew me at first, and I started talking with him. Still in hopes that he would improve and go with me elk- and deer-hunting to our camp in the Wasatch National Forest within a few weeks.

Soon I could see this was not to be. He drifted off and began staring at the ceiling. Then I could see that he was seeing something and watching them with a look of a hunter. "Look at all those geese flying over," he said. He had a little smile on his face. He was out somewhere in the country where he loved to be and was seeing flock after flock of geese fly over.

One time Bruce had to go see a doctor in Utah about his back, which he had injured at work sometime before and was still having lots of trouble with. It was during the winter, and he and Grandma asked if I would go with them. I had made a similar trip with them to Cheyenne before.

We went so that he could keep his appointment, but the weather was bad. Snow and blowing snow. They picked me up, and we headed out on I-80. The roads were open but not good. Bruce, who was a horrible driver, insisted on driving. Grandma did not like it but relented for now.

We were in his massive four-door car. A real battleship. We were going along pretty well when a semi passed, and Bruce lost track of where we were in the blowing snow off the semitruck. Visibility was zero. Instead of slowing and keeping the car going straight until we could see again, Bruce turned left, and you couldn't see, but you could feel that we had left the interstate gone a fairly steep incline and were still going forward in the dirt-deep snow median.

Finally, we stopped, and we could see again in the billowing snow and wind. We had come to a stop only a few feet from a stout barbed wire fence running between the roadways. Grandma was done. "Out, out, you are not driving anymore. You let Kenny drive." Bruce began to tell her he would be alright, but she was having none of it. I took over with hopes that we would not be stuck in the snow and be able to get back up onto the interstate.

I backed up and headed for the roadway. Never spun a tire in that deep snow and slick incline. We hit the road and took off. Bruce tried to take over driving again several times on the trip. But even with improving roads and weather, Grandma was not about to let him have another whack at it.

Bruce would drive me in an old well-worn car he had to services that I was to preach at in Big Piney sometimes. He would sing a special song for the congregation, which they enjoyed and were blessed by, and then I would conduct the service and preach for them. He would get to talking and singing and giving little attention to his driving. I had to watch him like a hawk. One time he turned his turn signal on, and it didn't cancel out. Actually, this was a common happening. However, this particular time rather than bringing his attention to the loud clicking noise the signal made with each flash and the flashing light in front of the driver's panel, I decided as we went down the highway with little traffic to see how far he would drive before he noticed all of this.

We had gone over five miles when I finally had become bored with the watch. "Bruce, your turn signal is still going," I interrupted his riveting tale or song with. He looked at the turn signal's light flashing on the panel like he was looking at some unusual sight seldom seen.

"That gosh dern thing, how did that happen?" He turned it off and picked up where he left off.

How many accidents he had I lost count of? How he kept insurance was always a mystery to me. I was never in the car when he had an accident, and in fact, it usually happened when he was alone—no one there to save him, I would guess.

I learned a good deal about hunting, trapping, fishing, and setting up camps from Grandpa Hamilton. I had a summer camp set up with Brenda and the dogs in the Bighorn years later when a seasoned cowboy-outdoors man and his wife rode past our camp. He apparently looked it over pretty good because we had gone on a little hike and met them a short way from our camp. We visited, and he made a point of telling me that that was the nicest tent camp he had ever seen. He was very impressed with it. If I was not moving around and had time to set camp in a spot for several days or weeks, it was always set up to Grandpa Hamilton's specs. Very comfortable and inviting to all. Always a tent camp, of course, no trailers or RVs for us.

Grandpa and I went three years in a row setting up nice camps in '77, '78, and '79 in the Wasatch National Forest at Whiskey Spring to elk- and deer-hunt. People would always invite themselves, and we only had parts of our time there alone. Chuckie would usually show up with a hooligan or two in tow. They did more drinking and sleeping in than any form of hunting at all.

Chuckie hunted there several times, and other than shooting one deer and me shooting a doe deer for him one time, I don't recall him ever taking any game home. But we wouldn't turn anybody away. Steve Reichel and a chubby kid that I barely knew came up one time too when Chuckie was there. We didn't sleep on cots but had pads or mattresses on the floor of the tent.

Grandpa was usually not bad for drinking when we were out and about. He would have a beer and kept a big glass gallon bottle of what he called his sacrament or red eye. It was red pop mixed with a large amount of high-content alcohol. It was as good as a paint remover. He would have a slug of this once in a while, especially if it was cold.

On this particular night, Grandpa and some of the camp company had been sucking down booze around the campfire that night. Everybody needed to sleep in the tent. So, we were sleeping across the floor stacked like cordwood next to one another.

Grandpa was sleeping next to Steve Reichel. He apparently got up in the night as described by Steve and seemed in a stupor as to his exact location. He unzipped and relieved himself on Steve's sleeping bag. Happily, he returned to bed and slept till morning.

Steve didn't worry too much about it, what could he do? He said it was a little damp but not bad. Might as well get a good rest, morning would soon be here, and hunting was on his mind.

Another time several of us were there, and Chuckie had pulled a camping trailer up, and he and somebody were staying in it by our tent. It was another social night around the campfire. Grandpa and a few of the visitors had a bit more sauce than they needed. Grandpa decided to get a big laugh out of everybody by throwing .300 rifle cartridges into the roaring fire. He would toss one in every so often, and we would all scatter like sheep while he stood at the fire and laughed like a fiend at us.

Usually, the cartridges just made a not all that loud *boom*, and that was it. But on the last one he threw in, there was a loud *boom*, and you could hear the bullet fly off and strike something metallic. The entertainment ceased. The bullet had gone through the top corner of Chuckie's camping trailer. He was laughing about it but really was none too happy about this.

Camp was just a good time of visiting, though, and having a nice time. Wild times were limited to just a few from my campers, and once I was putting up camp without Grandpa and started having fellow workers come up, the atmosphere was very different and settled. Not just because of Grandpa but because the whole makeup of guys coming up was different.

Grandpa was a hoot, though. A lot of laughs, not like a lot of old guys who want to sit around and talk about what doesn't work anymore and how many pains they have or what medications they are taking in full detail. He was tough and could take the cold like me.

The last year he camped with me at Wasatch, the weather started out that mid-October day a bit cool and rainy as we set up camp. Then it improved and was pretty nice. We had a young guy in camp that asked to come up, he and his young wife rented from my dad. He was from Missouri and was a decent guy. Chuckie set up camp on the next water hole up from us at Big Spring. He had a girlfriend with him, and they set up an old leaky catalog-store tent.

Chuckie had wanted a .22 pistol for Christmas, so I gave him a single-shot revolver. He was wearing this on his hip, and we kind of made fun of him for trying to be Wild Bill Hickok while deer-hunting. I seriously cautioned him, though, about this not being a good idea while deer-hunting with a rifle.

He paid no attention to any of this. He and the kid from camp went out with the girlfriend hunting for deer that afternoon. Grandpa and I usually hunted apart from one another up there. I came into camp that night just after dark, and there was no fire going or anyone around. This was strange. I unzipped the tent, and it was cool and dark. I spotted Grandpa all rolled up in his sleeping bag and woke him. I asked what was going on. He kept his head in his bag and mumbled that he was feeling sick as could be. I asked where everybody else was. He just nonchalantly told me that Chuckie had shot himself and the kid from our camp, Rich, and Chuckie's girlfriend had taken him to the doctor. This he related as if it were common knowledge and a usual occurrence.

I couldn't make sense of it, but I wasn't able to get much more out of my ill hunting partner. The next morning, I hunted and came into camp at noon. Grandpa was over his sick spell, and a short time later, Chuckie and the crew came in. He had a big cast on his leg and was no longer wearing the revolver.

He was pretty jovial about it but related that he and Rich had both shot nice bucks in the draw near Sage Creek. This was kind of a bushy spot, and as they were pulling out the deer uphill, some of the brush cocked the hammer back on his pistol, and it fired. The bullet hit him in the leg and broke the bone. Fortunately, no arteries were struck, or that would have probably been that, as they say.

Rich got the deer to the truck, and then he and the girlfriend helped the injured one to the truck when it appeared, he would live. They took off for Evanston and got him into the hospital there. Now they were back, but they had had enough.

Rich was only deer-hunting and had to get back for work, so he left with his nice buck. Grandpa and I went to Chuckie's camp and got it loaded up. Stuff was wet inside from the earlier rain. We sent them on their way then, and a good thing it was too. For the next day, it started snowing and snowed for two days. I never saw that much snow in that area at that time of the year before or since.

Several hunters had stopped at our camp on the way past before the season opened as they were going to set up camps too and hunt. Our camp was known to be friendly, and many people would stop as they went by just to chat, and it was known that we would help anyone with trouble. It was that way then, and it was that way after Grandpa was gone.

But one guy in particular was pulling a long camping trailer in and told us that he was there to stay. Boy, when that weather hit, you should have seen him and everybody else go racing back out! Not us. We had no weather reports and didn't know how bad it was to be, but we didn't care. Grandpa and I had no intention of taking off. We had at least another week to stay, and that was the plan.

We had the place to ourselves but wading in the snow and drifts was all you could do. The roads were impassable. Big buck deer were all over the place, and we had our choice of any. Strangely, the elk were hard to find.

As was typical, within a few days, the weather turned really pleasant and fall-like again, and most of that snow was gone. When we packed up a week or so later, everything was dry. In camp.

Just before we had to leave, I had been out hunting on foot for elk. Grandpa went out that morning, too, but said he was going to stay in camp that afternoon and fix his truck. The fuel line was leaking, and he needed to climb up in the old heap and tighten fuel lines up with a wrench.

When I came walking in to have lunch before I went out again, I noticed as I approached camp that there was a forest ranger's truck at the camp. Now, this was funny. Grandpa was standing in front of his truck, coffee in hand. The hood was up on his truck, and a forest ranger in uniform with his sleeves rolled up was hanging down into the engine compartment working on the truck. Grandpa could be heard regaling the ranger with some great tale of past exploits.

He had a big grin on his face when he saw me coming. I walked in smiling as he told me that he was in the process of fixing his leaking fuel line.

After we had been camped and hunting for several days, Grandpa would get a big load of firewood in his truck, and I would pull up wood from below camp where there had once been an old sawmill. We would have campfires in the evening and just relax and visit. Nice times, with fall weather and the big sky overhead with millions of stars that, the Bible tells us, God had given each one a name. The Big Dipper was very visible at camp as well as the Milky Way, or, as Grandpa called it, the Milkmaids' path.

Then within a few days, Grandpa would take a day off and start a big fire in the early afternoon. Then he used a huge pot and made a wonderful pot of mulligan stew over the fire. This stew was loved by most and was very filling. It had about everything in it. Sometimes you wouldn't ask what was in it as it was consumed. Who knows where the squirrel or the Canada jay that was hanging around camp disappeared to? Goodness, there were even badgers, field mice, and porcupines that would sometimes come too close to camp.

Once Grandpa was gone, I took over making the mulligan stew with the same recipe and techniques of making the nectar. That, along with stout cups of cowboy coffee, would put you on your feet to get you going or keep you going, no matter how tough the trip. The only ingredient that we found to be not so hot was one year when I added some deer liver to the pot. The stew was still good, but the liver chunks are not recommended.

Once the hunting was about done or in between getting elk or deer and taking a day off to just relax at camp, we would have a leisurely late breakfast at the table outside on a nice fall day. Eggs, coffee, and pancakes that I would cook. Very nice with meat hanging in camp and just enjoying God's great created beauty. I pity hunters that just have to be on a mission to get animals. I have hunted with a few of them over the years. They may have pretty good success, but they miss an awful lot of what it is all about.

Always had to have a good supply of ginger ale, root beer, and special cola in camp. Jan and Tammy would use their old grade school tin lunch pails, fill them full of homemade peanut butter and chocolate chip cookies, and send them with me.

We had a woodstove in the tent after the first year of hunting at Whiskey Spring. The first year Grandpa had this big radiating propane heater that attached to a big propane bottle. We would heat at night with that if it was really cold until getting in bed.

However, one night it was especially cold. Only he and I were in camp. He was cold at bedtime and wanted to leave the heater going. I didn't like this idea, but we did it. I would sleep with my head inside my bag if it was cold. It's a good thing I did. During the night, the propane heater went out but was still spewing out propane. Grandpa woke later and smelled the odor and called out to me. He said I just would laugh at him and lay in bed. He finally shook himself out of what felt like a cheap drunk and got me out of bed and outside into the snow and cold air. It was still dark and early. We survived that, but it could have been much worse. That morning we stayed in camp. We both had splitting headaches and felt not so good. *No more propane was run after going to bed, no matter how cold it was.*

We had pretty good hunting in this country, and I knew it like my backyard. It was a pretty spot. I had filled my first moose permit, shot a number of elk and many deer there over the years. I would go summer camping there too. Once in a while, Cottonwood or Sage Creek had some decent brookies in them, and I would catch dinner. One time I drove up there in January. There were tons of snow. I was able to just get a short way off the main road with my small four-wheel drive. Then it was such a nice day that I used my original pair of snowshoes and went from there to the ridge on Cottonwood Mountain. Spent the entire day in there. Not much for game with all of the snow but lots of birds.

Chuckie had this goofy friend of his named Charlie that he had run around with for several years. Charlie was loud and could tell whoppers like the best of them. He wore thick black-framed glasses, was plain as a mud fence, and was over six-and-a-half feet tall and lanky. He always wore heavy lace-up work boots and had about a size 12 foot, which was very large then for a person. He was funny to watch and listen to because he was so goofy.

Anyway, he and Chuckie came up to hunt with us for several days. They parked their camping trailer across the road from our camp. I guess Chuckie didn't want to risk any more possible bullet holes in the contraption! They would spend the evening at our camp and hang around the campfire.

The second night there, Chuckie and Charlie got horsing around the campfire, and Chuckie gave Charlie a shove. Charlie lost his balance and fell over his big clodhoppers. Grandpa had his truck backed into that area with the old heavy tailgate down. When Charlie fell, his forehead hit the metal piece where the hook in the tailgate keeper latched into. This was a stout metal hook that stuck up a couple of inches. Charlie rolled onto his back and laid there moaning. No one paid much attention to him, and Chuckie returned to the campfire. I thought I'd better make sure he was going to live, so I went over to check on him. There was a big old gash in his forehead and some bleeding. I got him some iodine and aspirin and helped get him laid down in their camp trailer after a bit. He had a terrible headache but thought he would survive. I comforted him with something like, "Well, Charlie, at least with your face, this injury can't hurt your looks too much." He didn't laugh.

The next day Charlie made it out to hunt and had survived the whack on his head. He was telling everybody about his great exploits in this forest. He had walked almost every inch of it. Of course, as I said, he had an unusually large foot, and his boot tread was distinctive. I made it a point to check on the little walking that he had in fact done, as he and Chuckie loved to ride around in the truck and road-hunt usually. Chuckie wanted to stay clean and always wore cologne and seldom wore a hat because he didn't want to mess up his hair. I found Charlie's few tracks in a couple of places. He never varied from the roadway. Truth be known, Charlie was afraid of his own shadow and was afraid of getting lost in the timber.

I had gotten my elk, and now I was out looking for deer. I was sitting up on top of the ridge where game often crossed, just enjoying the afternoon and watching for a deer to come through. An older man, probably in the late 60s or so, walked past me about one hundred yards distant. We waved, and he continued on toward the far edge of the ridge. About that time, a lone spike elk came running between me and the guy. The elk was making quite a bit of noise thundering past the guy's backside on the rocky dirt ridge.

I kept waiting for him to turn and fire, but he didn't. The elk crossed the ridge and went down into timber on the far side. I went over to the guy as he had stopped at the ridge top and asked what he was hunting. "Why, elk, of course." I then told him what had happened. The guy got kind of all puffed up and said he didn't believe me.

I said, "Well, that's what just happened." He was incredulous. Didn't believe that at all, and off he went.

Butch had been in the police department when I started but was now working in the oil field. He liked to hunt in the Hoback but would come up and hunt at my camp too. He worked for a company called Lay Right Pipe. They had a logo with the name and a naked woman lying on a side view on her back. He had a whole roll of stickers with this logo on it. Not at all a very nice item. Just to be the ornery one, the day before he left camp when I wasn't there, he stuck these stickers on all of my chairs, tables, and anything else they would stick to. It was funny, and many of the stickers stayed attached for years.

I hunted pretty light. Almost always on foot, I had my rifle, sheath knife, a cartridge carrier that was attached to the belt with a few cartridges, a few cough drops, and a small Snickers candy bar or two. If I could find it, I had the cans of shredded jerky that were popular in a plastic can like a chewing tobacco can came in. In later years I got used to packing a fanny or day pack some in Alaska and would do this sometimes too when I returned to Wyoming.

We didn't wear camouflage in the early years. Only a few people did. It was heavy carpenters' pants or fishing pants, bib overalls, and a heavy brown or tan shirt. I wore a duck-hunting jacket most times and an old flop wide-brimmed hat. A good pair of high-top hunting boots were worn, but in good weather, a pair of high-top tennis shoes were the ticket.

Lots of guys from work would come up and hunt with me or out of our camp. I wasn't crazy about some of them coming up as this was supposed to be my vacation to get away from town and work, but I never denied anybody and always made them welcome. I would tell them where and how to hunt a spot. Most of them were not very good hunters, but several cashed in on my advice and were able to get deer or elk.

The chief of police at that time, Hawk, was not a favorite of the police except with the new guys that had been brought in the past year or so. There was a lot of political trouble involved in the whole county at this time, but especially in Rock Springs. However, I was still serving as the head chaplain for the police department and, of course, as a full-time senior officer, etc. Somebody gave him instructions on how to get to my camp, and he came up for two years in a row while he was a chief.

He was a road hunter too and always had his much younger wife and baby in the truck with him. He made it a point to stop by camp when I just happened to be unfortunate enough to be there, and then he wouldn't leave. Mostly just wanted to be invited to sit around the camp table and visit over coffee. It was a lost afternoon, but I would accommodate them. I might add that, for the most part, he always treated me well at work and gave me full cooperation with the chaplain's division.

I had a friend from work hunting with me, Dave. We had come into camp to have lunch on a nice day when a forest ranger drove into camp. This fellow in his late 40s was officious and stern and introduced himself as the head ranger for the area out of the office in Mountain View.

We talked with him a few moments, and then he lectured us on the tenets of having a safe campfire and just very, very basic type of safety stuff that we had both learned as kids. He felt the need to hand out fliers that had additional information in them about how to put out a fire properly and so on. We took the flier and suffered through his little presentation.

Then off he went to save the forest from other campers-hunters. While we were finishing lunch and getting ready to go hunt for the afternoon, I saw this ranger walking on the road back to our camp. "Dave, look at who's coming. Now what?"

The ranger was really friendly now. No more high-and-lofty-attitude stuff. The smart aleck parrot had fallen from its perch! He had driven up the road a few hundred yards from camp. There the road had two passages in it for a short distance. One was a bit rough but obviously the route to take. The other had become a bog hole from recent melted snow, and only the most careless or greenest of outdoor travelers would have driven into it.

The head ranger that had just lectured us about how to build and put out a fire and so on had driven into the mudhole and was stuck. We were kind, but boy, what a time we could have had. We drove him back to the scene of the crime and used a chain and pulled him out. He was really sheepish. We privately had laughs about that little escapade the rest of the trip. We never saw the defender of the trees again.

One fall, the big topic in Rock Springs was that the program *60 Minutes* had been in town that summer and they were going to air the program they had made about "Sin City." It was supposed to be all about the great corruption, scandal, violence, and on and on. I had met the crew when they came to the police department that afternoon while I was working. Dan Rather was the correspondent doing the story. I thought he looked old and worn out then. I was not impressed with any of them and tried to avoid the circus. No question that the place was wild and barely controllable, but most of this media attention came about because of people with political ambitions, with sights on being a mayor, a governor, and so forth. A big oaf running the local radio station was one of the pawns also being used by the powers that hoped to climb the political ladder. I was hunting in Wasatch when the program aired and never saw it then or afterwards.

Another sort of work friend was a little middle-aged guy that had come to Rock Springs with his uppity wife from New York. He was likable but odd. I took him coyote-hunting once near Flaming Gorge, and he had asked if he could come up and deer-hunt at my camp. Okay, so he came up just for the day. I knew he was not much of a hunter, but he was hoping to get a deer. He wasn't particular about what he shot, and does were in season. I drove him onto the ridge above camp that afternoon after he had hunted in the morning by himself and had no success. I had seen him on the police pistol range. He shot okay, so I assumed he would be fine with his rifle.

As we went along, there was a lone doe standing broadside on the ridge at about fifty yards from us. I had him prepare to shoot. He got all set and began to fire slowly and methodically at the deer with his .30-30 lever-action rifle. Shot after shot never bothered the critter. Finally, he had emptied the gun of ammo, and the deer become annoyed at the racket and walked off.

His name was Orman. "Orman, I asked, "what are you doing?"

Well, he sheepishly replied, "I just bought this gun and had never fired it before, but it's a shooter, and it's broken in now."

"You never fired it before coming up here?"

"No, no."

"Didn't you sight it in?"

"No, I bought it brand-new and figured it was good enough." He wasn't the least upset over the results of using a quarter half a box of ammo in this fruitless endeavor. "It sure is a nice fall day," said he, and he just enjoyed me taking him around. He was good-humored, and it was hard not to like the guy, even though he would have been run off in most camps.

Neil Kourbelas, who was a good friend from work, came up and deer-hunted several times. He was from California. A rock climber and not too serious of a hunter either. I think he enjoyed just being out in this nice country mostly. I couldn't blame him, I did too. He always enjoyed coming to my camp and told me one time, "You know, this is really a ministry that you do here." I never really thought of it that way, although after Grandpa was gone, I ran a pretty booze-free and easy-going camp. Lots of fun but without the wild antics. Oh, I would let a guy have a drink in camp without any big production if they wanted, but that was about it. It was low-key. But I think over the years of being in that spot with all the different people that came along, I was able to show them what Jesus might have been like to some degree if He had been there hunting in that camp, and really, He was.

The camp was known as a friendly place but crawling with Rock Springs cops in the last years. It sure cut down on the seedy characters stopping by. An older rancher in the area always stopped by, and we would tell him where we saw his cattle that he was trying to round up, and if he had any sightings of elk, he would tell us. He was a paunchy little Mormon guy that drove a red flatbed truck or was once in a while aboard a dark-colored horse. I would always offer him coffee. He always refused. The last time I saw him, he had come down with throat cancer. He survived it but was now wearing a gauze patch over a hole in the middle of his throat, and his voice was weak.

Other hunters would just stop by for chats. One day a guy in his late 20s stopped by, and he was frantic. He came up to us in camp and said, "Have you seen my rifle?"

"What?" He was sure that somebody in the area had his rifle. He had got out of his truck on an old road to relieve himself. He set his rifle against the front bumper, did his business, got back into the truck, and drove off. A few minutes later, it hit him what he had done. He raced back to the spot. There was no rifle to be found. Someone had come along and hit the jackpot.

I think it was a really nice scoped .30-06 rifle, as he described it. He was pretty upset and acted like we had to know what happened to it. I told him we would keep an eye out but that we had all been in camp for lunch and had no clue about his misfortune. I never saw him again and don't know the outcome of his loss. It was probably bleak. I saw an ad he had placed in a shopper's paper about the missing rifle and some reward after I had returned from hunting that fall.

I often had people come to camp that had vehicle trouble or were stuck and helped them out. One old couple were about a mile from my camp one day as I drove past them. Something looked odd, so I pulled up and stopped. They had a moose permit, but their old vehicle had quit, and the battery was dead. In a matter of moments, I retrieved my jumper cables and had them on their way.

I was by myself one windy, stormy night. I had been forced into the tent with my woodstove and lantern due to the nasty weather.

I was having a late dinner and quite cozy when I heard someone approaching the tent and calling out. I opened the door and found three strangers in the dark. They had walked several miles over from a valley where they were stuck.

I closed down camp, and we loaded in the small four-wheel drive to go pull them out. I had a bigger orange-colored monster of an outfit that was a tank but thought the small outfit might do at this late hour. It was a little unnerving, these three guys in the dark, but what could I do? It wasn't long, and I had them on their way. They were grateful. Mine was the only camp in the area late in the season now. It would have been a long, tedious hike to the main road and probably no help there to come along at this hour.

I would not always but often come into camp for an hour or two break if the weather was warm. I would listen to Paul Harvey's news and comments and the weather on KMER radio out of Kemmerer. Do a few little camp chores and have lunch.

Lunch would usually involve me making large thick antelope burgers that I then cooked on my gas stove. "Cooked" is being used very recklessly here! They were browned on both sides. Boy, they were good. Probably close to a half-pound each. Then slabbed on white bread with a generous helping of ketchup.

Grandpa and Chuckie were in camp one afternoon when I offered them my fare. Sure, they wanted to sample my feast. I cooked us all burgers, and we ate them up. That night I came into camp. Neither one of them had left camp that day. They were both whining about they had been sick all afternoon, vomiting, and all of that good stuff. Those big burgers had about killed them, and they weren't going to eat any more of them. I guess that was the real clincher that was supposed to hurt my feelings. It bothered me not one bit. "Goooood," I said, "that just leaves more for me." I thought it was funny. If they had eaten them and couldn't take it, that was their trouble. I didn't keep a camp for wimps, and part of it was if you wanted my burgers, that was the only way they came.

I knew the real names of locations in the Wasatch, but we used other names for quite a few of the places due to events that occurred there. Moose Meadow I named for the location where I shot my moose. A big cow. She came charging at me from the edge of the woods while I was out in the open meadow with nowhere to go. She was mad. Throwing snot out of her nostrils and intent on stomping me. At full steam, she was almost on top of me before I could fire a shot. I had no time to aim. I simply pointed the .270 rifle at her and fired. She dropped like a rock. The bullet had hit her spine and broke it. Another inch, and it would have missed—*ouch* for me! I had to finish her off with a headshot as she was down but now pulling herself in my direction with her front legs and still mad as hops.

Jack Valley I named because I had camped there one night out of my old green Suburban when I was alone on a two-day hunt. I stayed in the back of the Suburban. I had stuff I placed around the outside of the vehicle to give me more room inside. This included a big old sheepherder's jack—high-lift jack. I put it under the vehicle to keep it out of any snow that might fall. The next morning, I hurriedly decided to go hunt another location, and, in my haste, I forgot about the jack under the Suburban. I drove back much later that night when I recalled not picking up the jack. It, of course, was gone.

Hickey Ridge was misnamed by Steve Reichel's dad the first year most of us started hunting in the Wasatch. He somehow apparently thought it was Hickey Mountain from a map of the area, but this mountain was actually to the northeast of what was actually Cottonwood Mountain, which really is more of a high timbered ridge than a mountain.

Buck Pond, named by, yes, me, was a nice little beaver pond in a chain of small ponds on Sage Creek. It was a pretty little spot all surrounded by pines and pretty colored aspen trees—in the fall. Steve Reichel and I had gone up to Wasatch for a day of a deer hunt. It was a delightful fall day. We hunted apart most of the day. I had not seen too much and finally, late in the afternoon, decided to just sit by the pond against an aspen tree and enjoy the sunshine and view and watch for game. There were game trails all around the pond. Apparently, Steve finally decided it was time to go home, and we had not been hunting too far from one another. He was above the area, probably several hundred yards. He began yelling my first name. I didn't respond or budge. I was in no hurry to leave yet.

After he yelled my name loudly several times, I heard something coming from between him and me that he had apparently got up and moving with all of his racket. I quietly watched. A nice buck deer was walking quickly toward me on one of the game trails. I waited until he was within about twenty-five-thirty yards and used my .270 to stop his escape from the above racket. He had no idea I was there.

Steve made his way to me after I had shot the deer. He had read some article in an outdoor magazine that showed a really neat way to pack out an animal whole. The idea was an old one, to tie the front and back legs to an aspen pole, and with each of us on an end of the pole, it would be a cinch to pack the animal out the several hundred yards to the old road. I didn't like the idea. It would be much quicker and better to just each get a front leg and pull the deer out whole. Nothing doing. It had to be done as recommended by the publication.

Time was wasted by quite a bit with all of the prep work of getting the right pole, tying, etc. Off we went. The deer swung side to side as we went along the old game trail to the road. It was hard to walk with the load and became quickly torturous. We undid this mess and dragged the deer out.

A ridge east of Cottonwood Mountain above Sage Creek Park was named by Steve as Reicheimer Ridge, using a combination of our last names. This was after we went there one unusually hot afternoon when everyone swore the elk had all fled the area and found a herd bedded in thick timber on the lower ridge. We each took an elk. Guys sitting in camp complaining about the heat were more than surprised when we drove in with a load of elk early that evening. This included Chuckie and Grandpa. You just can't quit because of weather not exactly to your liking when hunting and fishing.

The first elk that Steve and I took together in Wasatch when we were teens was something. We had little for equipment. We had borrowed his dad's old blue pickup, and we just had an assortment of stuff to barely get by with. We went to the area that we were only vaguely familiar with in late November.

We had hunted pretty hard for a couple of days for elk, but it was slow. The weather was pretty nice, with not much snow around.

The nights and early mornings were cold. The last camp we made was not bad. We hiked onto Cottonwood Mountain and hunted hard that morning but had no success.

We decided to go to camp and cook a limited lunch and decide what to do. We had been in camp only a short time, and the wind had started blowing pretty bad, and it had become cloudy. The weather was making a big change, obviously.

I sat on a big rock in camp, and Steve was firing up his dad's stove to cook some eggs. We were chatting about our next plans when out of the blue, a big cow elk trotted into camp between me and Steve. It was to Steve's back. The elk couldn't make sense of this situation for a moment, and it just stood there looking at us. I was so shocked that all I could do was jump up and make garbled sounds. This frightened Steve, and he jumped away from the stove and was quickly looking behind him for some impending doom. Then he spotted the elk. The elk had now come to life out of its shock as well and began running full bore out of the little camp and toward a nearby stream and small ridge. We ran for our rifles that were lying nearby, and as the elk ran up the small timbered ridge, we fired and got it.

You just never know what will happen. We worked at getting the camp picked up and the elk all taken care of and loaded up as the weather rapidly worsened. Boy, we were two happy guys. Just a short time after we were done, a tremendous blizzard hit. Raging wind and snow. We headed out. By the time we made it to the main forest service road, which was no small task, the side of the truck catching most of the wind had about a foot of hard snow plastered to it. It was a blizzard all the way back to Rock Springs. The temperature had dropped like crazy. Boy, did the Lord take care of us? We were not prepared with our little camp for such a storm, and the roads were terrible to get back on. The interstate was closed, and vehicles were off the road all the way to town, semis and everything else. We kept going as we dare not stop, closed roads or not. We made it home slowly but without incident.

When Grandpa and I hunted the Wasatch, we came and left together. After that, I would often have times when everyone else was either done hunting—successful or not, or had gone back to school or work. I was alone, and I didn't mind that at all. I have never been a lonely person and have always been very comfortable by myself, even in times of bad weather or touchy situations.

One such time was nice fall weather. I had been out on foot as I usually hunted all morning. It was getting late in the morning, and I was circling back toward camp but still a good way off and below of it. I had another hunter about my age pass on my left about fifty yards uphill from me. We waved at each other and kept going. I had only gone a few steps when a large four-point buck deer stopped in front of me on a rise about forty-fifty yards away and facing me. We locked eyes. He was on the move. Before he could take another step, I shot him in the neck with my .270. A big halo of blood mist appeared around his head, and he stayed upright and turned towards the hill that the other hunter was on and started to trot. I fired into his chest and hit right behind his front shoulder—in the lungs. He still did not go down. Instead, he spotted the other hunter above me and ran toward him. The hunter fired a random hipshot, and the deer lowered his head and charged uphill at the guy.

There was a dip there, and the guy threw his rifle down and laid prone as the deer with head lowered skimmed over the top of him. The deer then fell dead. The guy jumped up and went to the deer, and when I got there, he was getting his sheath knife out.

I asked him what he thought he was doing. He said he shot the deer and he was going to take it. "No, you're not," I told him before I looked at the deer exactly where I shot him twice, and then we looked at the deer and clearly saw what would have been the entry wounds in the deer, just as I said.

Further examination showed that his shot had hit the deer in the antlers as there was fresh damage there. He did not care; he was taking the deer. I made it clear to him in no uncertain terms that this was not going to happen. We stood only feet apart. He with the knife in hand while I cradled my rifle.

I told him if he had any doubts about this, I was willing for us to take the deer to the game warden and tell him the story and let him decide who the deer was killed by. He would have none of that. He stood there for a few minutes watching me as I prepared to take care of the animal, and then he began cursing and gathering up his stuff.

He said he was up here with his two older brothers. That they all worked in the oil field and that I could take the deer (oh, thanks so much) but that he knew where my camp was and that they would be paying me a visit. The threat was poorly veiled and intentionally so.

I was not having this. I informed my little friend that if anyone came around my camp for trouble, the results would likely not be to their suiting. In plain words, it was to the effect that it would not bother me to shoot any troublemakers, and that was what would happen. I believe when necessary, Theodore Roosevelt's logic can quench fiery darts before they do damage, that being "Carry a big stick and walk softly."

Later I had pulled the deer up to the road near camp and returned with my Suburban. I was loading the deer in when a truck stopped nearby. Three men got out and walked to within about twenty yards. It was the fellow that threatened me and his two brothers. They all appeared in good shape, but so was I. They never said a word, and I didn't either, I just kept an eye on them and prepared to load the deer into the vehicle. They looked it all over and returned to their vehicle. I never saw any of them again.

Another time before that, I was hunting on foot on Hickey Ridge with Chuckie, some pal of his, and Steve. It was a nice day, and it had been kind of quiet. Steve and I met on top of the ridge and then split up. Vehicles used to be able to drive up on the ridge. It is now closed to vehicular traffic. I was at the edge of the timber when a lone elk came running over the opposite side of the ridge in my direction but out 150 yards or so. I shot him, but he made it to the edge of the trees before he fell down.

Before I got over to him, a truck came racing up the dirt road and drove to the elk. Three men were in the truck and had apparently seen what happened and then decided they would rather steal an elk than get one of their own.

One of the guys jumped out and ran over to the elk that was lying dead and fired a shot. I ran up, and the other guys were getting out of the truck. All of us about the same age. I recognized two of the men as Mexican brothers from a rough family in Rock Springs that loved to fight.

Steve heard the shooting and joined me. One of the brothers said that they had their elk and acted like they were going to go ahead and take the animal. I told them that I had killed the elk and they knew it. I could see big trouble coming, but right is right, and this was no time to let a bunch of snakes have their way. They were used to outnumbering people and jumping them and intimidating people. I knew them well, and they knew me. I told them to leave the elk alone, that it was dead when they drove up to it.

They tried arguing about it and were milling around as I laid my gun against a tree and took my sheath knife out. I looked at Steve, who was standing just behind me and cradling his rifle. I said in a loud voice so that there would be no misunderstanding, "Steve, I am going to gut our elk, and if anybody tries to pull any capers, you lay them out with your rifle." Steve nodded at me in the affirmative and gave the three Mexicans his steady stare while holding his rifle at the ready port. The three told me that they were the so and so brothers from Rock Springs and that I would be sorry about this. I said, "I know who you are, now quit bothering me, I have work to do." With that, I knelt and began taking care of my elk. Teddy Roosevelt worked again. I did not like having trouble with people like that, and those are the only two times in all the years of my hunting and fishing that this kind of distasteful thing happened. The three loaded up and left cursing, and I never saw them up there again. I never had trouble with any of them at any other time in town either. They were pathetic road hunters at best. The kind of people that will start trouble, intimidate others, steal anything that they can, and shoot up road signs. I have no patience with people like that and would not allow them to run over a weaker person, so I certainly was not about to let them pull this on me and just embolden them to act that way with no repercussions. In either case, I was not giving vain warnings. These were battles that would have to be fought regardless.

Chuckie came up as the men were driving off, and we told him what happened. He said, "Yeah, but that is the so and so brothers," like their name held awe or something.

I said, "I don't care who they were."

I was alone hunting late one October. It was snowy and cold. Camp was empty, and hunting had been a bit slow. I was after elk. It was kind of a dreary day. I was about to walk back into camp when I encountered a guy my age aboard a horse. We had a good chat. He was looking for elk too. He said he had been everywhere up here and that there were no elk. "It is a waste of time to keep it up."

We parted a bit later, and I went into camp. Just before I got there, though, I noticed some large lone elk's tracks in the wet snow about one hundred yards away from my camp. It was kind of chilly and damp, so I went in and did a few camp chores and had a quick lunch.

I then went back to the tracks that had crossed the old road I had spotted them on. I began tracking the animal in the timber and quiet snow. I had gone several hundred yards in the timber when I came to a small opening. A five-point bull elk stood from this bed at the end of the tracks and prepared to bolt. I raised my .270 and fired quickly at him, and he dropped. I ran over and shot him again to finish him. Not all of the elk had left, as my fellow hunter had assured me. My first shot was to hit the elk in the rear of his neck, but I had shot just a half-inch low, and the bullet struck him at the end of his tailbone. It must have stunned him and caused him to fall down. The bullet then flew off and didn't penetrate, but it accomplished what I needed until I could further lead-poison him!

I was on a lone couple of days' hunts in the Wasatch with my green Suburban for elk and deer. I crossed a pretty rough creek in one place, and the battery was not properly secured in the engine compartment. It was a nearly new battery. The type with caps that you maintained with water when needed. The battery tipped upside down and spilled a good deal of the liquid out.

No problem, I up righted it and took some of the nice clear creek water and filled it back up. Not a good idea, I learned. Not too many starts after this, I found that the battery was dead and would not start the vehicle. Chuckie and some character that later ended up in prison for murdering a guy in Rock Springs were up there with his trailer hunting on top of the ridge. I was able to get him to jump-start me, and then I had to keep the jalopy running while I hunted that day and then head home.

Grandpa and I had gone on a late goose hunt in the Pinedale area. He said that he knew of a really good place at Boulder Lake for us to get geese. We got there late that evening and could hear the geese on the lake, but it was getting dark, so we stayed concealed behind the high bank with my old Suburban. He told me that we would get up early and sneak over the bank and that the geese would be right there for the picking. Wonderful.

We spent a quiet night at the vehicle and went to sleep. It got really cold in the night, and that old hack was not warm to sleep in. We defrosted ourselves that morning and crawled over the frosty frozen bank, all set for a jackpot. There were two disappointed and surprised goose hunters that peered onto the frozen, goose-less lake.

I could write another book, and I have an extensive hunting-fishing diary and photo books with many pictures covering many of the hunting, camping, and fishing adventures and escapes. So maybe someday, if the Lord delays coming, I may get really ambitious and give it another go.

High school was not one of the happiest times in my life as far as school was concerned. I liked to learn, but again, there was just too much wasted time, unneeded repetition, and the social club stuff was enough to make one vomit. Grandma Weimer used to tell me that school days were the happiest times in her life (she only was able to complete the eighth grade). I said, "Boy, you must have had a terribly unhappy life then." This would make her not too happy with number two grandson. She would say something like, "Oh, you smart aleck" or "It's a wonder that the sun can shine since you're so bright."

I was now spending friend time with Steve Reichel, who was a grade below me. I was friendly with a few kids in school, but it was just during class and nothing away from the school with them. I was bold about being a Christian and a young preacher. I would often spend time between lunch and the next class period sitting somewhere in the school reading my New Testament. This was a World War II military New Testament that I had found many years earlier. It was very durable, and I carried or took it with me most of the time.

We were reading some literature in an English class about African stories. The title used for preacher-pastor in the story was "unfun desi," I am not sure of the spelling now. Anyway, one kid in the class whose name was Dale had moved with his family here from the south. He would always make it a point to address me using that title and then smile. He was just saying hi that way, usually when he saw me.

In English classes where we had to give several verbal presentations. If I was able to work in anything on Scripture, the blessed hope, etc., I would never fail to do so. I was always given good grades on those presentations in class and was never discouraged by teachers in using that material. The class was always respectful and generally receptive to it, even though most of them were unchurched and more interested in other pursuits, both good and bad.

There was a rifle club in the school, and we had guns in our vehicles on the parking lots. Lots of trucks had rifle racks with rifles in them in the rear of the truck window. I often had a .22 in my car or four-wheel-drive outfits. We would go after school in the fall and hunt rabbits till dark just north of Rock Springs in the old mining camps like Dines and Winton. Rabbits were everywhere.

Drinking and partying were common in my class and others as well. Marijuana was popular as too. Other than redneck and cowboy types, most guys had long hair and listened to rock music.

Teno Roncalio was from Rock Springs. He was the U.S. representative for Wyoming. He had held this office for several terms. He was a Democrat. Wyoming was a conservative Republican state, but it did elect a Democrat governor and U.S. senator and/or representative at times. Sweetwater County was one of the few Democrat counties in the state at this time. It is now the twenty-first century and more Republican than Democrat.

Of course, then the Democratic party was more of a labor-working persons' party and not the radical, social mess that it has become. Roncalio asked one of our media classes to work on his reelection campaign. I was interested in civics and politics then. I and another student took the chore on for extra credit and got to make an advertisement for radio and television for his campaign. This took several afternoons after school. He was reelected in this Republican state, and we got a little experience in politics and some extra class credit.

I later worked for the local party during an election, just for one day. I was able to meet local state reps and was paid to help get people to the polls that day by rides or just a phone call reminder to vote. It was interesting, and I liked politics and elections as I understood them then. I was able to get extra credit at school for this and didn't have to attend class that day. They provided lunch. Grandma Weimer worked there with me too. Later, as politics seemed to become even more sordid and combative and I became more aware of how things really worked in government, I knew that politics running for office or being too involved with a political party was not for me.

I had a biology class with Mr. Anderson. He was a good teacher, and I really liked the class. There was a big sealed glass jar in the room that Anderson showed us once or twice that contained a little fully formed fetus in some liquid. This was a bit unnerving to see, but it was amazing to observe the detail of the little eyelids, fingers, and toes with nails. Little veins were visible. He had no certain information as to where the baby came from or who had preserved it. It had apparently been in the school for some years. I wonder what became of the baby. A little spirit loved by Jehovah—formed in His image. A real little person that for some reason didn't or wasn't allowed to live.

I took a Spanish class. The teacher was a strange little beanpole character who thought he was hot stuff. Most of the kids took him for a goof, but he thought he was admired. He didn't like me from right off. Named me Alfonso. I didn't care. Didn't bother me at all. Anyway, he didn't try to keep me in the class, and the more I was there, I grew to dislike it. I think I began to drive him crazy, and we finally decided that since it had only been about two weeks, it might be best for me to transfer to another class-subject.

I took an accounting class and liked it just fine. Just for the challenge and possible use of some of the subjects down the road, I also took classes like business machines, typing, and shorthand. I did well at all of these. Still liked history, civics, biology, and media type or offset printing classes best, though.

Gym I took because I had to and usually came off with C grades for showing up on occasion. I did take a weight training class in place of gym that I liked. It involved working hard with weights, running on the indoor dirt track—in the basement of the building, and stuff like that. We were graded on the improvement between the beginning of the class and the end, so it was to the students' benefit to work hard to improve to get a better grade. I had one of my best gym grades that I ever received in this class. I outdid most of the athletes in the class doing sit-ups. They couldn't believe how many continuous sit-ups I was able to complete. I just stopped after many repetitions of them because I had really helped my grade, but I could have kept going even then.

Steve played the guitar and liked John Denver and Gordon Lightfoot. He got me started listening to them. I liked them too, and they ended up being two of my favorites for secular music. In fact, a few years after high school, I was able to get concert tickets to John Denver's concert, one of the few concerts I ever went to, in Salt Lake City. Jan, my sister, loved his music too. I took her, and we made a long day trip to the event.

Denver, with his long hair and wire-framed glasses, put on a concert that lasted, as I recall, for about three hours. It that was almost entirely with only him performing. He was on a rotating stage, so it didn't matter where you were seated, the audience had equal time viewing him from all sides. The concert was great, we had good seats and certainly got our money's worth.

Steve got a job in a local neighborhood grocery store after school and on Saturday. He was working in the butcher shop. There were several bigger stores in Rock Springs now, but the town still had many of these little family-operated corner grocery stores. This store was located by the now junior high school—old high school.

Steve told me that the store had just fired the stocker/delivery boy and wanted to hire another. He told me to come to apply, so I did. They hired me right off. The store was owned by Ken and Patricia. They were people in their late 30s. Ken's mother also helped at the store, and their two grade-school daughters hung around too. They were nice people and good to work for. I stocked and bagged groceries and carried them out for people needing help. I also delivered our ground burger to a taco joint almost daily. Every week I had to make a dump run with the truck and haul off a room full of cardboard and other waste. One time I was making a Saturday dump run, and it was pretty breezy. As I drove through the south end of town headed to the dump, some of the cardboard started blowing out of the high sideboards on the truck. Before I knew it, I was being stopped by the police on the edge of town.

The cars then only had a red spotlight and were unmarked cars of various makes and colors. I stopped and was encountered by one of the old-time cops, Harry Cottrell. He didn't even check my license, although he really didn't know me. I thought, *Oh boy, now my first ticket.* He was pretty low-key. Just asked where I was coming from and told me to be sure to cover the load next time. We always used an enclosed van after that.

I worked at the store for about six months, and then the owners decided to close it and buy a bar in town. Ken was a tough guy—a boxer. He always treated me good. They bought the Astro Lounge, which was a rough place with dancers, drugs, pimps, prostitutes, and lots of trouble. It was a popular hangout for many locals and newcomers. This was not good for the family. However, I'm sure that financially it was much better than the store for them. Also, the small corner family stores were being replaced and soon to be a thing of the past. The transition was made, and they began running the bar and closing the store.

After the store closed, Ken asked me to come up that summer and paint the outside of the building, which they had turned into an apartment house, so I did that. I also put up a chain-link fence later for his mother at her trailer home. They all treated me well and paid me well. Unfortunately, we (Ken and I) were bound for a collision course down the road. He with his viper pit of a bar and me as a police officer.

Then Steve was working for a small corporation, which was a local fence company operated by Tommy. Tommy was a really good guy. Another old-time Rocks Springer! He was in his late 30s. He was short and wore thick glasses that darkened in the sun. That was unusual then. He was built like a tank and worked right along beside us younger guys. He had a boy that was fat and dumpy. He was kind of a slow kid and not to ambitious. He would come to hang out on projects when the mother must have wanted him out from under her feet but was more hindrance than help. He was junior-high age. Sometimes he was given a simple task to help with by Tommy. Of course, most of the time, within moments, the poor kid was having some major difficulty. Tommy would just look at him and shake his head and then look at Steve and me with a like "what can I do" expression. He was a likable kid, and he was big for his age.

I was in between any paying work when Steve told me Tommy wanted to hire another guy, so I went to see him. I had no experience in putting up a chain-link fence and the like. Tommy and I hit it off, and he put me to work that day. We put up a chain-link fence. Small projects as well as big ones. From small yards to fencing large areas. We worked after school and on weekends. Full-time in the summer. We worked hard for Tommy and would not slough off unless there was downtime, waiting for concrete or for him to complete some calculation or something like that.

One year Steve and I were doing a service at the Big Piney church when an old rancher tried to talk us into coming up that summer and helping him hay all summer. It was enticing to go up to that area and spend the summer. There would be some time to fish and prowl around, but mostly, it would be loading bales of hay out of the field manually, not using loading machines. Good hard outdoor work. That sounded good. The guy would pay a penny a bale and supplied room and board. We nearly decided to take the rancher up on this offer and skip that summer with Tommy—just for the hard work and adventure, but Tommy paid us really good wages, something like six and seven bucks an hour. We weighed this as well as Tommy being really good to work for. Also, this was good hard work, and it was outside work too.

We stayed with Tommy and turned the rancher down. He was disappointed and was looking forward to having two burly, tough

Christian boys working at the place. He was a nice Christian guy. The work for Tommy was not easy. We dug lots of post holes in the hard rocky ground with post hole diggers until Tommy got a drill on a tractor, but the drill still didn't work like it should have and required a good deal muscling it. Mixing cement or working with a cement truck, setting poles, installing, and stretching fence and barbed wire. We worked in eighty and ninety degrees as well as twenty below and wind.

I graduated from high school. The ceremony was held in the large gym. All of my family came except for Chuckie. There was a rumor that a streaker was going to interrupt the goings-on of the event. Streaking—almost always a guy would strip and run naked through a public place with only tennis shoes on—had become a popular thing to do all around the country during this time. It would occur at baseball games, parades, and public events. It only happened a few times in Rock Springs. Half of the year you had to be crazy to take your clothes off. You might frost some vital part! One guy tried doing this at the police department one day. He was in good shape, but apparently, the cops there that day were too. He got chased down and arrested.

Calling in hoax bomb threats to the junior high or high school occurred a few times too and caused the schools to be vacated while we had to wait out in the cold. The police and fire department had to check the building out with school staff, and then things resumed. This was copycat by some dummy as it had become something that was occurring around the country, and apparently, for whatever reason, it was thought to be needed in Rock Springs too.

The graduation was typical. Nothing unusual happened. When I crossed the stage for my diploma (obtained in half the time required—the rest was spent hunting and fishing, I would joke Steve and others that they could contact me at my office at the Flaming Gorge, this would really tick Steve off because his parents made him go to school all the time, he said I was hurting myself because who knows, I may have been a doctor or something like that if I had gone to school all the time, I would just smile at my envious little friend and tell him I had no interest in being a doctor or something as he watched me put hunting or fishing gear into my vehicle and he would go off to school), it was handed to me by Mr. Chady. He was a school board member but had been the high school principal during Chuckie's short tenure. He shook my hand vigorously. He smiled big at me and said he was glad that I had made it. Pictures were taken of each presentation by a local photographer. Mom insisted on me getting a few of those.

Most kids wanted a school ring, and they were really pushed by the school. I had no interest in jewelry and would rather buy something useful like a new fishing pole. My mother tried to get me to get a senior picture taken, but I resisted till she gave up. Only my name is in the yearbook. I thought all of this stuff was overkill. You already got ripped off for a stupid hat and gown that would never be used again and a yearbook that would end up in the dump. Mom did finally later convince me to go to a local photo studio and have a nice color picture taken of me in my security uniform. She was most pleased with the framed picture and kept it on a shelf in the living room for years at the old homeplace with other family portraits. She also had me get smaller black and white copies of the color photo. She had me take some of them, but she mailed most out to relatives and friends.

The church had the Texas pastor in Rock Springs take me to the Bible bookstore in town for graduation. They bought me a really nice leather-bound Thompson Chain-Reference Bible. I used this some for study and to preach from, but generally, I liked a white-covered Bible to preach from that was a Christmas gift from mom and dad. Then later, I had a red-colored Jimmy Swaggart's Bible that I used when the white-covered Bible was getting in poor shape from use. The Bible from mom and dad is what I first preached with as a boy preacher.

Work started slowing down with the fence company. Tommy was too nice of a guy to lay anybody off, but it was obvious now that there was more help than needed. Steve had one more year of school, and I was out now. I told him to keep the job, and I would find something else as I needed to work full-time year-round now.

I was eighteen, soon to be nineteen, and all of the talk around among guys was to go to work in the oil field. I had zero interest in this. Many of the guys I graduated with went to work at the trona mines and made well-paid careers from that. The other big opportunity was at the power plant being built near Point of Rocks.

Dad and Chuckie had been underground coal miners much of the time, and grandpa Joe had done much of this too. Dad kind of expected that I would go with them to the coal mines when I graduated. I like the outdoors and had no interest in confined mines, whether coal or trona. I didn't want to go to work in a local store or anything like that. I really was interested in public service and security-type work and was not too concerned with making big money. I just wanted a decent wage, but I wanted a job that I liked, not just a paycheck.

I started hearing about security guard positions at the Bridger Power Plant. They were hiring. Well, I wore a badge often enough as a kid that this sounded interesting. So, I prayed about it and decided to go check it out. All during my years of preaching, the positions were unpaid. I would often be given gifts, and an offering would be taken for me, but I would have to do something for a steady paycheck. Still living at home was a big help as living costs in Rock Springs had really escalated. The folks made no mention ever of me leaving home. When I finally did at twenty years old, it was my idea, not theirs.

Bruce Hamilton was needing a job that didn't require too much physical labor as he had a back injury to live with. He had his car, and somehow, we talked about the security job at the plant. It was decided that he would drive me out to the plant the next day and see if we could get hired. I didn't want to discourage Bruce, but I thought his chances were not good. He could only barely read and write and had only finished the lower grades. Then he was just a bit odd to most people's liking. He had a heart of gold.

We drove out to the plant on Monday morning. The place was a large facility under construction. Thousands of men and women worked there two and three shifts. We drove up to a security gate, and the uniformed guard directed us further down the highway to the main gate. This place was a mystery to us.

We told the uniformed guards at this gate that we had come to apply for a job with their company. They took our information and gave us a paper pass and directions to an office in the facility where the captain was located along with the large construction companies' security man.

We arrived at the small office and found Captain Reed inside with Joe, the security man, at a desk across the room from him. I completed my application and helped Bruce with his. They went over the paperwork with us and interviewed us for several minutes. They told me to report to the afternoon shift later that week and told Bruce that without reading and writing abilities, they couldn't use him. Only white security helmets and uniform shirts with badges and insignia were worn by most guards along with jeans. I would be issued these items when I reported for work. I was pretty excited about this. Bruce was disappointed, but I was afraid that that would be the outcome for him, but it was worth a try. Bruce usually did manual-type work, especially like a janitor and that type of employment.

I worked at the plant for about a year and a half. I liked it most of the time. Joe, the security man, was not easy to work with. He was very negative and critical. Kind of a boot-licker type with other company management. The turnover rate was high, and the captain was replaced just several months later with another man that seemed to cater more to Joe.

I received several commendations from the main Salt Lake City office while I worked at the plant. One for finding a truckload of the expensive hose and other material that had been thrown over the security fence in a remote area of the plant. I recovered this property before someone showed up to take it. We didn't have the staff to watch for the thief to return.

The other time was when I received a tip that an electrician was carrying his large thermos through the walkout gate with it full of stripped copper every day. I spotted the older guy just a day or two later as he walked through the inspection line. The inspection line consisted of all of the members of each trade walking out a particular gate at the end of the shift with their lunch pails open. A guard was standing at each gate and would eye each person over as they passed through. Hundreds of people would pass through each gate in just a matter of about twenty minutes. As the guy got up to me, he was passing by with his concealed load of copper when I stopped him. He was stunned. I pulled him aside and told him of my suspicions. I made him take the lid off the thermos. It was packed full of the copper, which he was amassing and would then sell at a junkyard—a recycling center, as they are called now. I took him to the captain's office, and there we processed him. He lost a high-paying job and could not work in any position at the plant over a few dollars each day of copper.

We had about thirty guards per shift. About half were assigned each day to foot patrols in the units being built, I think there were three completed and one still being built at that time. They were fourteen-story electric generating buildings adjoining each other. Massive structures.

Then there were a number of small gates about the plant that gave access to the roadways as well as the main gate where most of the traffic came through. Each vehicle gate had a guard stationed there. There were a corporal and a sergeant on each shift. The corporal usually was in the units while the sergeant was at the main gate and roved about in a security pickup truck. The sergeant also had access to a .38 revolver and could either carry it or keep it close by. The corporal did these duties if the sergeant was absent.

All vehicles had to have permission or a pass to enter and were searched upon accessing a gate and leaving. They had to have a detailed pass from Joe to take other than personal property from the plant.

I really liked this job, and it paid well and had benefits too. Many of the guards were young men and women home for the summer from college. Lots of them were off-duty highway patrol officers who needed the money as they were not paid well at that time. Quite a few were teachers, and then there were a number of older retired people and other young or middle-aged people that were interested in security work. There were some losers that were weeded out quickly, and there were some characters too.

Probably close to a year or so that I worked there, I was promoted to corporal. Then within several more months, I was promoted to sergeant. I was about twenty then. I learned a lot the hard way about supervising people of all different ages and personalities. I liked the job. It put me closer to Joe than I liked, but I was able to navigate him okay.

I worked the swing shift most of the time. I did one graveyard shift, and I was on the day shift for several months. Whatever shift was having supervision problems, I would be placed on as the captain and Joe trusted that I would correct the problems, which I did. This also was my fate in teaching Sunday school. Kids that were difficult were placed in my classes because they needed straightens-out, and other teachers didn't, couldn't, or wouldn't tackle it. I didn't have much trouble with these troublemakers or difficult persons, guards, or students. I just treated them like I would hope to be treated. I was firm with them and made it known right off what was expected and what I thought they were capable of. That was almost without exception the end of it. We got along just fine and accomplished the tasks before us.

I ran a very efficient shift and made several longtime friends along the way. Jim being one of them. He was an older guy—a veteran. I dated his older daughter for some time, and he and I often drove to work together. In fact, a number of guards would carpool as some didn't drive, and just as a matter of convenience and cost savings to get to work and back, it worked out well. Even though involved with Jim like I was, I still didn't favor him, and we had no problems with him working with and for me.

After several months he started wanting us and any others who wanted to stop after work at a local Rock Springs restaurant and have coffee and a snack before going home. We often did this. Usually, it was at the Renegade Cafe on the north side of town. One time it was just us two, and we had stopped downtown at the New Grand Cafe. It was his turn to buy, and we had finished. He was paying, and I stepped out of the cafe onto the sidewalk on the famous K Street. It was about 1:30 in the morning, and the street was busy. Bars, prostitutes, and food joints. Cars and people all over the place on this pleasant night. As I stepped out, I heard the loud report of a gun being fired just north of me. I stepped further out from the building and saw a man about one hundred yards away with a rifle. He went around the back of a station wagon that was parked parallel on the street and put the rifle into the rear passenger seat of the car. Then I spotted a man lying on his back on the street on the driver's side of this car. Obviously, the guy had just shot the other one on the street with the rifle and then hid it in the car.

People started swarming the area to see what happened. Jim came out of the cafe, and I related to him what I saw. About that time, three police cars showed up, and cops were all over the scene. A prostitute went up to the sergeant and was telling him what had happened before I could get through the crowd to do likewise. I stayed back and watched them recover the rifle and arrest the shooter. We left before the ambulance arrived. I learned that the victim survived the shooting by his friend, and the shooter was convicted and went to prison. It was a wild place. I would have gotten involved if really needed, but it looked like the case was solved, so I avoided a long night at the police station, etc.

I had become a keen observer of people and what they were doing from my involvement with security work. One morning Steve Reichel and I were in a Pamida department store in town buying something. As we stood in line at the checkout, I noticed that there was a long-haired guy a few years older than us in a cowboy hat checking out with a small item. He had on what appeared to be new cowboy boots, the right one still had a price tag on its heel. I pointed this out to Steve. We quickly checked out after this guy and found him getting into a vehicle by himself in the parking lot that had a Colorado plate on it.

We went up to the guy as he was seating himself in the car, and I told him I worked for the industrial in the area of security and was sure that he had just left the store with new stolen boots on his feet. We hovered right over his driver's door, where he was now sitting with the door ajar. He argued with us until we convinced him he needed to go with his "new Wyoming buddies" back into the store.

The store manager was super surprised and trying to figure these guys out. *What was in it for these two guys, bringing a shoplifter in?* could almost be read on his face. We explained what had happened and that we had no interest in this other than not wanting to see someone get away with what the Colorado "cowboy" had tried. The cowboy, who looked more hippie with just a tinge of cowboy in him, denied it until we all arrived back at the shoe aisle in the store and found lying by the cowboy boots offered for sale his old, dirty, worn-out tennis shoes he had donated to Pamida in exchange for a new free pair of boots.

We went to the office, and the guy was processed, and the police were called. He was arrested, and we gave our statements and left with a thank you from the store. I liked catching crooks. This was a bit risky, however. The guy must have been intimidated by us, and this was the unspoken and thrown-together plan. He could have easily fought with us, run, or stuck a gun or knife in our face. Ahh, youth live forever. Custer never dies! The guy later posted bail and plead not guilty. We showed up for his scheduled trial at the city court a few weeks later, but the guy forfeited bail and was a no-show. Case solved—case closed. The workforce usually cooperated with the guards as they did not want to lose their high-paying jobs. There were three shifts working at the plant most of the time, with the majority on the day shift. There were rough and all types of people thrown into that huge project together. Actually, for all of the mix of humanity in fairly close contact, there were not a lot of problems. Theft and vandalism were the main concerns. Also, there were always people wanting to come into the plant to see it, and this was not allowed. Absolutely no trespassing was permitted. There were trailer courts near the plant where many of the workers lived. These were wild places, but we did not patrol them. This was the problem of the sheriff's department. I was sent one time to patrol the construction company trailer court near Reliance, Wyoming, for one day. Speeding in the trailer court had become a problem. I stopped several people and took their data for the captain and gave warnings, but mainly just the presence of a uniformed guard in a vehicle seemed to be warning enough for most. Workers at the plant did not want to encounter the wrath of Joe, the security man, who was able to send them packing quicker than a jackrabbit can mate on a date for crimes or workplace safety violations. Violators were easily replaced by the union halls. All jobs were premium with pay and benefits.

Old Joe was a real negative guy and not easy to work for. About every two months to as long as one year, he would find a reason to get rid of the guard supervisors and then lean on the captain to have this accomplished. Of course, the current captain was in fear of replacement, so old Joe didn't have to lean much.

Some of the supervisors needed to be replaced when they were, but most were good men. There were female guards, but only men were supervisors. Before I was promoted to corporal, the sergeant on my shift was a chubby Southern guy in his late 20s. I didn't like him, and he and a Mexican guard that was his little minion didn't like me and several other guards. His minion was a skinny little guy in his early 20s. Just had a snake's or wormy type character. The type of guy that you wouldn't want behind of you with a sharp object. We did our jobs, but the sarge would still be really snotty with us and pick at us with his little minion in tow. They both thought they were pretty hot stuff, and it was known that sarge was one of Joe's, the security man, pets.

One evening I was at the main gate with another guard. Just after dark, the sergeant drove into the main gate but didn't come into the office. Then we heard pistol shots. This nut had gone over to a portable outhouse and shot it full of holes with the duty pistol. Then he came over to me and the other guard and threatened us that we had better not speak a word about this to anyone or else. He was not hinting so much about our jobs as to implying that he would hurt us. He made for a very unsettled atmosphere at best when he was present and now worse. He and the Mex were yuking it up.

I knew that this property damage would be reported by the day shift, and I had no intention of covering for him, come what may. The next morning the captain called. I had made a note in the logbook about the incident. He had this and the day shift's report.

"Tell me about this, Weimer." Well, of course, I told him. This was not only horribly unprofessional but dangerous and criminal. I never saw this former sergeant or the Mex again. Pets or not, Joe could not abide anything even close to this.

I had been at the plant for about a year and a half. Things were fine, but I had been there as a supervisor longer than most, and my time had run out with Joe. It was just as if he would get bored with staff supervisors and want a new face for no other reason than that. I was the next one to be replaced. I was on patrol, and the pickup truck had gotten stuck on one of the muddy roads I was to check. I tried to pull it out with another vehicle, and it got stuck as well. This was a common occurrence with most of the trucks of all the companies when it was muddy or deep snow. It was a simple matter to take a machine on-site and pull out the disabled vehicle in a matter of minutes. Well, this was enough for old Joe.

However, I was well-respected by the assistant manager of the security company in the Salt Lake Office, and when I was sent packing at the plant, he put me out with another sergeant as a co-head of the small construction project at a soda ash project west of Green River. I worked there for another six months when this project was completed and everybody was being laid off.

The security company I had been employed with wanted to keep me and offered me the head supervisor position as a sergeant and promotion soon to follow at the large coal mine in Kemmerer, Wyoming. I prayed about this and really considered it as if I passed this up, the only other opportunity would be to leave the state with Burns or be done with them.

I wasn't ready to move from Rock Springs and, for sure, not out of Wyoming. This had been one of the reasons for not being interested in joining the military. In addition to the fact that when I was old enough to go see the old bitty at the selective service office and register, Vietnam was over, and Nixon had made the military all-volunteer.

I, against the advice of Mr. Tadd, the assistant manager, turned the offer down. I wanted to work security and still had my eye on law enforcement in addition to actively preaching and teaching pretty much now in churches away from Rock Springs.

I lived at home until I was about twenty, and then Steve Reichel and I rented an apartment on A Street. My brother Chuckie had gotten married and moved out a few years before me. He was still in need of my training while still at home. He was in his late teens, and I was six years younger.

He would come in from a late-night drunk party and thought it would be fun to pull me out of bed. He did, but he got the dirty end of the stick repeatedly. One time he pulled me out, and we were in the middle of our carpeted floor wrestling. I got the best of him and ran the side of his face up the carpet. He had a dandy rash and was ready to quiet down. Grandma had gotten up when he came in and was trying to pamper him. As long as he had the drop on me, she didn't mind, but how quickly that changed when the little brother put the hurt on him. She would try to pull me off and say, "Don't hurt poor Chuckie." It bothered me not one bit. I wouldn't want her trying to pamper or baby me.

We had bunk beds. I was on the top bed. I would lay up there with an uncovered wall lamp and read. Chuckie on the lower bed thought it was hilarious to put his foot on the bottom of my bed and push up and down, tossing me all about on the mattress and springs. He did this several times and would just laugh when I would tell him to knock it off.

There was a dresser mirror on the opposite wall of our beds. I took the lamp off the wall and watched him slowly raise his foot as he got ready to give me another routing. I quickly reached down with the lamp and put the hot one-hundred-watt bulb on the top of his foot. Oh, did he howl! Now I was laughing. He was out of bed, hopping around and really belering. Too bad. He had a dandy blister to try to put a work sock and boot on the next morning for work in the coal mine. Voilà, no more rousting of my bed after that. Old granny was mad as a wet hen at me. "Poor Chuckie, look what that Kenny did to him." He got no sympathy from anybody in the house but granny.

191

Chuckie and I weren't very close due to age and lifestyles, but we still got along pretty good most of the time. He went to church for a while during the boom with all of us, but he was older than most of the older teens, single and younger than the middle-aged people, and kind of like a fish out of water. My dad put a lot of pressure on him to not go, and this did the trick. My dad tried at times to discourage me too, but I paid no attention to him. I knew he was messed up in his thinking and so I couldn't let that affect me. Other times he would brag on me to other people but really for his own benefit because he always made a big part of this about what a great job, he had done in raising me to turn out this way, ha, what a giant laugh this was. My dad was a Jekyll and Hyde character but usually the worst when drinking too much.

I ordered a mimeograph machine from Sears to print a weekly paper with for the Rock Springs church. I put this paper out for over probably a year and a half or so. It was a three- or four-page 8.5×11-inch paper. I called it *The Trumpet*. As in the return of Christ. The trumpet will sound at His return after a shout according to the Book of Revelation. *The Trumpet* was sounding out good news and information. It was well received by the church.

The mimeograph machines were a mess, really. I had to use a ribbon less typewriter to type up a carbon page and then put this page on the drum, and with an inky mess, I would roll the drum manually with a handle and print one page at a time. If a mistake was made typing on the carbon page, it was a mess to correct but had to be done.

Steve and I ended up in this big apartment that was actually the second floor of a big house that faced B Street. It was owned and occupied by a dentist and his older girlfriend. This guy was an oddball. But the place was pretty nice, and we settled in. Steve had graduated from high school and was now working for a company putting up metal buildings. The way into our place was through a driveway off A Street. Funny, I started out on A Street in my first home, and now here I was again.

Our moms gave us kitchen items for the place. I took my stuff, and dad gave me several guns to have officially as my own now that

I had been using over the years. The .270 I used so much was my grandpa Joe's gun. It was a Husqvarna. A nice rifle. He also gave me a nice semiauto .22 and grandpa's shotgun with a damaged stock. Several other guns were included too. I would go out and shot rabbits for my dad because my mom would cook them for him, and he just loved them. He would stuff himself before he quit. I liked them too but not to that extent. Until I got married, most of the animals that I got went to the folks' house where they had a large chest freezer. I would still go to the house often to visit and have dinner or coffee from the large urn my mom and dad kept going almost twenty-four hours a day.

The Reichel's got me hooked up with Martha, daughter of Jim that I worked security with. Jim had never mentioned her to me. I had girls that I was friends with, but I had never really dated. They assured me that Martha was interested and was a nice girl with only one drawback. What…she had an extra arm or three eyes…no, she just talked a lot. Steve called her Martha Mouth. I didn't follow up on this info right away, but they kept urging me to contact her, and I finally did.

She was a nice girl. Attractive and a nice personality, but boy, she could talk. They had not described that attribute to me, no small wonder why! She had dated a good deal, even though she was only a couple of years younger than me. She was a little "fast," but I tamed her down in short order. Jim was most pleased when we were dating, though he never involved himself in our relationship. We went on quite a few dates, including to the Baptist church that the Reichel's were now going to and also to the Assemblies of God church. Lots of nice dinner dates and more casual times too.

I liked her, but she was much more attached to me than I was to her. We dated for probably six months or so until I just didn't want to spend that much time involved in that lifestyle, and I just wanted to be friends. So, we broke up. She was pretty upset over this. She even talked with mom and asked her to talk to me about us staying together. Mom told her that "Kenny makes up his own mind." She couldn't influence me about something like that even if she tried.

Jim and I still worked together much of the time while I was still at the Bridger Power Plant and carpooled. Nothing really changed. Jim was a real nice guy and pretty low-key. Really likable. He would have liked to have me for a son-in-law but he never said anything about the breakup.

That is about the extent of my love life. So, dear reader, you won't have to read about soppy stuff about the loves of my life! I did have single dates with a few gals, but no big deal, and I always treated the girls nice. There were several that tried to date me, but I pretty much shrugged them off. I will write a bit more about some of the interesting ones later. I did meet the love of my life, Brenda, later. She was the one for me, even though I was too dumb to pick up on that at first or too afraid to.

I left industrial security employment with no immediate job prospects. Still preaching for churches, but that didn't generate much income, and I didn't do it for that reason anyway. For the only time in my life, I applied for unemployment and drew it for about two months. During this time, I was job-hunting, hunting, fishing, prowling the dumps, and spending time with Grandpa Hamilton in many of these pursuits. It was late winter and early spring, and I had rent to pay and expenses of living on my own. Steve had changed plans and was going to leave in the summer for Bible college, so I was facing the prospect of all the housing expenses being my own. I wanted no roommates to replace him with, and I didn't want to pack up and go back home with my tail between my legs.

I was interested in applying for law enforcement, but I was still too young. Twenty-one was the requirement. Well, I was getting closer. I learned that a small security company called Bronx-West was wanting to hire an experienced industrial guard to join their staff at a construction project in the soda ash trona fields by Green River. Close to where I had worked the short time at my security company after leaving the Bridger Plant.

I applied and was hired. It was a good-size construction project but only a small security staff. Two on day shift—both sergeants (go figure), and a single guard on the swing and grave shift. They usually had me work the swing shirt. It was all foot patrol and similar work as at Bridger. Keeping trespassers out, searching workers and vehicles leaving the place, and general safety patrols for all other perils. They provided a nice brown uniform and a duty belt, etc. It was unarmed security, even though in a remote area. If help was needed, call the sheriff's department, and with any luck, they would show up in about a week. It was a busy place with all types of people but not the problems as at the Bridger Plant. It was really pretty trouble-free as long as our presence was there. Another older guy was hired about the same time as I was. His name was John. He was a middle-aged heavyset Spanish guy with a nice family. He was a talker. We had sort of a friendship. They were Baptists, but he would have some awful bouts with depression and just lay in bed when not working. It was tough on his family.

They lived in a trailer court out of town on the west side. They had me to dinner one night. Nice kids, and his wife Daisy was a very nice person. However, her sister Jan was a middle-aged single woman that had been invited to dinner too. She was a nice person. She had been on several extended periods of time' missionary trips to Africa. She was at least twelve years or more my senior. Not overly attractive and a much different personality than myself. It was obvious that one of the main purposes of the dinner was to try to hook us up. I didn't bite.

Steve had a girlfriend. An attractive, lively soul. The day after Steve left for Bible college in Washington, she was at my door to visit. Poor old Steve's footsteps had hardly cooled off from the front steps when she was fishing for another guy. This was after Martha. I visited with her for an hour, but beyond that, I didn't bite.

Summer was beginning. I would be twenty-one this August. I could now apply for the police department and knew that I had to. So, I began the process. I completed the lengthy application and provided all of the required documents. This was a civil service position, so it required a long-written test. I showed up that summer night with about half a dozen other guys. The exercise took place in the city council chambers of the old city hall, which was the current city hall, police department, city jail, and other city offices, with the attached number one fire station.

Adjoining the city building was the Eagles Hall. They were having a big dance that night. The music was blaring. It was like taking the test while sitting on the dance floor. The test took several hours, and no one said a word about the loud music. Part of the process. The completed tests were turned in to the police civil service commissioner that had monitored the testing. We would receive results later by mail. I thought that I had done pretty well on the test, but you never know. It was timed, so you didn't have all night to think about things or figure for too long.

When the testing was completed, we were to be interviewed separately by the full commission. Four men. I knew all of them but not well. They knew my family but didn't know me too well. Most of the guys had long interviews and were grilled by this group. I was in there about five minutes. They were a stern bunch but just talked with me really generally. They asked the group then if they had any questions for Weimer, and no one did. It was a long night. About half of the applicants were from out of town.

I only knew one of the guys I tested with, a black guy named Delbert. He was my brother's age. He had been in the police department for a short stint and left. Now he was trying to get reinstated but had to go through the whole process again.

Happy day! Several weeks later, I received a letter from the commission that informed me that I had passed the testing and interview with a good score. Now my name would be placed on a hiring list. Oh boy, that could go somewhere or not. I continued to work for Bronx-West. They were good to work for, and the pay was good, but it offered no benefits. I waited, hoping to hear from the city, but who knows. They were hiring often on the now expanded police department. Most of the old guys that I had known growing up had or were retiring and being replaced by mostly young guys, many from out of town and state. The highway patrol was hiring, but it would require moving in the state, and the pay was low compared to the police department. Also, they only worked traffic as a rule, and I wanted to do that but criminal enforcement too. The sheriff's department was an option too. It didn't require the testing, but I felt I had to wait for something to happen with the police department, so I did.

It was only a matter of weeks, but now getting into late summer and early fall when the city contacted me. I would have to take a physical with a doctor now, that was not my own family doctor. In preparation for hoping to get in the police department, I had gone to Salt Lake City to get a pair of contacts that were supposed to be a much better deal than getting them from a doctor in town.

I had a two-wheel-drive blue step side pickup that I had traded for in town and gotten rid of a lemon of a nearly new foreign-made four-wheel-drive vehicle that I had earlier traded my big old green four-wheel-drive outfit for. This was a nice truck. I made several trips with it to Salt Lake City for various reasons. On one of the trips, I had parked it in a busy large parking lot. It was early afternoon. I was away from the vehicle for about an hour. Upon returning to it, I saw that the driver's side wing window was now open. The door was shut but not locked. It had not been that way when I left it.

Inside I found that my CB (citizens band) radio was gone. I also had a pair of real handcuffs covered on the bench seat that Steve Reichel's dad had given me when I worked at the Bridger Plant where he was employed as a pipe fitter. He had the cuffs and black open leather case from when he was a reserve conservation officer in Pennsylvania. I cherished these more than the radio. They were gone. Ripped off in Mormonsville in broad daylight with people coming and going in the area. CB radios were hot items during this time and were constantly stolen out of vehicles in Rock Springs too.

I had my .38 pistol in a holster under the driver's seat, and it was still there. Wow, I hated to lose my radio and the cuffs but was sure glad that the quick-moving thief had missed the gun. I looked around the area on foot but to no avail. I had someone contact the police, and a sort of disinterested patrol officer came and took a report.

I was now wearing contacts along with glasses when I could. With the rough and tumbling work in the police department, if I was hired, I knew that glasses would be a problem and never last. These contacts just didn't seem really clear, though. I went to a local eye doctor; he was a really nice guy. I had seen him before for an exam and glasses. He explained that the contacts were cheap material and could not be improved on. He was happy to hear that I was facing good prospects of becoming a local officer. He gave me the exam and a new pair of contacts at no charge since the Salt Lake people had really sold me an inferior product. I stuck with him after that.

I reported to the hospital and took the physical exam. Submitted that to the city and then didn't hear anything for a few weeks again. Out of the blue, I was called by Lieutenant Overy from the police department. He had been there for a long time. I knew him but not very well. He was, of course, well acquainted with the other males in my family! I was offered a probationary patrol officer position. Yes, I would be happy to show up. One problem, though. I was to report on October 1st. I had drawn an elk permit for Little Mountain south of Rock Springs that also opened on that day. In most cases, I would not have been given an option as to when to show up to begin a new career/job. Show up or else. No, Lieutenant Overy, who was second-in-charge of the police department, was also a hunter. I explained my dilemma to him. "No problem. Show up on the day shift at 07:00 on October 5th if that will work."

"Yes, yes, I will," and I did.

I arrived in civilian clothes at the police department that frosty morning in the old city hall building on Broadway and C Street. Some of the cops who had been there for some years and knew the family kind of gave me sideways looks, but I was treated good. I could see right off that I had a lot to learn. My security experience helped a good deal, but this was a different world. I would work that day with Sergeant Mark. Funny, he didn't remember me, and I didn't bring it up, but he was the officer that showed up and arrested our shoplifter at the Pamida store the summer before.

He had gone to high school with my brother, but not much was said about any of this. Which I was glad about. I am not my brother or my dad. None of the police had ever really had any memorable contact with me in the past, so nothing was said about any of this stuff.

I talked a few minutes with the lone "meter maid" that morning. Gordon. He was an old skinny guy that wore a police uniform and was allowed to wear a cross-draw revolver on his hip. He rode about the downtown area in a little covered police scooter. He wrote parking tickets and helped collect money from the parking meters.

He was friendly. I was a little gun-shy of him at first. He didn't, of course, remember me and some of my pals from a few years earlier when he yelled at us and cussed us. Riding bikes was not allowed on the sidewalks downtown. We did it anyway most of the time. It really wasn't that big of a deal. Except for Gordon. He would spot us and open the door on the scooter and began to yell threats, and when we rode away from him, still on the sidewalk, he would really get hot. Then he would cuss and yell for us to stop. Of course, that made for an increase in the speed of the bicycle for some reason. He even tried to run us down with the scooter once, but we escaped through an underground walkway between Front Street and Broadway with railroad tracks overhead.

I spent the day with the sergeant. I liked it. A guy came into the station to report a theft. The sergeant had me take the report while he observed. He was happy and surprised at what a good job this young skinny kid did. I used their forms, and with a little direction, I was on my own to write up the report. This was not a problem for me. I had some training and a lot of experience in writing up reports from working with industrial security. Sergeant Mark was pleased and amazed at the report I had completed. I heard him telling other officers that day of the job I had done.

Maybe I would be a keeper, but there was a long way to go. At this time, if a person was hired, they worked with experienced officers and had a one-year probationary period. A number of people had not made their probation and had very short police careers for various reasons. If you made the probationary period, then you would be sent to the Wyoming State Law Enforcement Academy in Douglas, Wyoming. There you would receive your basic training to be a police officer. You would be expected to attend every day and not miss classes, even though we would be traveling home on most weekends and had to be back by Sunday night for Monday classes. Every portion of the training would have to be satisfactorily completed. Then you would be a permanent officer in the department.

Day one was good, and they told me to report again the next day. Same place, same time. I had a duty belt that I had purchased in Salt Lake City along with cuffs and minor equipment. The police in Rock Springs wore a uniform identical to that of the Salt Lake police, but I had none of that. Money was tight for a guy my age who had not gone to big money being made in the area. I could only afford to buy so much at one time. The officers talked with me in a small group at the end of the day shift and figured out that they could come up with different uniform parts and pieces for me to have till I could get my own.

On day two, I was assigned to work with Officer Jim, who had been a highway patrolman for a number of years and left that for the police department due to its low pay. He was a talker and didn't like to get interrupted by radio calls or anything like that from his constant patrolling. I guess that came from his years of covering lots of highway miles as a state patrolman. He made a point of wanting to put as many miles as possible on the fleet patrol car as possible as this seemed to be his goal of having completed a successful day.

Day two ended with me going into the small cramped office shared by longtime Chief of Police Muir and Lieutenant Overy. I knew the chief. I remembered when he came to our sixth-grade class in Washington school. He never wore a uniform. He was a big man and wore a badge on his belt and a gun on his right hip. I never saw him in a uniform until years later, when he had retired and worked a few years as a deputy in the sheriff's department. In the class that day he was very friendly. It was Halloween Day. He brought popsicles for the class and reminded us that he did not expect any vandalism or trouble to come from us on this special day.

He was friendly but all business when he had me stand in the small office and raise my right hand. He did the same and swore me in. Then I was issued a patrolman's badge, a brown wooden nightstick, and a city ordinance book. If probation was completed, the city would provide me with funds for uniforms and equipment other than a handgun. Until then, it was part of your obligation to have a full uniform and all required equipment and soon.

I was then to report the next day to the midnight shift at 23:00. This was to be a new and very different world from the day shifts I had just completed. I had purchased my handgun locally. I paid about 200 dollars for it, which was a fortune to me at that time. It was a .357 Magnum revolver. For another twenty-five bucks, I could have bought the better-grade gun. This was too much at that time, and I went with the cheaper gun. The choice of weapon was at the officer's discretion. Some carried .38s as did Muir. Others had the popular .357 Magnum; a few carried .44 Magnums, and then there were a few oddballs that had the .45 Autos. Revolvers were still the main choice in these years. Autos were thought to be too undependable in a crunch by the majority of the staff. I still have the .357 Magnum and carried it for many years, and when my weapon was not provided by a department, even after using different revolvers and autos of different calibers, I usually came back to the old revolver. It never failed me. I used it to pass basic firearms training at the police academy, and many years later, when out of Alaska, I was sent to Oregon for firearms instructor training again, it was my old friend the .357 Magnum revolver that was my choice. I was given my Aunt Marylou's .357 Magnum from when she was a deputy in California after she passed away. It is a nice gun, but I have never fired it.

Four other guys were hired from the recent testing process, this did not include Delbert. Most were from out of town, and we were placed on different shifts, to begin with, or worked apart from one another. There were going to be a good deal of challenges in this new career endeavor, but I liked this. It was what I wanted to do since I was five years old, in addition to preaching the gospel, which I was also called to.

There were benefits, which helped with the low pay. It was several years before the city did the right thing and started paying us a competitive wage. Many of the married guys with family loved the job. They were honest guys, and they worked extra or part-time jobs to make ends meet. Women were not working out of the home so much at this time, but some of their wives worked to help with the bills.

Dad and mom didn't say much about my new career. Chuckie thought it was great, why? Well, a popular activity for kids and young adults then was to cruise around town for hours in whatever heap or junker they had. Some had nice vehicles, like him. He said, "Wow, you can ride around town in their car and don't have to buy gas." The light was on for Chuckie, but obviously, nobody was home!

Grandma was angry about me being in the police department. She was happy about Marylou in California carrying a badge, but Rock Springs cops...those old cops she would begin her tirade with. The reason she didn't like the local constables was solely because she thought they had nothing to do but make my dad move the numerous cars he had parked all over the streets by our place for long periods of time, but even worse was that they just spent their time picking on poor Chuckie. Poor Chuckie, I would remind her, had wrecked several really nice cars by this time and racked up tickets as he drove like a fiend. This really got her. "Oh, you smart aleck." Then the remark would follow that she didn't know how the sun could shine with me around when I was so bright. I would laugh, and she would give me dirty looks.

Several years later, she would offer to dry-clean my uniforms at a reduced price and had decided that life wasn't the catastrophe she had imagined with her grandson in the local police department.

Grandma worked hard for her money. She liked to work out of the house, but being a clothes presser in a hot full-service laundry on your feet all day was not easy work. No matter, Chuckie worked most of the time, too, but he would whine to her about some big challenge that had complicated his life. Then the next thing was that they would huddle together in her bedroom where she would be handing out twenty-dollar bills to him like a pill-pushing doctor to a drug fiend. He had no shame about this.

My sisters were proud of their brother. The Hamilton's were not happy about it. They had accepted without too much effort me being a guard. This was different in a big way. The main cause of their unhappiness was due to reading the local *Rocket-Miner* paper and taking it for the gospel. The papers were becoming full of stories of corruption in the local government and wrongdoing by police and city officials. Most of this was the same tripe as on the local KVRS radio station's "news" programs. The local media was being badly influenced by people wanting positions in government, as I described before. They needed to discredit and root out people now holding office if this was to be accomplished.

There were cases where the news reports had truth to them, but most, including the *60 Minutes* story on national TV and other national-regional papers and magazines that ran articles, were a fabrication and just wrong. The southwest area of Wyoming had just experienced a massive migration of people from all over the country and the world. Quite a few of them were rough and just plain bad people. Quite a few were coming from hard times and having low wages and now just the opposite. Big money for doing about anything and lots of ways to spend it for things other than needs. Living costs were high, too, compared to what they had been prior to the boom.

Some of the officials and the agencies were not at all prepared for all of this change and disruption, including the state. Many of the Wyoming people were enjoying the money flow but hated to see the crime, trouble, and crowded conditions. Too many jokers out in their hunting and fishing spots. Lots of them had no idea of how to hunt or fish in this country. Poaching of big game animals was happening all too often. Sometimes they were just shot and left in the field to rot. Too many strange faces and weird characters. Lots of troubled people and families showing up. People carousing night and day. Prostitutes on the streets. Drugs, alcohol, and violence in spades. Congested streets, cafes, and stores that were not able to handle all of this overflow and increase. People living in camping trailers, tents, motel rooms, vehicles, and much of this in bitter, cold weather. Rent was high if anything could be found.

It was, in reality, an invasion and took time to adjust and respond to. State and local governments had not been given much notice of the impending conditions about to befall them. Then when they were overwhelmed by the carpetbaggers hoping to obtain political office and the media that loved the newfound excitement and attention, they imagined many opportunities for themselves, and they smelled blood in the water. People's lives and careers were ruined or at least caused all kinds of heartache and trouble that should not have been. There are always dishonest people. The vast majority of government officials and law enforcement that I was involved with were not among this description. I, as only a small example, did okay with my remuneration as a patrolman. But I could have easily followed most of the guys I went to school with and gone to work in the trona mines, the oil field, the Bridger Plant, the strip mines, and so on and made much more money than being in law enforcement. Certainly, those jobs would not have been the grief or requirements that being a police officer was. I am simply saying this was a calling, as is the ministry. A career that I and others did it because they wanted to, not because they had no other options or abilities. Most made sacrifices of different types to protect and serve. I hoped to keep Wyoming more like Wyoming than what it was trying to evolve into. To protect the weak and keep the peace. To right wrongs as much as one could and to stop as many bad things from happening to people and businesses as we could. To me, there were no places like Wyoming and especially Sweetwater County and areas within one hundred to 150 miles of Rock Springs.

Steve Reichel and I had just completed our first antelope hunt in the Big Piney area. We were hooked on this stuff. We had taken the bucks to the pastor's home near the town and processed them that afternoon and then went to church that night.

The next day we looked around a bit for deer, but it was time to head home. We headed toward Kemmerer to enjoy a different route home. Only a few miles out of town, the truck his dad had loaned us began to act up. It would start trying to quit and wouldn't run well. It had little power and would slow and start making little hops down the road. We stopped several times and looked it over. Nothing obviously wrong. We would pray for the old heap and go till it demanded another break at the roadside. The weather had turned cool and looked stormy. This was going to be a long drive home at this rate. We decided we had better stop in Kemmerer and have a mechanic look at the thing.

We finally made it there and pulled into a local garage. They were busy, and the mechanic/owner looked kind of suspiciously at these two kids that came to his shop. He agreed to look at it and put it on a diagnostic machine. When he was able to, he finally got to us. He described some ignition-type work that needed to be done. We explained that we had to get home right away, and then he gave us a rather stern and questioning look and said, "Well, just the cost of the diagnostic machine on the truck was twenty-five dollars." *Gulp!* We put our heads together and told him that we only had about ten or fifteen dollars among us. *O*, he was not too happy.

He kind of chewed us out but took pity on these two kids with a truckload of antelope meat, standing before him in their dirty blood-stained hunting garb from a recent escapade out in the prairies. Maybe he remembered a time like this in his days of carefree youth. We gave him what we could and promised to mail him a check for the balance when we got home. He was trusting under the circumstances. Fixed the truck, and we were on our way. Of course, we mailed a check to him that week. That was the Wyoming way.

Nothing doing, though. We needed to get home and had had enough trouble up to now. As we went along the highway headed toward Rock Springs, we encountered a long-haired biker with the front wheel off his disabled motorcycle at the roadside. We stopped to see if we could give him a ride.

He was not the type of guy you would want behind of yourself with a sharp object. I felt pretty uneasy about him, but we would still help him. However, we didn't have an excess of time or gasoline, and he talked Steve into loading up the cycle and hauling him on the other side of Rock Springs to the little ghost town of Superior where he was staying.

This was not a good idea in my estimation, but Steve thought we had to do it, and it was his truck. Loaded up, the guy was far grimier than both of us put together. He was a big talker and told Steve that he was short on money right now, but that when we got him to Superior, it would be no problem to get his money to give Steve enough to fill his gas tank for our kindness. Boy, he was sure happy that we came along and appreciated us and on and on. We now had an overflow in the bed of the truck with a broken-down motorcycle, a bunch of antelope meat, head, and hides, and camping equipment.

After a too long uncomfortable ride to Superior with this wacky character, we arrived and unloaded his disabled machine. He said, "Hey, thanks, man," and handed Steve some worthless paper card from his wallet and disappeared like a puff of smoke in a strong Wyoming wind into an old shaky-looking place in the dilapidated village. This was *not* the Wyoming way. Good to be a good Samaritan, yes, but sometimes putting a target on your forehead is not the best idea. Nuff said, Steve, old buddy! We barely made it back to Rock Springs on the gas that we had. Fumes and a strong wind at our rear got us there.

Steve had drawn an elk permit for Little Mountain and went up there to hunt by himself. I was working and would go out on the pleasant evenings after work and hunt bunnies north of town. It was nice dry calm fall days. Just a pleasure to park and walk the hills and gullies and pick up bunnies with the .22 rifle. If Steve hadn't arrived back in town with an elk by my days off, the plan was for me to meet him on the mountain and hunt.

Several days passed, and no Steve. I headed up there and soon enough located him. It was still very nice weather. We had a nice night camping out. The hunting had been slow for him. We decided to hunt this deep canyon. He was to work toward the bottom of it on the opposite side of me, and then I would go down my side of it and try to poke an elk toward him.

I enjoyed the view and waited till he was in position. Then I went as planned and tried to make some noise and usher a critter or two his way. In this particular canyon, we had seen lots of elk. Numerous big bulls. One time there were over a dozen big bulls just lying together on a summer day.

Steve would like to have scored on a big bull but would be happy just to fill his tag and have the meat. Especially now, his hunting time was about used-up. The only elk that moved was a lone big spike bull. It went toward Steve, crossed the bottom of the canyon, and just started toward him when he shot it.

Great. Two happy guys. One problem. We now had a bunch of meat to get over to the side of the canyon I was on and back up over the steep hillsides to the top where our vehicles were located. Well, that was just part of the deal. We began to gut and prepare the elk for the arduous chore that now loomed ahead of us. It was later morning, so we were looking at an all-day job at least. Maybe could have it completed by dark if we really got to hoofing it.

We had only been at our task for a short time when we heard somebody helloing us. *No* one had been around in this deep place, but here came Al on his horse Cindy. Cindy was a gentle mare that he kept in a corral by his trailer home east of Rock Springs. He would allow Steve and me to come out and saddle her up and ride her around the prairies when we wanted to. He liked to ride but being a pipe fitter at the Bridger Plant kept him busy. So, we liked to ride her, and she needed the exercise, a win-win for all.

Al's wife was a heavyset sweet lady who was a little mixed up mentally but very likable. She was not accepted too well by the few female neighbors in the small trailer court and had no way to get into town except when she went with Al. You could tell that she was very lonesome and not too happy about being in this rough, windy country. Like many others who landed there.

We would always make it a point to stop and visit her after our riding. She was glad for company. She always insisted on fixing lemon-flavored ice tea for us. Steve rather liked it, I didn't like tea of any type, and just to think of it all these years later as I type this makes me almost heave. Anyway, it was always a large glass, and then she would stay right there and visit till the mixture was consumed and we had to be on our way. No way would I hurt her feelings, so I would force the stuff down my gullet and try to keep from showing any sign of nausea, passing out, or anything like that.

Al was a heavyset balding guy in his 50s. He and his wife came to our church and were friends of the Reichel's'. They were transplants from the back east and, like most, had come for the big-money jobs. They were odd to the area, but Al had befriended guys at the church and become interested in horses and elk hunting. He had drawn an elk permit like Steve and was up here looking for one on his days off.

Al was sure glad that we had an elk. This would be no problem. Cindy was an excellent packer too. We could load the elk on her, and in one trip, she would be topside in short order. Wow, was that ever a big blessing! We visited and finished our chore in short order. Soon we had Cindy packed up and at our vehicles just a little later that afternoon. Al didn't mind missing the hunt to help us. He wouldn't use up time riding that canyon since I had worked it pretty good for Steve's elk. Now he would go try another nearby spot. Thanks, Lord, thanks, Al, thanks, Cindy.

Al later offered me Cindy for a good price. He and his wife were splitting up, and she was moving back to something more civilized. He had found him a livelier gal and was going to stay in the area with her. So, he would liquidate the horse if he could. I wanted to buy her, and she was a great animal, but I had to weigh the cost of feeding and caring for her. This was more than I wanted to invest at the time.

Steve wanted to take me back on a trip to Pennsylvania to see where he was raised until they moved to Denver and then Wyoming. All of their family on both sides lived in the Meadville-Erie area. I had a vacation coming with my job in security work, so we took off in his little green hatchback car. I met most of his family. The Reichel's were all nice, easy-going folks. Steve's mother's family were a tough bunch of close-knit Polish folks. We stayed with his mother's folks. The area around their old home was sort of rural, and it was nice, but only the type of place that I would care to visit, not live.

We went to the fair one night. Among our activities was riding this horrible carnival ride that stood a person on their head and spun around. As soon as I got off that torturous trap, I made a quick exit to the outside of the fairgrounds, wobbling like a drunk, I was so dizzy. I puked up my socks. Then I heard somebody behind me doing the same. Steve, old pal, wasn't that fun!

The best part of the trip was largemouth bass fishing on a little secluded pond not too far from his grandparents' home, called Georges Pond. Nobody else was ever there. Nice big two- and three-pound bass could be caught in short order with just a worm and a bobber. Then his grandmother was an expert at filleting them and frying the fish. We had several of these feasts. Steve would want to go visit some more of his old friends or family, and I chose to return to the pond and fish while he went off.

Steve's Polish grandfather was the tough matriarch of the numerous brothers. His grandmother was a chubby bespeckled apron-clad lady with a big smile. She would grab me and hug me like she had known me since I was a child. They loved to polka, and she and grandpa would dance to the lively music they played in the kitchen while she was busy preparing bass for dinner.

We were en route to Pennsylvania and somewhere in Indiana when we stopped for gas. Attendants pumped the gas at most of these places. The buck antelope that Steve had shot on our first trip to Big Piney had been taxidermized, and he was taking it back to give to his grandfather. The critter was in full view in the large rear window of the back of the hatchback car. The attendant was pumping the gas and staring at the animal. We could see that he was curious but didn't want a couple of kids giving him a biology lesson. He finally asked, "What kind of deer is that?" That was a chuckle.

My family liked Lagoon. It was and still is a nice park in the Salt Lake/Ogden area of Utah. Most of the park is permanent carnival rides, but there are exhibits, games, shows, gardens, and lots of eating places. The weather was usually nice, and we made many summer trips there and would spend the entire day or more.

We had been going there most summers at least once for several years. I was probably fifteen or sixteen one time when Chuckie and I got onto this spinning cup ride. I was usually picky about the stuff I rode even then as I hated to get sick from them. I threw caution to the wind, and the cups began to spin as they rotated around a circle. There was a steering wheel in the middle of the cup. The riders seated around this could spin the wheel and make the cup spin even faster. Well, we did. The next thing I knew, they were stopping the ride. I was out like a light and lying in a heap on the bottom of the cup. Sick as a dog for most of the day. Just the smell of a corn dog nearly set me off again!

Steve and I had been installing a chain-link fence all day. I had been invited to preach the evening message for a sectional youth meeting at the Green River church. The church was packed that night with about half to them teens. The district superintendent, Brother Beard, was there as well as a number of other preachers from around the district. We had a great meeting. Brother Beard, who liked me anyway, was a big white-haired man with a big smile. He had been a big supporter of me, along with Brother Griffin, in getting my minister's credentials at such a young age. He was so pleased with my preaching that night and the success of the meeting. I preached on Joseph as a youth and how that he could not be stopped and never quit. We had a tremendous prayer/altar time with mostly young people that night. Steve sat on the front row while I preached and kept trying to make goofy faces at me with the hopes of cracking me up. I saw him out of the corner of my eye, but I never would acknowledge him with a direct look. He didn't mean any harm. We just messed with each other sometimes like that and wouldn't pass up a chance to pull a dirty trick on one another.

I was at Steve's folks' home one night when they had a trailer home on the north side of town before it was moved to the company trailer court later when his dad went to work at the Bridger Plant. Steve, his dad, I, and an older man that had come to Wyoming to work at the Bridger Plant were all outside in the yard looking at some equipment of some type. The older guy was a short little man in his late 60s. He was also a preacher and had spoken one night at the church. He was a nice, quiet little man from the back east somewhere. He was stout for a guy his age, however.

For whatever reason, I still don't know to this day why, but all a sudden, Steve decided to take him on. He jumped on the guy and was going to take him down to the ground. His dad and I just stood watching. We couldn't believe what was going on. In a flash, this little man turned on Steve, a young guy in good shape, and had him down, and Steve couldn't get up. He was pinned. We both started hooping and laughing at this turn of events. We cheered the victor on. The guy enjoyed pinning a young troublemaker who had gotten too big for his britches. Steve didn't do it to be mean, it was supposed to just be a funny little wrestle. Well, it was funny to everybody but Steve. Brother Paul was the older man's name. He let Steve up once there was no question of who won the tussle. Steve was so humiliated when he jumped up, he was red in the face and never said a word as we all laughed and hooped it up. No mercy with this bunch over that kind of showing off. Steve beat it into the trailer home and was not seen again that night.

When Steve and I were renting the apartment on A Street, we got to wrestling on the enclosed porch one evening. We were both on our feet shoving back and forth like two rams in battle when we finally fell over. I had a military metal ammo box on the porch. When we went down, I whammed the back of my head in full force on the box. I hit so hard that Steve immediately heard the loud thump and jumped away from me. He probably expected a dead pal or at least one that was knocked out. My head is too hard for that. Oh, it hurt, but I was immediately back on my feet. I had quite a lump but no cuts, no blood, but that was the end of the wrestling match for the time being.

I began the graveyard shift on the Rock Springs Police Department on that fall night. It was busy. The roll calls were informal. There were about six officers working that night, including Sergeant Matt. The dispatcher for the shift was George Wales. He had been there since I was a kid. He always worked the grave shift. He was called Hornet, a name given him by Sergeant Matt. He was a fun-loving, nice guy but could turn really taciturn if he was pestered too much by rookie cops or crossed by somebody. He was hunched over and walked that way. He had suffered some type of birth defect but was now in his late 40s or maybe 50s.

Most of the guys on the shift with the exception of Sergeant Matt were young guys. I was assigned to ride with Lester, called Butch. He was an Oklahoman with military experience. He was three years older than me and was just toward the end of his one-year probation. He had not been to the academy yet. He had a huge opinion of himself and saw himself and another young guy on the shift, Neil, as Starsky and Hutch type of cops. Neil didn't buy into this but would humor Butch. Some of the prostitutes would refer to

Butch and Neil as Starsky and Hutch. Butch loved this and wouldn't discourage it like Neil or other officers would.

Neil was the only working friend that Butch had in the department. No one wanted to ride with him when we did two-man cars. I guess this was my first acid test to see how I coped with Butch. He thought himself to be too good to work uniformed and expected to be a detective. He knew lots about being a cop, so he would tell anybody who would listen.

Butch thought I was a dummy, which was what he thought of most people other than Neil. We were in the car only a short time and going from call to call. I couldn't touch the radio, shotgun, or lights and siren controls, not that I wanted to, it was all a mystery to me at this time. He immediately let me know that people from Rock Springs were all crooks. I told him that I was born and raised here, but he quickly detected that what would normally insult and infuriate most went off me like water on a duck. No matter, he would repeat this "known fact" often. The chief and the lieutenant, the mayor and on and on were all crooks. I wondered to myself, if he really thought this, which at that time I am sure he did, why did he come to work here or care to work for such an agency?

I was made his regular partner most of the time. He wanted himself and Neil to ride together. Neil really quietly resisted this, and the supervisors wouldn't allow that to happen at any cost. It would be easy to dislike the guy and not have a thing to do with him. He would go out of his way to be obnoxious with fellow officers. They avoided him or dished it right back to him.

One night later, I was assigned to ride with Neil. He was a young Greek guy from California. Loved to hike and climb. This was what brought him to Wyoming, in addition to seeing relatives in Green River. He had college degrees and could have been anything but a police officer. He had long hair, which was allowed but really frowned on. He was about four years older than me. His parents were very unhappy that he had remained in Wyoming and especially that he had become a rookie cop in such a wild place as Rock Springs. They had designs on him of being an electrical engineer or something more along that line.

Neil was easy to work with, and though he held me at arm's length, he was friendly compared to Lester, whom Sergeant Matt called Lester P. We were all given nicknames as time would pass, usually either by Sergeant Matt or Hornet. This was readily accepted by most as it meant that you had passed their muster and were one of the group. Plenty of guys had been rejected and ran off and just couldn't be part of this police department and particularly the grave shift.

I, of course, was later called Preacher, or Preach for short. Neil was not surprisingly called Greek. If you were one of the dependable ones that stayed, you were given a name. One young guy's name was Forest. He, of course, was called Woody.

The first night I was assigned to ride with Neil, another guy that started when I did was put on the grave shift for a while too. He was assigned to Butch. He was likable and had come from Colorado for this job. His uncle was the chief, but he didn't receive any favor from this and didn't make a big deal out of it. It was just a known fact. He had ridden with Butch on several calls, and maybe they had been together for an hour when he was brought back to the station, located on the main floor of the old city hall. He refused to ride with that so-and-so Lester. He was pretty upset over Butch's verbal digs and heckling. Butch was not upset. He seemed rather pleased with himself that he had got to the guy. The new officer was hot. He would walk before he would ride with Butch again. Sergeant Matt took him on for the night and had Butch ride alone. Butch was constantly wanting Neil to meet him, car to car somewhere, every chance he had. Neil would humor him some but seemed to want to keep Butch at arm's length as much as he could…probably the only way the friendship would survive.

Butch was one of the few married younger guys on the shift, but he made not much effort to make this known in making plans to do stuff with the single guys or if some flirty female was around. I learned some from Butch about the career, and we became close friends later as he metamorphosed into a better person. Pride is an awful thing, and it did no good for Butch.

Sheryl was a dark-haired Christian girl that I knew from Big Piney. She had moved to Rock Springs with her family. She was attractive and just a few years younger than me. I was friendly with her as I knew her from the services I had been to in Big Piney.

It was obvious that she was interested in me. She made a point of running into me around town in the daytime. I liked her, but I was far too busy to start dating a girl. She began working as a waitress at the restaurant on the west side of town. This was a chain restaurant that was open twenty-four hours. We would take our brief and usually interrupted lunch breaks there on the grave shift. Sheryl was working then and would make it a point to wait our table.

Butch immediately picked up on her interest in me and that she had none in him, though this he couldn't figure. He was far more handsome than me or Neil (his opinion). He would challenge me, "Gee, what's a matter with you? Don't you see that she likes you? You ought to date her." Letting me know that he wouldn't pass her up, no way. I didn't answer him. I would just smile and laugh at him. This would really drive him up the wall. Most of the time, to everybody's wonder, I was able to put up with Butch when only his wife did because I have never been a person that allows themselves to be offended. Yakking, threatening, and insulting remarks don't bother me.

Butch had met his match. He couldn't ruffle me, but I could him and pretty easily too. I would just not bite on most of his jewels that would enrage most other guys. The presidential elections were going to take place. Carter and Ford were running. My family and I were Democrats then. I thought Carter, being a Christian man, would make a good president, and I was not too happy about all that had occurred between Ford and Nixon, though we had supported Nixon for president till it was learned that he had really done some bad stuff.

I was going to vote for Carter for the first time I was able to vote for a president. I did, in fact, do this. Boy, did I later regret that? What a dud he turned out to be. He was the only Democrat that ran for president that I ever voted for after that and not for his reelection either.

Anyway, Butch hated Carter. It wasn't that big of a deal to me, and I would rather have avoided the subject of presidential politics with him until I found that by praising Jimmy Carter and talking down Ford, I could really drive him crazy. I mean, he would get worked up about it. That was what I wanted, so, even though I didn't feel that strong against Ford, I wouldn't let Lester P. know that.

Hornet and Sergeant Matt would also call Butch "You dumb Okie" when they were upset with him. It was kind of welcome relief for me and others when Butch and Neil went off to basic police training at the academy.

As time went on, I became good friends with Hornet, Neil, Butch, Sergeant Matt, and others. Bonding was an important thing to have among as many officers as possible, especially on grave shift, to keep from being hurt or killed. It made for a more cohesive unit that could be successful in getting the job done. Not everybody was part of this cliche, even if they worked on graves, and hardly anybody on day shift was thought to be of any use, and only a few guys on swing shift. Most of these opinions about the ability to be an effective officer were pretty accurate as they related to these officers. I still got along with just about anybody and everybody in the department, even though I became increasingly considered a graveyarder. I did work later on other shifts, too, mostly the swing shift.

After two changes in department leadership in just a short time, Butch did finally get his shot at being a detective. He played it to the hilt. It was short-lived as the next change in another short period of time in leadership put him right back in uniform. I never worked much with him, though, when he returned in uniform.

Some of the graveyard guys were back together when Butch came back into uniform. Neil and I were in a two-man car on this particular shift when Butch typically wanted to meet us. We did. Butch had a young guy with him, Forest-Woody, that had only been in the department for about a year. They were all excited about some new patrol cars that were being painted and readied for use inside of a body shop on the north side of town. They wanted to go see about looking at them.

Neil and I told them no. We weren't going to do that and that they didn't have to either. It was a bad idea, and we were busy anyway. After some talk, we parted. Only a short time later, things really hit the fan for Butch and his partner. They had gone out to the shop and used a folding knife that some of the officers carried to try to enter a walk-in door to look at the new patrol cars.

Unbeknownst to them, an employee stayed in the building and had heard someone at the door and found them there trying to open it. This guy was a rough character and disliked cops anyway, so he made a big deal out of it. All a sudden, they were burglars. Going to steal tools, money, etc. The politics were in full swing in town then, as I previously described. Chief Hawk had only been in place for a short time, and he was supposed to help clean up all of the "corruption." These guys had not a chance. They were fired and had no future of being in law enforcement again after the media catered to the politicians getting lots of mileage out of this event. Yes, it was a stupid thing that these guys had done, we told them it was before they did it. Of course, we didn't know they were going to try to enter the building if they didn't find an open door. They didn't deserve what they suffered from this, however.

Butch went into oil field work after this, and we remained friends over all of these years. Butch turned his life over to the Lord, who saved him from divorce from his wonderful wife and children, most of the pride went, and Butch became a much more likable person.

When I was in security at the Bridger Plant, I had a big stretch four-wheel drive. Green in color with windows along the side. It was a goer. It was similar to an orange stretch four-wheel drive. I later had. They were tanks. They put modern four-wheel drives to shame. I ran around most of the time in country in a two-wheel drive that modern four-wheel drives would have a very difficult time negotiating. Seldom did I have to use a four-wheel drive, and when I did, it was usually to pull out another vehicle that was stuck. The International was even more of a tank than this.

I would often stay in the back of these vehicles on hunting or fishing trips where I wanted to be more mobile and wouldn't have to mess with a tent. However, in nicer conditions, if I was alone or with Grandpa Hamilton, we usually just threw down a tarp and slept on it in sleeping bags with another tarp over us out in the open. It was great, even if it sometimes rained, frosted, or snowed some. The fresh air was nice, and before falling asleep, the coyotes singing out and the stars in multitude made for a very special bedroom.

Grandpa Hamilton and I were fishing at the Firehole side of the Flaming Gorge. We stayed as usual all day but ended up even late into the evening on this spring day. We had gone in the green stretch four-wheel drive. The drive home was through open range once out of the Flaming Gorge area with cattle scattered about it.

Grandpa loved to drive like a maniac and would often give his passengers a white-knuckle ride as he sailed along. I usually followed the posted speed limit or close to it. On this night, I decided to see if I could get him on the nervous side. It was pitch-black as we roared down the narrow state highway. Suddenly, a large Hereford cow was in front of us, and I mean directly in the middle of the highway and just barely moving to the right. She had no concern about the head-lights about to overtake her.

Grandpa had been sitting silently for some time as we had talked about most subjects that could be discussed through the long day. He came to life when we saw the cow. He reared up in the seat in a sort of standing position with his back still against the back of the seat. He made some loud noise, but I have no idea what he said. It looked bad. I couldn't slam on the brakes on this tank, it would send us spinning down the highway, and we were too close to the old heifer to do us any good now anyway.

She took one slow step to the right, and I turned sharp to the left. Had to be careful. If we went off the highway, we would prob-ably roll. In a flash, we skimmed just past her rear end and missed a terrific chance to harvest a load of beef (already tenderized too)!

Grandpa sat back in his seat. Noticeably shaken but trying not to let on about it. All he said was, "I thought we had it that time!" Mission accomplished.

I was by myself in the same tank one winter day at the Flaming Gorge just hunting for rabbits and predators and prowling around.

I decided to take the steep county road out of the place, back to the highway, late that afternoon. It was the Big Firehole road. It was snow-covered, to start with, but got increasingly slick and snowy as I went up the steep incline. I didn't like this, but I had gone too far to turn back now, and there was nowhere to turn around anyway.

It turned into sheer ice, and I was barely getting up the road in a two-wheel drive. I dared not to stop and turn the front hubs in so that I could engage the four-wheel drive. Had I been in a four-wheel drive, I would have had no difficulty, but the road became far worse than I had prepared for. Suddenly, on the steep hill, I could go no further. To my right was a bank. To my left was a deep canyon immediately alongside the road. The tank then started slowly sliding backwards down the hill and picking up speed. This did not look too good. If I went into the canyon, it would most likely be curtains.

I had only one slim chance to escape this little problem. There was a clear patch of bare ground for several feet at the edge of the road that I was approaching. If I turned the vehicle so that it backed into this spot and gave it full power, it might flip me back downhill and avoid this fender bender! If not, I would go over the edge and fall down and go—*boom*—into the canyon. All of this happened in milliseconds. As the back of the truck came almost to the dirt spot, I turned, and it immediately slid back on the ice, and the rear wheels hit the dirt. I mashed the gas pedal to the floor, and the motor roared. The tires spun on that little patch of ground, and the four-wheel-drive tank turned and bolted back downhill. I went sailing along the icy road until I came to a spot that was level, and I could wipe the cold sweat out of my eyes. Obviously, for anyone other than a full-blood skeptic, there had to be an angel on duty moving that big vehicle about and averting sure disaster that day.

Another spring day, I was out prowling the Firehole area as I loved to do. I drove up near the edge of a canyon below but parked far enough back that I could sneak up to the edge and look into the precipice on foot, hoping to spot game animals or predators below. There was an old road at the bottom of this wide canyon. I crept up and peered over. I left my firearm in the vehicle as I was only looking for now.

In the bottom of the canyon, there were two vehicles parked and three men standing and talking. They were probably 400-500 yards from me. Well, nothing to see here, so I stood fully up and was going to take one short look at the scenery before I walked back to the vehicle. Suddenly, at least two of those guys below were looking up at me and pointed rifles in my direction. Then they began firing. The bullets went whizzing close by, and they kept it up. Sounded like .22s. Like a scared jackrabbit, I was racing away from that mess. They kept firing a number of shots even after I had left their view. I have no idea who these guys were, but without question, I had wandered into some kind of a drug deal. I left there in a hurry and expected that this was not over. At least when these guys met me somewhere on the road systems, I would be able to return fire. I never saw them again. I kept angels busy in those days and still do, I think. Not usually by intention.

At the Bridger Plant, we had just completed our swing shift and were onto I-80 headed west just after midnight in-route home. Traffic was light, and I had a vehicle full of guards that had carpooled with me for the day. As we rode along talking in the dark, we noticed a vehicle coming at us eastbound, but it seemed far too close to us. Moments later, this truck passed us like nobody's business. Going around the speed limit in the westbound lane of traffic. That was a close one too. I put out a message about it on the CB. There was no highway patrol out usually after midnight. The guy was either badly disoriented or drunk. He continued on down the road.

Steve had gone to Bible college in Washington. There he met his future wife in only a short time. They ended up transferring to a college in Florida and then decided to marry there. I was asked to be the best man. I was able to take a few days off from my short time at the police department to fly down there and back. I had never flown before. I flew out of the small Rock Springs airport and then connected and flew onto the Tampa area with the now-defunct well-known commercial airlines that commonly served that area.

I had never been to Florida. There was not much time for anything but the wedding, but they did drive me around Tampa some and the small nearby town where the wedding was to take place.

It was alright but no place that I would care to live. Some months later, Steve had enough of college. He moved his bride back to Rock Springs and went to work for a company putting up steel buildings. The thing was, they were pretty tight for money. They asked to stay with me in the old apartment I now occupied alone on A Street. I wasn't crazy about this arrangement. Having newlyweds in the one-bedroom place. It would work for a short time, what could I do? They had no money to pay the high rent in town until they were able to work for a bit. I didn't know his wife very well, only from the wedding. All she really knew of me was the wild and crazy stories that Steve had told her about our escapades over the years. She must have thought she was moving in with some crazed halfway mountain man. The only redeeming thought was that at least he was a police officer and a minister, so he could not be completely whacky.

This arrangement worked for the short term. I was working graves and would sleep only a short time in the day. They were usually gone working during this time as his wife, Carrie, who was a very quiet and gentle soul, had found employment at the library.

Poor women. It was a difficult spot for her, I know. Besides, she had never been to Wyoming. She was pretty much a Southern gal and had really no interest in Rock Springs. I let this arrangement go on for several months. However, when Steve gave no hint of finding his own place, we had to have a "come to Jesus' meeting."

The landlord and his girlfriend decided to marry. She had been living in a small two-story house in front of my upstairs apartment, directly on A Street. He lived in the house underneath me. They decided to open up the apartment and take over the entire house and offer me the small house where she had been living. This I did. Moved into 507 A Street shortly after they married. It was a pretty good place. The one drawback was that the street was a pretty good incline with a lot of traffic. I had a one-car garage and still could park in the driveway alongside the house too.

I had been in the police department for only several weeks when one grave shift, I rode with Officer Gary. He was married and in his late 20s. Had several years in the department and had moved to Rock Springs from the Lander area. He was a nice guy. Quiet and easy to work with. He liked to ask me questions about the Bible, and we would have discussions as to why the Ten Commandments would not save him, as he claimed he followed them, at least he tried to. He thought he did pretty good in his efforts.

Among the wild mess that town had turned into, there were a number of particularly bad bars or clubs. Dotsies—The Townsend Club was allowed to stay open without restriction. Once the bars closed, most of the carousing partiers went there until daylight or after. The Twilight was on the west side of town, and it was a wild disco bar. Downtown was the A&D bar, Jake's Bar (mostly a Mexican hangout), on the north side of town, there were two big cowboy bars that were problems often. The Kasbah and Haddocks.

On the east side of town was the Astro Lounge that my former employer from the grocery store had bought. All of these were pits of trouble among all of the other pits that covered the town. Lots of churches but far more bars occupied the scenery.

We would make bar checks as much as possible during shifts if time allowed. Seldom would one officer do this alone, and it would not be wise to either. We had a break in the action, so Gary decided that we would do a bar check at the A&D bar on Front Street. It was a seedy place. No windows on the front of the building. On another night, while doing a bar check in the place, there was a young wom-an-dancer completely naked on a table on all fours. She was enter-taining four men seated around her. I was about to make an arrest for indecent exposure. Whoever I was working with that night would not let me do it. The city judge had ruled that this was not illegal under our city ordinance if it was in a bar with no view from the street. I was not happy with this and would have made the arrest if it was up to me and taken my chances at a trial with this judge if the parties even contested the arrest.

Fortunately, all of the dancers, though nearly naked in the var-ious bars, were never again seen to be fully in their birthday suits by me. But not to be distracted completely from the night that Gary and I did this particular bar check, the place was a good-size build-ing. It was packed with mostly guys from the oil field, the Bridger Plant, and the like. It was wild. Loud music and loud voices. I was to remain at the front of the bar while Gary worked through the crowd toward the back and then would come back to the front.

It was elbow-to-elbow. Suddenly, this short black guy that was seated at the bar and occupied with his back to Gary apparently spotted Gary passing by. He turned on the barstool and leaped off it and attacked Gary. I could just barely see them begin to fight. I started forcing my way through the crowd in that direction while pulling out my nightstick. Before I had gone more than a few steps, several of the crowd grabbed me, and we started wrestling. I never had less than four guys fighting with me at a time. One of them got my stick away from me, and someone was pulling on my holstered revolver, trying to remove it. I had to fight like mad to keep this from happening. Barely able to move, we fell to the floor, and I was being hit in the arms and back as I wrestled with several of them. I was able to get back up, and they started backing away from me. Many of the crowd had started fighting among themselves, and it was just one big free-for-all. I made my way to the bar where I was going to make the bartender call for help. The bartenders had scurried away. No phone could I find, but here was my nightstick amazingly laying on the bar. We had no portable radios then. I retrieved my stick. I couldn't see Gary with all of the pandemonium, so I made my way to the front door and onto the sidewalk.

Unbelievably no one was on the street as I was going to commandeer someone and send them to a phone or to the police department for help as it was obvious that we had a mess to bring under control.

Only the driver of the patrol car carried the car key then, so I had no access to the police radio. I quickly tried the doors. We always locked them, but in hopes that maybe one was unlocked, I tried all four. No dice. Still, no one in view on the street. Well, just going to have to play Custer and face the battle badly outnumbered. I headed back to the front door to go in when Gary stepped out.

His uniform, like mine, was all askew. His face was bloody. The little black guy was wild and had punched him several times in the nose as they fought. He had a broken nose. The black guy was in the bar fighting with others now. Gary was going to the car to call for backup when suddenly somebody got the idea that we had been out of contact for too long. Sergeant Mark, who was now working some graves when Bider was off, came rolling up and saw both of us kind of battle-worn. Gary far worse than I.

He put out the call for help, and in we went to get the black guy and put a stop to this mess. If you were in a police uniform on this shift, whoever was with you, almost without fail, would not leave you in the lurch. It was one for all and all for one. We fought to win, we had to. Bar fights are not like the westerns on television. They are vicious and violent. Some of the people in the bars are just bored and angry or otherwise. It was common for guys to have sheath, folding, or pocket knives. Although illegal then for anyone that was not law enforcement or had no permit from the county sheriff to carry a concealed handgun, we knew that it was done often. It could be great fun and entertainment to fight with the cops. Others were after blood and were really violent people or had no intention of having someone (like the police) interrupting their fun. We often arrested people wanted for all hosts of things on NCIC (National Crime Information Center) with felony warrants from all over the country. Also, the horse tranquilizer PCP was a preferred drug during this time as well as marijuana and cocaine. Booze of all types flowed without restriction. The PCP was especially a problem, though. It would cause hallucinations and violence. Cops in California were having big problems with it. They had developed nets to throw over PCP people to bring them under control without so many injures to the police and maybe the PCP nut as well. The black guy had just taken a hit of PCP as we entered the bar. When he saw Gary, he went nuts and stayed that way till well into the morning.

Help was limited. We only usually had three to six officers working on a shift. The sheriff's department only had one or two deputies out in the large county. They often were not in town and usually quit anywhere from 10 p.m. to midnight. The few highway patrol officers stopped at midnight. So other than the police department's grave shift, it was almost always wide open. It was probably around 01:00 (1 a.m.) when this started. It was a weekend, and fortunately, two highway patrolmen and a deputy had not gone in yet.

The highway patrol would be bored with constantly working mostly traffic and were all too happy to have a reason to help the police department with action going on. When the call went out, within a few minutes, we had our half a dozen guys, the patrolmen, and the deputy. Still badly outnumbered, we were going to clean that mess out. We did in about twenty minutes. Many of the crowd still wanted to fight and had no intention of going easy. Very few people had left out either the front or back door. I guess many of them just didn't care and went back to their carousing, and a good few of them probably figured they had run the cops out and they wouldn't be back any time soon. These were rough times in the state. Not too long before I started in law enforcement, the chief of police in a small department in Mountain View, Wyoming, had been run out of town by a couple of toughs, and nothing happened to them. This was a little town about seventy or eighty miles southwest of Rock Springs in Uinta County. It, too, was affected by the boom, however, being near us, Kemmerer and Evanston. These guys worked the chief over one night and told him to leave town. He did. It was in the papers, but nothing really came of it. People just didn't care or were too busy with life to get involved. Besides, it wasn't them that got worked over.

The fight was on. None of us really got injured other than Gary. Torn this and that and cuts and scrapes, but we did the hurting till it was over. People were marched or dragged out the door, and each patrol car was piled full of arrestees. Neil Kourbelas likes to tell people a story about me. He was inside the bar at its front. He was handcuffing somebody, I think, but saw me come back into the bar after returning from putting somebody in a police car. I was standing in the doorway of the open door and had turned to face the sidewalk. He saw somebody in the crowd give me a shove. I went out the door. Then the guy who shoved me stood where I was. He saw my hand reach back through the open door and grab the guy by his shirt. Out the door he flew. Neil has that jolly look and laughs every time he tells this.

The bar was emptied, and the old jail, which is what a jail should be, was packed overflowing. We had to put the black guy in a small cell by himself. He was like a wild animal. He had violently fought and was now in the barred cell screaming at the top of his lungs. He would climb up the bars and hang from the top of the cell bars, screaming. This went on for hours till the effects of the PCP and booze wore off. There were more fights in the booking room as people were taken out of cuffs and restraints to be booked and placed in cells. A few of them still had not had enough at the bar. One high-way patrolman just about put a guy's head through the wall because he wouldn't quit. No one was hurt that didn't have to be, though. They just had any and all necessary force applied until they quit. We had to keep control. If we ever let the hordes take over, it would be an unmanageable situation. There were many, many such brawls but not usually quite this wild.

A few nights later, Lieutenant Overy had been out of town, and when he returned, he got on the radio and publicly commended me for all to hear. He heard about this brawl and wanted to let anybody on the radio and all the people with police scanners of which there were many, scanners and CB radios were the rage, that Weimer, the new guy, was alright. I was a little embarrassed and tried to play it down in my reply, but he repeated his message again. He wanted it known.

Quite a while after this, we had the first female officer the town had ever had. She was from Rock Springs like me. I didn't know her very well, but she was only a few years younger than me. She was a small woman, and I found her and most of the women that later joined the department to be quite worthless and not able to pull their weight. We ended up with about five or six of them in my eight years in the department. One or two of them were pretty good, and in a more peaceful setting, they would probably have been okay for the most part.

One night this female officer was riding with me. We went into our old stomping grounds at the A&D bar in doing bar checks that night. It was a weeknight, not that it made any difference, the bars were busy and packed most times. Just as we stepped into the crowded bar, we encountered people immediately inside the door. There was this Latino-looking guy that had his back to me, and he was intently talking quietly to a guy in front of him. He, without a doubt, had this guy's attention. I saw the Latino guy's right hand that was by his side, he was holding a big sheath knife and obviously getting ready to stab the guy in front of him in the gut. I quickly told the officer behind me and grabbed the guy's knife-hand. The fight was on. We wrestled for a few seconds till I had him under control. The knife finally dropped, and my partner got it. He was cuffed and went to jail. The guy that just barely averted assault was white as a ghost. He and this guy had gotten into it, and the Latino meant business.

We had a woman sexually assaulted, and, in the process, we had her in the interview room for her account of the incident. The sergeant thought that this would be the ideal situation to have our female officer who was working take the statement. Obviously, the women would feel more comfortable with telling this to another female. The female officer came out of the room after just a few minutes with the victim. The victim did not want to talk to a female. She preferred to make the statement to a male officer. *Okay?*

I had the female officer with me one late evening on the swing shift. We were called to a big apartment complex on the west side of town for a loud domestic disturbance. We located the apartment on the second floor and entered after knocking and having the door opened to us. A middle-aged man and a woman were having it out verbally. I had them nearly quieted down when the female officer just started screaming at the people. They immediately blew up and really started yelling at each other and us. We nearly had to arrest them. Finally got it stopped and had them separated for the night and referred to outside agency assistance.

We got back in the car to leave. I was not happy one bit about how that scene blew up for no reason. I called the officer's first name and said, "What was that all about, why did you start screaming at those people?" She knew that she had really screwed that call up.

She sheepishly said, "I don't know, Weimer, I just thought it would help."

"Not that I need to tell you this if you have a brain at all, but *don't ever do that again!*"

She was assigned to me one cold night on graves when we received a call of a man down on the sidewalk in front of a bar that wasn't usually a hot spot. We had very few calls to this bar. The only previous thing I could remember of any consequence that had happened there was late on one night after the bar had been closed (they had to close by 2 a.m.) for some time, and no one was around, I was on patrol with Matt Keslar. Matt was from Cheyenne, where his family lived. His twin brother had joined the police department there. Matt was just a bit younger than me. He was new at this career too. He was dependable and a top-notch guy. We became good friends. Anyway, as we patrolled down the dark, almost empty Pilot Butte Ave section of this downtown street, two guys came running out of the bar with their arms full of bottles.

They nearly ran into the police car. We jumped out and grabbed the first guy and were going to chase the second guy down that was running ahead of the one we grabbed. He just made it into a nearby alley as we secured the first character, and as we went after the other one, I guess he figured what's the use. He came right back out of the alley and up to us and gave up.

Either the alarm didn't work or hadn't been turned on, and these guys had broken out the front glass door. Gone into the front liquor store of the bar and filled their arms with all they could pack out and were making a run for it. The timing didn't work for them. Sure, did for us and the bar. Everything was recovered, and the two burglars went to jail. I caught lots of them. In fact, many considered me to be one of the best at catching burglars, and several of the defense attorneys in the area called me the "King of DWUIs," drunk drives. I arrested more of them than several cops put together, and they very, very seldom could beat it in court.

Anyway, the female officer and I responded to this call of a man down. Sure enough, the middle-aged guy was lying on the sidewalk and was unconscious. There were no immediate signs of injury, and he had the smell of alcoholic beverages on his person. He had been in the bar earlier. Nobody's around to say what happened. Maybe drunk and fell, maybe assaulted and rolled/robbed. I told the female officer to stay with him and keep an eye on him while I called for an ambulance. It would typically take twenty minutes for an ambulance to arrive at this time of night. I was seated in the car with the window down and calling for an ambulance and standing by the radio. Then after just a few minutes, the female officer casually wandered over to the open window and said, "Weimer, I don't think this guy is still breathing." *What?* I jumped out and went to check him. She just stood over us looking like any Joe Blow would. No, the guy had quit breathing. I got him into position and started mouth-to-mouth resuscitation. This was before there were any kind of devices to put between you and the victim. Wanted to avoid this, but there was no choice. It was definitely lip-lock time. Glad that the police academy made this a part of the curriculum. It was not encouraged or taught that much then except for law enforcement and medical people.

I swore to protect and serve, and this was part of it. Just as a side note, my first partner Butch would just get really irritated at this. He was not a public servant. He was not a slave. Well, I'm certainly not a slave, but I am here to protect and serve. I used to really get him going with that line of conversation, too, as you might imagine. I finally got her to help with chest compressions, and I stuck with the breathing because I knew she would not do it or would not put any effort into it.

We get the guy breathing again. He was alive when the ambulance got there, and they took over with advanced care. They were a very good service; they didn't just scoop victims up and haul them to the hospital. The guy finally died in the emergency room. He had major blunt force trauma to the back of his head. It was not easily visible, but something had really hurt him.

This was investigated, and we suspected two young thugs that had been in the bar of hitting the guy in the back of his head and taking most of his money. He was from out of town. Came there to make his fortune, and now, like many others, he had died instead. He could have hit his head on the sidewalk in a fall too. Nothing could ever be proved one way or the other.

Later as I was this female officer's chaplain, she presented me with a beautiful pair of praying hands that she had made in the class she took. I might bump heads at times with other officers, and there were some that genuinely hated me or disliked me for various reasons. I never was offended or carried grudges. There were officers I didn't personally like, but that was the extent of it. I could work with anyone and be a chaplain-minister to anyone that was willing.

There were probably around forty prostitutes working in Rock Springs. Most were on the streets and at the bars that would allow them in. About half of them stayed most of the time, and the other half or so were on a circuit from Salt Lake or Denver and would come and go, and faces would change. Nearly all had black pimps. There were young girls at the age of eighteen and nineteen to mid-aged gals in their late 30s. They were black, white, and Latino. We even had one or two that were in the process of sex change and were a mix at the time. They had no problem staying busy either! Most of them avoided the police and trouble. Some had mean streaks and were just trouble. Some were thieves.

The laws made it difficult to stop what they were doing. So, if we couldn't arrest them for prostitution, we used whatever law we could to keep them off the street and out of business. Otherwise, we would just herd them on if they got too comfortable hanging out in places. Seldom did they not comply. The pimps were low-key and tried to stay away from us.

As a young officer still in my first year, we would take short lunch breaks at a chain restaurant that stayed open twenty-four hours. One night two of the girls that had not been in town too long came in and asked to sit with me and whoever I was with. One of the girls was named Rose because she wore a rose in her hair. She was a pretty girl, probably about nineteen or twenty. They were friendly, so we let them visit. Then Rose wanted to ask me something. I went off to the side with her. She didn't want to keep doing this. She wanted to know I was single and wanted to know if she could come to stay with me! She was sincere, and I didn't want to hurt her feelings, but no.

She showed up by herself at the police department the next grave shift and asked to talk to me in the hallway. Again, she made her pitch. Nice girl, and I hope she was able to change her life, but *no*, she could not come live with me. She left town shortly after that. What became of her, I do not know.

I finally had my year in, and I was scheduled for the academy in October. "What, not October, Lieutenant Overy. I have a two-week vacation I can take," and I really wanted to hunt with Grandpa Hamilton in the Wasatch Forest for elk and deer in October. Lieutenant Overy was really good to me always.

"No problem, we will reschedule you guys to go in January." Great. Only two of us had made probation out of the five. So, it would be me and the chief's nephew going in January to Douglas.

We went and along with us were two Green River guys and a deputy sheriff. The deputy was the only one I knew out of this group. His name was Rich (Richard), and years later, he became the sheriff. The academy operated on a temporary location in the state fairgrounds. I knew this area well. It was where we would have our church camps and do the trail rides a few years back.

The academy was overseen by the director, George Nimo. He was one of the tough old sheriffs and had been the sheriff of Sweetwater County when I was a kid. There were a lot of politics going on statewide, and a grand jury was being impaneled for the state to look into all of what the media and people with their political ambitions thought were travesties of justice. There was probably some wrongdoing anywhere, but nothing like the media tried to cook up. This was affecting the academy, and Nimo was somehow implicated in some of it. He was there when we first arrived. He welcomed us. He was a thin older gray-haired man. He wore glasses and had a prosthetic eye. It was shot out as a kid by a BB gun. Truly a case of the old Red Ryder curse, "You'll shoot your eye out, kid." You could sense that he was a tough person. He was gone then, and the assistant director took over. Nimo never came back, and the assistant became the longtime director. Ernie Johnson, he had been a Casper cop. He was a mid-aged Latino-looking guy. Very fit and professional but friendly. He made an excellent director.

Our basic academy was five weeks then. It seemed like an eternity. I and my counterpart from Rock Springs were single. The other three we had come to the academy with from the area were married and wanted to go home on the weekends. So, we rode along. It was long trips on these wintry highways with a cold, nasty winter in full force. We left on Friday afternoons as soon as we could and had to be back on Sunday night.

There were two men to a room in the dorms. I roomed with a deputy from Teton County. He was a Christian guy and really pleasant. It was a large class with officers, not highway patrol, from all over the state. Quite a conglomeration of humanity. There were guys my age and younger to guys in their late 40s.

There was a large shower-bathroom area. One morning as I went in to clean up, Deputy Rich was already at a sink. He was a Mormon. This I knew, but I didn't know much about a lot of their customs otherwise. He was wearing a sheer one-piece garment as he shaved and so on. I couldn't help myself. I said, "Hey, Rich, what do you have on, your wife's underwear?" He did not like this, especially the laughing that accompanied the quip. He told me that this was his holy garment and was not one bit happy with me. We got along fine, but I didn't razz him anymore about his undergarments.

The courses were pretty challenging and good. I was finding out why we did some stuff I had been doing and what the legal basis and restrictions were. The meals were huge. There were three meals prepared by a staff of local ladies that were used to cooking big meals for ranch hands. Really nice older women. The young guys ate with a vengeance. Lots of the older guys had to really pull back. They were gaining too much weight. This was the same kitchen and dining hall where we had our church camp meals. It was like an old home week.

There was a group of officers from Gillette. About five of them, and they pretty much stayed to themselves. After the first week, they started all hanging out late in the bars at night and then coming into the darkened, quiet barracks where most of the guys were asleep, about 1 or 2 a.m. They would come in banging on the walls, yelling, yuking it up, and so on. We put up with this for a couple of nights until it appeared that they planned to make this a nightly occurrence. A bunch of us got together with them and let them know if they came in one more night like that, there was going to be a blanket party for them. That stopped it.

We graduated. The ceremony was held in the dining hall. A number of the officers had family members attend the luncheon and ceremony. The chief's nephew I was at the academy with had made it known to Ernie Johnson that I was a minister. Johnson asked me, in addition to graduating, if I would do the benediction. I did.

Back home, not much had changed. Several of the guys were asking me about being the chaplain for the department in addition to a working officer. I prayed about this and was sure I had to pursue it. There were no law enforcement chaplaincies in the state, so this would be the first. I obtained materials from the General Council of the Assemblies of God for chaplain programs in other locations.

I would need to be a licensed minister rather than having an exhorter's permit. As I explained in the previous pages, I did indeed receive this license. I much later became ordained but not with the Assemblies of God as their thinking was that a person should be full-time in order to be ordained. I worked full-time in ministry or near that often, but I never received my livelihood from ministry.

I began the chaplain's program alone but began efforts to recruit interested local clergy. This was not an easy chore. The bad media had most of the preachers gun-shy about being involved with the police department. I also soon discovered that some ministers were not really interested in being in jails with criminals or in being out on the street dealing with seedy, troubled people and especially outside of typical office hours. Mentally ill and violent people seemed to turn some preachers away like rain stopping a picnic on a sunny day. Too many of the ministers investigated being a chaplain, that was about as far as it went. A meeting or two in a nice office was okay, but having to mix it up with rough cops, criminals, and the like was not to their taste. That was a good thing too. Because it is not for everybody. A person must be called to that ministry to start with, not just putting their toe in the water to give something a try, wishing to obtain the title of Police Chaplain, or satisfying some kind of curiosity as to what happens outside of a church building. This is not to demean anyone. It is just a true fact. Ministry of this type is often not pretty. It involves risk, and one must be willing to get dirty.

About this same time, the city had decided to make the position of public safety director for the department. Chief Muir, who was just not up to trying to run a department in the conditions that had developed, would still be the chief and Lieutenant Overy still under him. However, this new director would run the department.

Clyde Kemp, a middle-aged cop from Colorado, was hired. He was all for the chaplain's program and fully supported me in every way he could. So did Chief Muir and Lieutenant Overy. I had no resistance at all except with the local clergy. That was okay. This would not be a nice, cushy ministry. If you weren't called to it and had no interest in it, I really didn't want you. However, the city wanted me to try to make it inclusive for all the ministers that could and would join.

Kemp had a difficult time. He tried to make changes, and he did implement some, but his time was short, and he was soon gone. Another director would have to be hired.

A statewide grand jury had been impaneled, and their investigators were all over the state looking for dirt on public officials and so on. They had a particular eye out for Rock Springs. This was unfortunate. All of the boom towns in the state were having big problems like we were. We just had a bunch that intended to get good for themselves out of this and bring down those in office. Besides, it was a boom for the local media. Papers were selling, people were listening to the local radio stations more and on and on. Mayor Wataha had been in place since I was a kid, as had Chief Muir, and there were plenty of enemies that wanted to get rid of them for starters.

I couldn't get any chaplains to start with. I would minister to officers, in the jail, and to people that came into the department or were brought in for help. I was going most weekends to preach for the Big Piney—Marbleton church or the Green River church. I would work graves and then take off right after work in my little blue hatchback car for the one-hundred-mile drive to Big Piney. I would preach there on Sunday mornings as they were without a pastor. I began recruiting my sisters, Jan and Tammy, who were teens, to practice a good song. They would go with me when they could and sing a song for the congregation before I preached. Green River had pastor Griffin, and unless he was away, I would usually preach for them on Sunday night. I would be worn out by the time I got back to Rock Springs in the late afternoon from Big Piney. Then back to work that night on graves. I usually only slept five or six hours anyway, so I did okay.

Sleep I did too. I mentioned the time at my folks' where I slept through a guy shooting a big game rifle right by my bedroom window and never hearing it. Well, I was that way for many years. When I slept, I was in a coma. I had a loud ringer phone right by my bed, and I would seldom hear it ring. The Bible tells of the beloved of the Lord having rest and sleeping well. I have no doubt that I had to be one of them!

I was provided a chaplain's nameplate to wear on my police uniform. Often, I would be wearing the uniform when I ministered. There was never a conflict or question about whether I was acting as an officer or a chaplain. It worked out perfectly.

I really liked to spend time off prowling around on Little Mountain about fifty miles southeast of Rock Springs. It was a pretty timbered area. Lots of elk, deer, and sage chickens. Antelope in the lower areas. I knew it well. I would go there often when I wasn't going to the Wasatch in Uinta County or up north around the Big Sandy Openings, New Fork Lake, and so on. I would take my sisters and a friend they chose to take on two- or three-day camping trips to these places. We had wonderful times. Camping, hiking, and fishing. Poor Jan was a large girl. She never complained to me, but I know I must have about killed her on my long hikes we would take. Usually up steep hills and trails.

In nice weather, we would just do the Grandpa Hamilton thing and sleep out in the open on tarps with bags. One time we were coming back home from the north country. We were nearing Farson. All loaded up in my monster bright orange four-wheel drive. We were rolling along on this very windy afternoon, just having a nice ride home. *Whoosh.* In an instant, the hood flew up. Hit the windshield and flew over the top of the vehicle going about fifty-five miles per hour in the opposite direction, fortunately, no one was behind us when this heavy metal hood dropped from the sky onto the highway.

Oh, these things would happen. We retrieved the hood from the highway and put it in the back of the vehicle. We sure drew some unneeded attention by passing motorists. On we went with further trouble. The hood had a few scratches and minor dings, but I had it bolted back in place and in just fine working condition the next day.

I had taken Jan in this same vehicle on her first antelope hunt. She was able to get a nice buck in the Farson area. The next year she had a permit for the Daniel area, a bit further north. I was taking her there one dark early morning in the four-wheel drive. We were rolling along about fifty miles per hour. It was really dark, and the headlights on this tank weren't really bright on the road. The area was fenced along the highway, but deer, antelope, or some other critter could easily be in your path. Had to watch it.

We were having a nice visit as we rolled along when a car from Colorado went roaring past us. I told Jan that guy was driving way too fast on this dark highway. We'd find him up the road in a wreck from running into a deer or something. Yep, no doubt she agreed.

We were just north of Farson. Jan had just handed me a cup of coffee from my thermos bottle, and things were just peachy. Suddenly, a large black Angus cow appeared in front of us on the highway. Somebody had left a gate on the prairie fence open, and the cow had left the herd this early morning in search of the old "greener grass."

No way to get past it. We were going to hit. I threw the cup of coffee behind me and yelled, "Hold on." We had no seat belts, of course. *Boom*—we hit the cow directly in her side. The impact wasn't bad. The cow went flying out of the way. As we passed her, she let go of her bowls on the side of the vehicle. I was thrilled that my window was up.

Then the ride got really exciting. The vehicle went into a spin down the middle of the highway. I was fighting the steering wheel like mad to keep the vehicle from rolling over, and thank God that there was no other traffic. We spun three full circles down the highway. Jan had been thrown off the passenger seat and was lying on the floor with her back against the door, looking up at me with our junk piling up on top of her as it flew all around the inside of the rig.

We finally came to a stop facing the opposite direction, still in the middle of the road. The front end was crunched in some, and the radiator was steaming. I was able to drive off to the side of the road, and the cow got up and went to the roadside. She went down there and died a bit later. Wow. What a ride.

It was starting to get light by the time that we got Jan off the floor and figured out that we were a little shaken up but no worse for wear! We got a ride into the Farson cafe. The people there were really nice Mormon folks, we had coffee and settled our nerves while we waited for a highway patrolman. About an hour later, Steve Watt, a patrolman from Rock Springs, arrived. We knew each other. Steve was a prince of a guy.

He took us back to the vehicle and made his report. We gathered what we wanted from it for the time, and then he called a tow truck from Rock Springs for us. We rode back to town with Steve. The injured four-wheel drive was taken to my dad's house and put it in the yard there with his collection of wrecks.

The old bright orange four-wheel drive was tough. Done, no. It wasn't like the plastic, fiberglass stuff we drive now. I located a new radiator at a wrecking yard east of town, and with that in place and a chain and padlock on the hood, it was a little unsightly but good as new. About a week or so later, Jan and I were at it again. We went to Daniel area, and she got her antelope. We had a fine trip. I drove that old wreck for many miles and years after this. I finally had to leave it when we moved to Alaska. I still wish I had that old wreck. I was in places that any other four-wheel drives would have been thoroughly mired down in. Not the Binder. If it didn't break down, you would keep going, usually not even in need of the four-wheel drive. In fact, one of the few times that I used the four-wheel drive was in the Wasatch. The rear driveshaft broke. I had to use the front end the rest of the time to get around and get home at the end of my hunting trip until I could get it in the shop for repair.

I had found this jewel of a vehicle, which people like to razz me about, in Salt Lake City at an auto dealer. It has just been freshly painted bright orange and traded in by some lug when I came upon it, looking for a good one. I latched onto that baby, and no matter who laughed and poked fun about it, I would not have traded it for anything.

Grandpa Hamilton and I had decided to make a several days' trip onto Little Mountain in early September and camp up on the top in a nice little aspen patch. The sage chickens were thick up there, and we were going to have a go at it.

He took his old truck with an old cab on its bed. We were going to stay in it, and I had my stretch four-wheel drive—the cow killer. It was just terrific September/fall weather. The kind of magic Indian summer days that you wish would never end.

We were setting up camp when I began crawling into the cab on this truck, getting stuff out of there that we needed outside and to make a sleeping room. He had the thing full of stuff, including a number of fishing poles with hooks dangling on them. Before I knew it, one of the number eight barbed hooks had caught in my left ear as I crawled in and out of the cab.

Ouch. I came out with the fishing pole in hand. Grandpa wasn't too bothered by this revolting development as much as I was. We cut the line and discovered that the hook was completely in, bedded in the lobe of my ear. Only the eye of the hook was visible.

Grandpa said, "Well, I guess we'll have to get you into town to the doc to get that out." He wasn't too thrilled about having to make this trip. I was far worse.

"I didn't come up here to just go back home," I told Grandpa.

"Okay then. Let Doc Hamilton help you." He set me down on an old plastic milk crate and got his pliers and a few other various hand tools out of the passenger floor of his vehicle.

The plan was for me to hold steady, and he would get a hold of the eye of the hook and yank it out. He said something like, "Hold on tight now," and he gave it a big yank. Oh, felt like my year came off. "Fine, fine." The trouble was the hook didn't budge. He gave me a blank look and was kind of amazed that I hadn't howled and carried on like most people with any good sense would have!

"Now what?"

"To town, I guess," he said.

"No way. Try it again."

"Okay if you can take it."

"I have to. I came up here to stay for three days and camp and hunt." He got a hold of it again and gave it a yank with all of his might. Out it came. Blood flying all over the place. "That's all right, I'm fine now." He had an old bottle of iodine on the floor of his truck and dosed the ear good with that.

I couldn't sleep on that ear for about a year, but otherwise, we had a terrific time. We had great hunting and saw lots of wildlife and hardly anybody around on these weekdays that we preferred. We had as many sage chickens as we could get. We did have to change ammo, though. We had a couple of boxes of a well-known brand of 4 Shot twelve-gauge 2¾ inch shells that should have been fine. They were worthless. They wouldn't kill a chicken at twenty yards unless it scared the thing and it dropped from a heart attack.

We used my rig to get around in, but most of the time, we would park and walk areas. However, one time while en route to a spot, we came along a hillside where there were probably sixty chickens sitting all together in the low sage. We stopped and got out on the passenger side of the tank of a vehicle. They wouldn't fly. Okay, this was going to be murder. The big plan was at the same time, we would both fire into the mob and slay a bunch before they flew and then keep at it till they flew away.

This was going to be good. They were watching us and only about thirty yards away. We fired when he gave the call. The whole bunch jumped up and flew off. We never saw a feather even fly off any of the birds!

We always had a ball. I tried to keep weekdays off so that we wouldn't have the weekend warriors to contend with out hunting, fishing, and so. This worked well because most people wanted the weekends off if possible.

Grandpa and I would hardly miss a summer week of fishing, usually up north in the Squaw, Chicken, Grass Creek areas. We were in his old truck on one trip and driving from one place to another to camp and fish. He had taken the cab off the truck and had the bed loaded in our stuff and all kinds of other "treasurers." He wanted to drink beer on this hot day and just enjoy the ride, so he had me drive. We were going along a county road at a reasonable clip. He had been smoking too and threw the butt out his window as we went along yakking and just enjoying the area.

We had driven four or five miles when he gave me a funny look and said, "Do you smell something like old rags burning or something?"

I said, "No, no, I don't."

He said, "We'd better stop, maybe that butt went in the bed of the truck." I pulled to a stop at the side of the dirt road. As he began to open his door, the smoke flew up from him. He jumped out, yelling, "I'm a fire, I'm a fire!" The seat cover under him was smoldering too. I jumped out. We had no water with us. I spotted a big glass jar that was full of pickle juice with a few large pickles in the bottom of the jar in the bed of the truck. He had picked it up at one of the dumps he had prowled earlier that week. I grabbed the jar, got the lid off, and ran him down at the roadside, where he was hopping about in his smoldering bib overalls. I doused his smoking right rear with the pickle juice. Instant relief. We put the seat out and were good to go. He chuckled, and said something to the effect of, "I guess my rear end must be dead. I was burning up and couldn't feel it!"

Back at work. We had two young guys shot that summer, as I recall. Not that that was unusual. Murders, sexual assaults, robbery, assaults, shootings, and knifings were all common events that we faced. The responding officers and their shift were expected almost without exception to handle these calls and resolve them. There was no on-site crime lab, herds of detectives, SWAT teams, and all of that stuff. It was uniform officers taking care of almost everything. This was good in a lot of ways. It was the chance of a lifetime to learn how to take care of serious crimes from start to finish in most cases. To gain expertise in these exercises. An officer would never get this experience in uniform in a large department or in a quiet little place.

Both of these young guys had gotten into arguments with their girlfriends at bars in different locations. The enraged females happened to put their mitts onto a pistol in the vehicle in each case where the argument had progressed to, and *wham!* Both males were completely neutered with one shot.

Another time a guy took his wife in their car to the north side of town to the old fairgrounds area. She was a nice-looking blonde woman. She stayed in the car on this summer evening and was reading a book or something while he went off a way into the prairie and target-practiced with his pistol.

The guy was busy shooting, and the car was just out of his view. He returned a bit later when he had finished shooting and found his wife yelling and a big black guy raping her in the car. The black guy saw the husband coming and changed course and made a run with his pants barely up to his nearby car.

The husband raced to the car, and the wife was yelling that the black guy came along and started talking to her and then attacked her. The husband had no ammo in his gun but got more in the car and reloaded and gave chase with their car.

The chase ensued back into town. The black guy parked in a hurry in a parking lot by a large two-story hotel (a boarding house) near the south end of Elk Street and, with himself exposed, made a run for the hotel. He made it to the front step when the husband had stopped their car, jumped out, and fired once at the guy. The black guy fell at the front door. That's where he died, laying in a pool of blood with his pants down and his lower atomy exposed. No charges were brought by the county attorney. The husband had stopped a violent fleeing felon. The guy was one of the many workers from somewhere out of town.

Another night I was on swing shift. It was dark, and I was called to one of the malls on the west side of town. A woman had been sitting in the passenger seat of the locked car waiting for her husband, who had gone into one of the stores. While she was waiting, this big black guy came up to her door and started pulling on the door handle. He told her to unlock the door. She began yelling for him to get away. He persisted a few more times and then quit. The husband came out, and she told him what happened. The black guy was now just walking in the lot and acted innocent.

They called us. I had them all come into the station. Took statements. No other witnesses could be found, and it was her word against his. He acted very refined and denied having done this act at all. Very insulted that he was being accused of this nonsense and didn't know why the woman had it in for him other than she didn't like black people. He had simply been walking in the parking lot at the mall before going in to shop when this all started.

The present chief was not supportive of the longer-term officers at this time, so the guy could easily make noise about being harassed, and the chief would bend over backwards to cause me grief. I had nothing I could do. What current law was broken even if I could prove this happened? I gave the guy very strong warnings and let him know that I tended to believe the woman and that we would be watching him. He was from out of town.

We tried to keep tabs on him, but nothing happened for several weeks, and we had to drop it. A few weeks later, there was a bad head-on crash on the highway going north of town near 14 Mile Hill. It was dark, but the weather and roads were good, and no particular reason for the accident. It was investigated by the highway patrol, but I looked into it when I learned that two people in the car going out of town were this same black guy and a married woman. She had been driving the car and turned it into the oncoming vehicle. They were both killed, and the occupant of the other car was badly injured. There is no doubt in my mind that this guy had succeeded in abducting this woman in a similar case as the other he was involved in attempting and was taking her out of town for his pleasure. She must have decided to take her chances and collide with the vehicles rather than suffer the fate otherwise before her. Too bad.

A really cowboy type of guy would come into the station once in a while on the early grave shift. He spoke mostly with Neil and Butch while we were all in the station. I didn't know who he was. He wore a beat-up cowboy hat, a duster, jeans, and boots. Western shirt and a sidearm. Western-type mustache. He had a kindly but worn face and was soft-spoken. I just remember hearing part of one of their conversations one night as I walked past them. They were telling him that somebody got away, and he was assuring them that you couldn't catch them all, but at least they had their hooks in the water.

I then learned that he was the undersheriff. This was different. The second-in-command of the sheriff's department is usually a political-type animal that would not be caught out on anything other than the day shift. This guy looked like the real thing.

I never saw him again until a few weeks later, after Clyde Kemp had left. He was leaving the sheriff's department after only a brief time there to be our new director of public safety. He was a tough character, and I became friends with him and learned to admire this much-underappreciated man.

He was a crack shot and a speed drawer of his sidearm. He had been an Indiana state trooper when he left that with his family and came to Wyoming. He loved horses and cattle and the west. He loved hunting and law enforcement. He had been a Wyoming highway patrolman for many years and had been a lone range detective working for the cattlemen's associations to stop and catch cattle rustlers.

He began making changes and insisting on dedicated police work. You just knew that this man would back you to the hilt if you even tried to do your job. He liked me and fully cooperated with me as a chaplain and the chaplain's division too. His name was Ed Cantrell. He and I went one afternoon and met with a group of ministers at the college. The purpose of this was to recruit more chaplains. This group didn't know how to take this soft-spoken cowboy. The response by them was not overwhelming.

That's okay. The chaplain's division was only staffed by me for some time, and until much later, I never had over one or two assistants. This ministry put you in jails, on the streets, and in dirty, nasty, dangerous situations. Dealing often with desperate people and the worst members of society. It is not a ministry for people unless they are called to it and willing to roll up their sleeves and be ready for this unconventional service. Some of them only wanted to be involved during the daytime. That was nice, but a chaplain is like a cop. Needed at inconvenient times, holidays, and bad weather.

The department leased a building further down the street to be used as well as our area in the city hall. We now had about twice the space to operate in than before. The jail and dispatch and some of our offices were still there too.

Back then, we had no evidence room. There were lockers downstairs in the old city hall. Each officer had one or two lockers that they were responsible for to keep their evidence in. It was your responsibility to maintain its chain and integrity. Mine was packed full of guns, knives, booze, bongs, drugs, and related materials.

Ed's office and some of the guys' he made detectives were located in the new leased building. Butch finally got his chance at it. He played it to the hilt. One night he asked me to come down to the office to see him when I came on shift. I thought he wanted to talk business. He had a feeling he was maybe getting to a spot of kind of headed toward going off the rails. We talked heart-to-heart as a chaplain to a cop. We had talked for a while, and it was getting late when Ed came into the building around midnight. We wrapped it up then, and I spoke just a few minutes with Ed. He had a desk further back in the building. On the wall over his back was a large bighorn ram that he had got. It was a beauty with broomed horns.

Forrest-Woody had been hired on before Ed came on as a nineteen-year-old. The law and regulations had changed to allow this. I think he was the only nineteen-year-old to ever be hired in the department. He was a kid in many ways, but I and at least a third of the department or more were not much older. He was taller than me and likable. He wore fairly thick wire-rimmed glasses and had kind of a John Denver type haircut. Not long but longer than most of us.

He thought Butch was what a cop should be, and he tried to ride with Butch if he could. The trouble was they kind of brought out the worst in each other and could be headed for trouble. Butch also gave him too much leeway for a new rookie.

The department still, like many of them, had people work a year before they went to the academy. A new academy was going to be built in a few years, and the fairgrounds would not be utilized any more. This was a long wait for some of these people that were hired and had no police or security experience at all. The department put on a week of orienting training for new hires in the meantime. Woody was among the first in these classes. I taught report writing, and I had received special training in Cheyenne and was the technician-supervisor of the chemical testing equipment. At this time, it was a complicated gascomatograph instrument that was used to test intoxicated people. I trained officers and recertified them on the equipment from the highway patrol, sheriff's office, and our department.

Woodie was not thrilled to ride with me, although we got along fine and liked each other, I just wasn't Butch. Like a hungry teen, he would ask to stop as often as we could at a convenience store and load up on eats. He would get back into the car with hot dogs, pop, and anything else he could hurriedly buy. I would make it a point to make sudden take-offs or stops and listen to him howl about the stuff that had just got all over his uniform.

We were called to a bar on Pilot Butte Ave one late night. Woodie and I were together, and Matt Keslar met us there for a call of some unknown problem. The bar was only about ⅓ full, but the problem was my old friend Joe from church. Joe had gone off the rails since we were friends a few years ago. He had married a girl that wasn't a Christian. They had children and were separated or divorced. She and the kids lived in another state now. He was back in town and hanging in the bar and just carousing and wasting his life away. I think he was working in the oil fields some.

Joe was causing enough grief to the bar that they wanted him out, and he wouldn't go. He was about half-drunk and was by himself at a pool table shooting pool. He eyed the three of us over as we entered the bar, and I talked to the bartender.

We started toward the back pool table at the rear of the bar. I told Joe that he had to leave. He stood at the rear of the pool table with the stick in his hand. "No way."

"Yes way." He refused, and I told him he would go to jail if he didn't comply. He was a tough guy, and he didn't feel like leaving. So, as we advanced, he backed toward the wall and began swinging the pool stick at us with every intent of doing damage. This went on for about half a minute. The three of us trying to get past the stick and grab him. He would not let up. Finally, I was able to jump behind him and put a carotid control hold on him, which was taught and a commonly accepted and used method in the "good old day." I used it often on fighters, as did other officers, and never had a problem with it.

In second, the stick fell to the floor, and Woodie and Keslar moved in. In the tussle, Joe got hold of Woodie's glasses, and he started to yell, "My glasses, my glasses," as they went to the floor. He was trying desperately to retrieve them before they were stepped on. Very few officers wore glasses just because this was what happened to them far too often and worse.

I had Joe out now and was going to drop him to his haunches on the floor, but he slipped away and fell on his face. We cuffed him as he came to, and off to jail he went. He had enough. He was tame as a lamb now. That morning he looked like he had been hit by a truck, and I never had to fight him again.

I had one other problem with him later at the A&D bar. Someone had fired six to eight rifle shots into the front of the building one night. The bar was packed. Amazingly, no one was struck by the bullets that went from the front of the bar to the rear interior of it. One guy was seated at a table. He was wearing a baseball cap, and one of the bullets had passed through the ball cap and just over the top of his skull without injuring him. That was close.

I was in the bar collecting evidence by myself, and Joe was there. We were short-staffed, and whoever was working the call with me was busy outside looking for the shooter. Joe was high and had been drinking too. He kept following me around the bar as I worked and was making little comments that I paid little attention to. I was keeping an eye on him, though. He was brewing for trouble, and I didn't have time to mess with him but did expect that there was going to be a battle before I was done. He kept trying to hover behind on me as I worked taking measurements, photos and digging the bullets out of the walls and so on. I just kept ignoring and downplaying him. I completed the task, and we parted without further trouble. A few years later, Joe was somewhere in Idaho, I believe. He was desperately trying to get his wife to take him back, and she wouldn't. He called her from a phone booth and was giving her an ultimatum. She didn't bite, and he shot himself to death. A sad waste of what could have been with Joe.

Another grave shift Woodie came out to join me in the patrol car at the start of the shift. Officers were allowed at that time to bring a rifle of their own with them if they cared to for their shift. Only a few did this. Woodie had his Mini-14 with him. These were very popular semiauto .223 caliber rifles at that time. Not only by law enforcement either.

Just a few weeks earlier, Woodie was in a hurry to go to work. He was in his apartment house with his wife in the process of gathering all of his work stuff, he picked up the rifle, and it fired into their waterbed. Quite a mess in an upstairs apartment house. We had all heard about this. Even so, Butch and others still let him bring the weapon to work.

I stopped him as he opened the passenger door. "Woodie, where do you think you are going with that?" I challenged him as I obviously look at the gun.

"With you to work," he said, and he got ready to put it and himself in.

"Nope. You take that gun and put it right back in the building."

"Preacher," he moaned.

"No, do it and hurry up, we have to get going." He was not happy with me and stomped back into the station, complaining all the way and to anyone that will listen to him about this travesty. Hornet and others just chuckled. He returned sans the long gun. He mopped the rest of the night. Too bad. If anything could happen, it would be with Woodie, and I didn't need myself or my car shot.

We would drive up to businesses and get out and check doors, windows, and general building security later in the shift as we had time to be sure all was secure. Burglary was a common occurrence, so we did all we could to thwart it.

One winter night Woodie and I pulled up to the rear area of a country-Western clothing store on the west side of town. The building was on my side of the car so I would get out to check doors and so on. The procedure was for the second officer to exit as well and stand near the patrol car and cover the officer checking the premises and just watch the general area.

I hadn't heard anything unusual, and after I checked the building and turned back to the patrol car expecting to see Woodie standing near the open passenger door, all I saw was the car with both doors open but no Woodie anywhere. I stepped back to the car and called out Woodie. No answer. Then I heard the weak voice of Woodie call me. I didn't see him, and I called again. He answered. I called out, "Woodie, where are you?"

He shouted as loud as he could, "Help me, I'm under the car." I looked, and there flat on his back was long, tall, stretched-out Woodie. I went around and pulled him out by his outstretched arms from his dilemma. He was all roughed-up and dirty and complaining about what happened. Well, what did happen? The instant he stepped out of the car to cover me, his feet flew out from under him on the slick ice, and he slid under the car. Once I pulled him out and saw that he was alright, I just had to keep laughing, especially as he whined and complained. This laughing did not help his attitude, but I couldn't help it. This could only happen to Woodie.

The veterans of foreign wars (VFW) club on K Street and Pilot Butte Ave was a troubled spot at times. The club let anyone and everyone in. The bar was usually busy but not often the problem spot of some of the other local pits. However, late in the morning, at the bar closing, we were dispatched there on report of a bunch of people fighting on the street in front of the club.

Several of us arrived about the same time in three patrol cars. Woodie was with me, and there were three or four other officers. The car with lights going all stopped surrounding the horde of people fighting and brawling on the street. There were probably thirty people really going at it. We started breaking it up. Some of the fights complied. Others had to be stopped and arrested. Then a few of them decided to fight with the police now instead of each other.

I encountered one such person. He quit fighting and turned on me. Instead of complying with my verbal commands, he came at me ready for action. I had my nightstick in hand and began letting him have it. I started at his shins and worked up. He slowed immediately. During this quick process, for reasons that made sense only to Woodie, Woodie was watching this and decided I needed his intervention. He jumped in and started to grab the guy with his left hand on the guy's throat. About this same time, I was striking that area with the lightning-fast nightstick. *Whack*, Woodie got it on the fingers with my stick. He immediately jumped away and was hopping around in the street, howling about his hand. I completed my stick action with interruption on the guy's forehead and started back down his front. He dropped to the ground and held his hands up at me. "I'm done, I'm done," he shouted. He went to jail, and Woodie went to the ER. He had one or two broken fingers. This was a very worthy exercise. In one arrest, the guy learned it was not good to fight with the police, and Woodie learned it was a really bad idea to jump in the way of a striking nightstick.

In combat, I used the nightstick often, which I still have, the one taken from me as a young rookie in the A&D bar and that I recovered minutes later (it was never taken again). I used the carotid control hold often and mace in the face, this was before pepper spray. These were common tools and methods used by most officers then. Pepper spray, stun guns, PR-24 sticks (which I detested and never carried), and expandable batons came later. We also had "saps," but I never used mine. Otherwise, verbal commands and just plain old street fighting would be deployed. Neil and Butch carried nun chucks, and Neil was good at karate, but these methods and tools were not common in the police department.

I almost without fail prayed for blessing, wisdom, and protection on each shift that I worked and for those I worked with and ministered to. Many times, I would be in a situation or going to a call and be in prayer about it as well as fully alert to what I was doing at the time and planning steps to take when I dealt with the situation that I was in or soon would be.

The Lord took good care of me and led me to successes that only He could. I was never badly injured at work. During arrests or investigations, I was bit on the leg twice by dogs and on the forearm twice by people. The people's bites were the worst. I did fail while crossing a railroad track in the dark one night while chasing a thief. Tore up my knee and uniform pants. Lots of bruises and scrapes but not much else.

I carried a variety of handguns and, of course, police shotguns over the years. Usually, my own handgun of choice, but a few times, the departments I was at supplied the weapons. I had to put a gun on people many, many times and was ready to shoot them if I had to, but they always complied, some just in the nick of time, so I never had to shoot anyone.

The closest that I came to shooting a guy one night would have been justified, but I am glad it didn't happen. I responded on a dark swing-shift night with a female officer to an apartment house. We arrived in separate cars on report of a prowler at the rear of the older one-story building. The other officer was to go around one side of the building, and I around the other. We would meet at the back of the building on opposite ends. The area behind the building had bushes just several feet away from it and was very poorly lit only by what light emitted from apartment windows.

I came around my side before the other officer did, and I saw this guy several apartments down from me, maybe forty yards, and he was standing at the back of the building. Probably peering into an apartment, with an open window, but who knows.

I stepped into this view in uniform and announced myself as I trained my flashlight beam on him in his mostly dark clothing. He was told not to move and put his hands up. He did this immediately. I began to slowly move toward him, and he dropped something shiny and metallic onto the ground that he had concealed in one of his hands. He then bent over and picked this up. All I could see was a shiny metal object in his hand as he rose up. I had my 9mm on him and almost fired, but I hesitated. Lucky for both of us.

He put his hands back up and in, then I could now see a big wad of keys. He was the manager of the apartments and was check-ing the buildings, or so he said he was? The guy was trembling as he realized what a stupid move, he made in leaving his surrender posi-tion to pick up the dropped ring of keys. He couldn't even explain why he did this but was sure thankful he wasn't shot.

Woodie was with me the fateful night that changed everything in the department. Ed Cantrell was a hands-on director. He was not an office cop. He would be out with us and giving a hand late at night if needed. He handled things the old way. He was honest and hard-working.

Rusa was not known to us. He had been hired in the department by Ed. He worked undercover and had made a number of drug cases. The understanding between Ed and Rusa was that at the conclusion of these cases, Rusa would come to work in uniform as a patrol officer. The cases he made concluded with arrest and search warrants. Rusa was introduced to the department, and we spent several nights doing search warrants at residences and arresting people on warrants and for drug possession during the searches.

Then Rusa, who was an arrogant, hot-tempered Puerto Rican, was allowed to work with us at night for a bit while still in plain clothes and with his unmarked car.

One night we had a call of someone chasing a guy down Front Street with a shotgun. We got there and found Rusa chasing this guy down the street who had come out of a bar and broke a window. Rusa happened to be there and jumped out of his car, and the chase was on. The guy didn't know Rusa was a cop. Rosa was all worked up. You would have thought the guy had committed some heinous crime. The suspect was glad to be apprehended by the uniforms. He was expecting this long-haired wild man to shoot him as they ran down the sidewalk.

Rusa treated uniformed officers like dirt. He did not want to be in uniform, even though this was about to happen. He was a married man with several kids. Not much older than me. He never spoke to me or other uniforms, even supervisors, if he didn't have to.

The night of the final event with him, I was in the station by myself, getting ready to go to my car. Rusa was hanging outside of the dispatch room and went out of his way to talk to me. I was surprised. This was out of character for him. We chatted for a few minutes, and I had to go. I didn't know till later that he was hanging around the dispatch then because the female dispatcher working at that moment was a girl I had graduated from high school with. A nice girl from Rock Springs. Anyway, they had gotten involved with each other and were messing around pretty often. Big mistake by her, well, him too.

That night we were busy. It was a Saturday, I'm pretty sure. Ed had his fill of Rusa. He was resisting going into uniform. Ed didn't want to fire the guy if he could help it, but the days of Rusa running around like this were over. Things really had soured between them. Ed got Sergeant Matt and Sergeant Jim, who were some of our small detective force now, to go with him and call Rusa out of the packed Silver Dollar bar on the north side of town. Rusa was in there doing more partying than anything. He was not happy when the police department called the bar and he was told to meet the three outside. He eventually went out and got in the rear seat of an unmarked car with the three. In the end, Rusa and Ed had strong words, and hot-tempered Rusa went to pull his gun on Ed. Ed was too fast and shot Rusa in the head.

The statewide grand jury was in full swing in Cheyenne, and Rusa was one of the persons that were subpoenaed to testify there soon. I had to go there myself. I went with Lieutenant Overy, who also had to testify. The media made hay of this. They made it into a big plot in which Ed stopped Rusa from making it to the grand jury, where he had the information, they were sure would blow things wide open. This was utter nonsense. The trouble with Rusa should not have been handled the way it was, but that was Ed's old-time cowboy way that usually was successful. To not string a problem along and to face a problem directly. No need for formal action and daytime office meetings. He, along with two detective supervisors, could put a stop to Rusa being a loose cannon, he thought. Ed would get him to work in uniform as was agreed to start with. It backfired.

Woodie and I, along with Neil, were running around like crazy that night. We started hearing Neil being requested to go to the Outlaw Inn parking lot—across the street from the Silver Dollar bar. With Rusa obviously dead, the men drove across the street to get out of this packed parking lot. Absolutely the thing to do. Secure a crime scene and avoid attention from the public and possible interference.

We had a hit-and-run case then in the Silver Dollar parking lot that involved the deputy county coroner being the suspect. While in the area investigating this, we noticed the coroner and other officials being called to the Outlaw Inn parking lot. It was perplexing. Something bad had happened. As we continued to work that night, we later saw Rusa's unmarked police car being towed by a wrecker. I told Woodie I thought Rusa must have died.

Ed ended up being arrested and locked up later that morning in the county jail. The county attorney was going to get good mileage out of this. He and several of his deputies that were defense attorneys saw big headlines and fame for them in prosecuting Ed. Things were working out better than hoped for by the forces working to oust current officeholders and officials.

Things just worsened. All a sudden, the media liked the police, well, one man only, I should point out. Rusa. He was a saint, and his testimony at the grand jury would have been instrumental in stopping the corruption that they were sure was taking place. The dispatcher having an affair with Rusa was devastated. This foolish affair harmed her life for years, especially when it was made public.

The county attorney saw this case as an easy slam dunk. A cop with few resources to defend himself. This would be a first-degree murder case, and nothing less would they accept. It was an additional boom for the papers and media in the area. People were drawn to this constant news coverage like files to a fresh cow pie.

Rusa and his family had a big German shepherd. After he was killed, the family left their trailer home in the trailer court in town and left the dog for several days alone in the place. The dog finally jumped through a large window and ran off. The next big allegation and headline were that the corrupt police had broken into the home via the broken window. The purpose was to go in and get secret files that Rusa had there for the grand jury. All of this made our jobs almost impossible to do. The entire police department was now criminalized. Much of the town knew better, but it was constant attacks by the media, politicians wanting to make hay out of this, and the local prosecutors who planned on this being their ticket to fame and upper mobility. Several of these deputy prosecutors did not like the police, to start with, and would do a poor job on cases unless they had an interest in them. I had at least two run-ins with the county attorney myself. He was a longtime know-it-all Rock Springs attorney and had been the country attorney for a long time. He would not prosecute favored people or made sure they were treated with kid gloves. He was a rowdy hard-drinking character, and I nearly arrested him one night when he was drunk in the OK bar on K Street and being belligerent and disorderly. The arrest was narrowly averted when he backed off. He was brewing for a fight with us that night.

The deputy that was to be the head prosecutor in the Cantrell case was a prideful, arrogant loudmouth. I had many cases with him in later years when he was back to his comfortable defense-attorney career after his loss to Ed and his eventual loss in the election to be the next county attorney. He disliked me and was a bitter, nasty person. I won almost every case I had against him and his clients along with his associate, who was just like him. They despised me and could not stand losing to me. They played dirty, so you had to really watch them.

Ed was kept in the State Mental Hospital in Evanston for thirty days of observation not long after his arrest. He told us later that with all of the yelling and screaming that went on all night at that place, he nearly lost his mind. He was then returned to jail but was able to get out on bail.

Then things didn't work so well for the crack prosecution team. Ed was able to get Gerry Spence from Jackson Hole to defend him. Spence did not want the case to begin with. He said he didn't defend murders. But after he talked more with Ed and his son and looked into the case, he changed his mind.

Spence was a nationally recognized attorney and had handled big cases. He was able to move the case for trial from Sweetwater County to Sublette County, and it was held at the old courthouse in Pinedale. Pinedale people were anti Rock Springs people, but Ed had a much better chance at a fair trial with these western-leaning people than could ever be in Green River. The trial went on during the winter. Matt Keslar, Neil Kourbelas, and I drove up one day and watched the proceedings. Spence made the Rock Springs prosecutors look like amateurs. We spoke with Ed. He looked pretty good for all he had been through. Ed didn't talk about his troubles and situation. He, in his low-key, welcoming way, asked how we were doing. Just a prince of a guy.

In the end, Ed was found not guilty. He had been ruined, and his family suffered unspeakable trials. Years later, I was working in Newcastle, Wyoming, after having returned from eight years in

Alaska. Ed knew that I was there from an old highway patrol officer friend of his that was working there too and knew me. They were cruising around the area of my home, not just sure where I lived, when they ran into me in a park, walking a dog.

It sure was good to see Ed. He didn't look much different. Looked like an old cowboy. He had come to the area to hunt whitetail deer. He said that he was pleased that I had come back to Wyoming. I was able to visit one-on-one with him for two days during this time. Took him out and showed him an area that he could shoot in that I liked, and we had him to a family dinner one night.

He liked our little dining room table. He liked our little dining room. Only compliments. Fine dinner and all. My wife and children enjoyed him. I asked him during one of our one-on-one visits if he regretted shooting Rusa. He gave me a little smile and then, in a low serious voice, said to the effect of, "If I knew where they buried him, I would go dig him up and shoot him again."

I left the state again a year or so later and never saw Ed again. He became ill some years later and passed away in a Salt Lake City hospital. They don't make many like Ed anymore, and the world is at a loss because of it.

After Ed was gone, the department was headed by Chief Muir again until other arrangements were made. Mayor Wataha was not going to seek reelection again so it would be a new mayor and who knows what.

Butch was back in uniform, and on shift with us (graves), he was working alone most of the time. One snowy, wintry night, he was the senior officer and in charge with no sergeant on that night. I often did foot patrols and would check areas better that way and then just sneak around. I often caught burglars this way and saw and found all kinds of stuff that never could have happened from a patrol car. Neil liked to do this, too, but most cops didn't want to get over fifty yards from their car.

So, he and I were going to patrol on foot for an extended period of time. We had on black snowmobile boots due to the bad weather. Butch, who would not venture far from his car, would not allow this. "Go home and put on regulation leather boots or shoes." We laughed at him about this and then argued with him, but he was serious. He wouldn't budge. We told him we were not going to put other boots on. He said that he would call Lieutenant Overy and make us. We told him to go right ahead. He called. A short time later, he was pretty quiet. Didn't want to talk about the footwear anymore. We made him tell us what happened. Reluctantly he said that the lieutenant said, "If they are going out on foot patrol in bad weather… what's the problem?" You think you know a person…

One early grave shift, we were short on patrol cars, and I was assigned Lieutenant Overy's unmarked car for the shift. Around 3 a.m., I was dispatched to the downtown area where a person was in the process of stealing a vehicle and about to drive off in it. I was on the north side of town, and traffic was now very light. I came racing in with the dash bubble light and car emergency flashers going. I just came up to the traffic lights at Elk and Center Streets and had the green light. There was no traffic at the large intersection. Suddenly, as I was just about to enter the intersection, this old truck appeared. It ran the red light and was in front of me. To avoid a bad crash, I steered around the now-scared and mouth-open driver as the truck kept going. I had to go into the lanes to my right and pass around traffic light poles and a traffic island, then back to the left and into the southbound lane of Elk Street again. I nearly made it without incident. However, as I made all of these evasive moves, the car struck a telephone pole with its right rear quarter panel and was dented in. It really showed up on this yellow car with its brown roof.

Too late to mess with the light runner and the car that was still in the process of being stolen, and no one else was closer than I. I went on and stopped this theft in progress and handled the call. Then it was the damaged car. I made the reports and all that was required. The next shift or so, Sergeant Mark was at work and told me that I was going to have a two- or three-day suspension over the damage to the car, despite the circumstances. The next day Lieutenant Overy wanted to see me at the department when I came in. He had read my report and asked me about it. We talked about it more, and I told him that I had to take a suspension as Sergeant Mark told me. He said, "Forget about it. These things happen in this business." I never heard another word about it.

When we had time, we tried to put pressure on the prostitutes and pimps. We would herd them off the streets or out of areas where they had taken up posts. We arrested them and wrote tickets at every chance we had, anything to curtail their activities and income. We would chase the men—Johns—away and also arrest them or write tickets for whatever reason if they were persistent.

They would give us very little trouble as a rule. There were a few of them that were knot heads, though. There was one young attractive black girl that had a nasty attitude. She didn't want the police telling her what to do. I wrote her numerous tickets and messed up lots of her business.

One summer night, she was seated in her car working the street. She did something, and I had stopped behind her car and wrote a ticket for her. She was mouthing off when I had her sign the citation and gave her a copy. She took her copy and tore it up and then threw it out the window at my feet. I told her she was under arrest for littering. "Get out of the car." She wouldn't. I got a hold of her before she knew what happened. Out through the window she came. In cuffs and off to jail she went, all the while cussing and raving. She gave me a wide berth after that.

Another time a big tall black pimp was in the Astro Lounge playing pool with other pimps. He was being loud and obnoxious and ticked off the bartender with his antics. She ordered him out, and he wouldn't go. We got there, and he was immediately aggressive. Probably had been snorting coke as well as drinking. He was from Denver, as I recall, and was only in and out of town. I ordered him out, and he wouldn't go. He mouthed off and kept playing pool. The fight was on. I and he went at it in the crowded bar for a few seconds until I had him on the floor kicking and yelling. He kept spitting and fighting after I cuffed him. He was bigger than me and wouldn't get up from the floor. Just kept kicking, struggling, and yelling. Cussing like mad. I got him by this big bunch of gold necklaces and his shirt and dragged him from the bar, to the sidewalk, and into the patrol car. Gold necklaces were breaking and falling off him, and he just kept resisting. He went to jail. He never gave me a minute's trouble after that.

Another time I arrested this older huge black pimp. I got him to the jail okay, but then no one was there to assist me when I took the cuffs off him to book him in. He decided he wanted to fight. I had enough. Called another guy in, and while we waited, every time he got up off the chair, I blasted him in the face with mace. He yelled and cussed and sat back down. This was repeated several times with mace flying off the brim of his hat and all over his shirt. Another officer got there, and he stopped. We locked him up without any further trouble.

A few weeks later, this same pimp was brought in to see me as a chaplain by officers. His girlfriend had been murdered that day in town. He was all upset and bawling like a baby. I met him in the chaplain's office by the jail. We had a good time of counseling and prayer, and he left doing much better. There was never a question of what role I was playing at a time by even pimps or prostitutes. It was either all cop or all chaplain.

Neil and Butch had put out some effort one night to act under-cover in their own time with some prostitutes that didn't know them and make a prostitution case against the two women. So, they were feeling pretty good about having made these arrests together. The next week, not because of what they had done, I came back from several days of camping and fishing with Grandpa Hamilton.

I was wearing an old flop hat, bib overalls and was dirty and smelled of fish and campfire. It was around 9 p.m. I had stopped at mom and dad's and left them some brookies from our catch, had dinner with them, and after visiting and having numerous cups of coffee, I was headed home. I decided to make a pass down K Street in my large ugly (only the opinion of some) stretch four-wheel drive before going home to see what it looked like.

As I drove the busy street, I saw a Utah-plated car parked. There were three women in it, and they were waving and yelling at passing men. Obviously brazen prostitutes. They summoned me as I drove slowly past. I went on and parked nearby out of their view on North

Front Street, I walked back down the sidewalk. Once near them, they started yelling for me to come over.

They were three prostitutes from Salt Lake. All young, attractive women. They had only been in town a few minutes and were desperate for business and needed to make money. We talked through the open car windows until it was determined what services they would provide for the low cost I negotiated them to, of ten dollars apiece. Then the shocker. This dirty bumpkin-looking young guy pulled out a Rock Springs police badge. They were shocked and very unhappy. They complied and got out of the car. I marched them like prostitutes on a single-file parade down the sidewalk. They had better not try to split and run, or I would have my hands full. I kept really tight verbal control on them. I marched them into a little building that was a taxi cab dispatch office. The male dispatcher was stunned. He didn't recognize me and had trouble making sense of this. I told him who I was and ordered him to call the police department and tell them I had three prostitutes for transport to jail. He dropped what he was doing and called in a flash. I had the girls sit down, and I remained blocking the only door.

In a short time, a patrol car drove up. The officer was senior to me. A big tall red-headed cop who was kind of comical. He just looked and shook his head as I told him what happened and loaded his car full of the girls.

Neil and Butch couldn't believe it. It took them most of one night to get an arrest each, and I got three in a matter of minutes! It was the talk for a few days. Nobody could remember any officer making three arrests for prostitution at one time by themselves. I have the record, and it was never surpassed. Hornet thought it was hilarious. He kept making comments for days about it being a good thing that I arrested them before they got me and wore me out.

One night there was this tall black prostitute that had only been in town a short time that I encountered on duty. She was taller than me. She kept working a corner with a few others, and I got out of the car and herded them on. She wouldn't leave the area and started getting really bold and mouthing off. I kept at her, and she got mad and started cussing me. Then she got even louder and was yelling and cussing. People were looking at her, and this made a disturbance-of-the-peace case. She went to jail. Just being nasty, cussing, yelling, and spitting. I got her in the booking room. At this time, we had started only housing male prisoners in the old city jail. Females had to be taken to the county jail in Green River. Another officer had to go there, so he offered to transport the woman for me. Great. I was booking her in for transport. She remained loud and nasty. I noted that her hands and feet seemed overly large and brought this to the attention of another officer out of her presence. I never saw a woman with such large hands and feet. She was dressed in a nice dress, jewelry, and heels.

Off to the county she went. Once there, the matrons were searching her and booking her into jail, including putting her into a jail uniform. Orange-colored for men, and blue women's suit for her. Then I got a phone call from the county jail. They were laughing but wondered what kind of trick I pulled on them. I hadn't a clue for sure. They said the matron nearly fainted while doing the strip search on this "woman." The prostitute was a well-endowed black man with a large female breast. What color suit did they think I had to put on our prisoner? Without a thought, I said, "Why orange on the bottom and blue on top!"

Working one afternoon, it was a nice summer day. A call came of little boys trapped in tunnels they had dug into dirt banks on the north side of town near a grade school. Three boys about ten years old or so had dug tunnels and were in them digging further when the wet sandy dirt dried and became unstable and buried them. When I arrived along with Sergeant Mungo right behind me, we found parents, neighbors, and anyone else with a shovel, hands, or whatever could be used, digging frantically, trying to locate and recover the boys.

After about ten minutes, we pulled one boy out. He was breathing but full of dirt. I threw him and his mother into the rear of my patrol car and went Code 3 to the emergency room at the hospital. This boy survived. His two friends who were found and recovered several minutes later were not so fortunate.

This type of incident happened another Sunday afternoon on a nice sunny day a few years later. Two boys had dug into a high bank on the Bitter Creek on the west side of town near the sewer treatment plant. We had trouble locating them, and when we finally got there, it was a similar scene as before. Parents and neighbors in this semi-remote area frantically trying to dig the boys out. They pulled one out as I arrived. He was not breathing. EMTs followed me in an ambulance, so they crossed the flowing creek and attended to the boy. He could not be revived. The other boy was pulled out minutes later and was also dead.

Over and over again, I dealt with sudden and tragic deaths. Sometimes people just died in their sleep, but usually, when we were called, it was for a suspicious or violent death. Shootings, knifings, beatings, many vehicle deaths, falls off cliffs in town, drug overdoses, and incidents like these—little boys just having an adventure that turned horrific. Suicides by the gross. These had to be investigated as homicides, so they were time- and resource-consuming. Most suicides were males and by gunshot. The other preferred method primarily for males was asphyxiation by carbon monoxide, using a motor vehicle in a garage or more commonly driving to the edge of town on some old road and attaching a hose to the tailpipe and then into the vehicle interior. We would be checking a suspicious vehicle or get a call about one and find the person in the car dead and cherry red in color. Usually, women took pills in a "suicide attempt," but it was really a call for help. They would usually call us or someone and tell them what they had just done. Then it would be the oil of Ipecac syrup and off to the hospital with them.

I watched many people die as we waited for help or were trying to revive or assist them. Sometimes taking a dying declaration if it was a criminal case and death was imminent. Some people died peacefully, and others were violent, nasty deaths. It was always a bit unnerving to see a person thrashing about and fighting in death throes. Cursing and yelling. Calling for help, but they were beyond any human help, it was too late. I could sense regret in some of the young guys that were dying when we arrived. They had shot themselves over usually a lost love, and now they realized it was too late to go back. No one could save them.

I had one particularly nasty suicide that I have never forgotten among most of them. You can pass reading this if you have a weak stomach. It didn't bother me so much as it was just unusual. It was a semi-quiet Sunday afternoon when we were dispatched to a shooting in Blairtown, which is an old part of town on the southwest side.

I was the first to arrive at the small older home. A woman came dashing out, she was hysterical. She quickly told me that her husband was inside a back bedroom and had shot himself with a shotgun. I entered the now-quiet home and carefully moved to the back room. Handgun out.

As I looked in the open doorway of this room, I saw a man, fully dressed but with the front half of his face and head missing. He was kneeling on one knee and had one foot on the floor. There was face and brain material all over the wall and ceiling behind him. He had the shotgun in one hand with the butt of the gun on the floor, and he was using it for leverage, trying to raise up onto his feet. Kind of a gory scene. I told him to stay where he was, that an ambulance was on the way. Could he hear me or did he have any sense of what was going on? Not likely. If he got up and kept going, I would have to stop this bloody mess where it was. I didn't think he would get up, but he was sure trying to. No way could I let him have the gun or go outside if somehow, he tried to. This was impossible, of course—to help this guy.

After about fifteen seconds, he toppled over and stayed down. He appeared dead now. Another officer arrived, and then the ambulance. EMTs confirmed that he was dead. No need to transport. We would investigate further and dispatch—call the coroner's office and have them respond as well.

The guy and his wife in their mid-30s were in the process of separating when, on this nice sunny afternoon, they were having an argument. In the process, he had had enough.

Death happens so easily and quickly. Unexpected for most. It behooves a person to make certain that they are prepared for eternity because this life can fade in a flash. Some people surprised us at how easily they gave up and died. Others fought but lost. Somebody crossing a street in a crosswalk, out for a good time, driving—often too fast, high, or drunk, out for a motorcycle ride, or just in a bar having a drink. Out for a meal or for a walk down a sidewalk. Somebody eating a meal at the family table when a heart attack strikes them down. Boys digging a tunnel to play in. Young, healthy people, not thinking about death, just living when it all comes crashing down.

I saw so many accidents, injuries, deaths, hit-and-run accidents, and property damage by the thousands of dollars that were caused by drunk and/or drug-impaired drivers that I had little mercy for them. I probably had the record for arresting the most DWUIs and estimated it in later years during my tenure in Rock Springs at somewhere around 500. This would be brought out by the former prosecutors of Ed Cantrell, who were now defending someone silly enough to pay them for their "services" in drunk-driving trials. The lawyers would grill me about this and try to act incredulous about what I testified to. Inferring that this was hugely exaggerated or an outright statement of perjury. It was nonetheless true, and I stood by it, to their disappointment. The juries and judges didn't doubt it when I gave an explanation as to how this could be as the defense attorneys stood there glaring at me in the witness chair.

A pimp was shot on a downtown sidewalk by another pimp with a .44 Magnum pistol. Shot in the forehead. This call you just knew was a murder. We arrived to find the average-size guy standing and fully conscious. He had a nasty hole on his forehead. The bullet was fired point-blank by the angry shooter who had fled. The large chunk of lead had traveled from his forehead completely around the skull just under the skin and back out near the point of entry. He had a terrific headache. The shooter took off, we learned, out of town in a hurry and headed for the interstate toward Rawlins. He had a lead on us, but driving a big fancy car, he was most likely to keep going down the interstate. Certain that he had killed the guy and that if he could get away from us, he would be home free. It's hard to outrun a police radio, even in Wyoming. We put out the all-points bulletin (APB), and he was stopped and arrested for attempted murder in Rawlins.

Several times on the late swing or grave shifts, we received calls from one of the local game wardens. He was north of town and had tried to stop a suspected violator with his game and fish patrol truck. They ran, and he was in pursuit but not able to catch them. No problem. We were waiting at city limits, one time to their surprise and another time at the guy's house.

On a swing shift one afternoon, we were standing about in the squad room by dispatch at the old city hall just about to deploy. These were our informal briefings we would have on occasion. The supervisor was Sergeant Mungo. He was a large tough cop. In good shape. Loved high school football and sports in general. He had been in the force since I was a kid, but he wasn't that old, probably late 40s. He was good to work for. Just expected that you would do your job and he didn't need to babysit anyone. He pretty much left you alone unless you needed him. He was a friendly man with a kind face for a guy that had been a cop for so many years. I liked him.

We were getting people from all over the country, especially California, that were being hired. Most locals could make so much money nowadays in this area that they had little interest in law enforcement. There was this one young guy that was from Anaheim, California, that we called the Anaheim flash. He thought and acted like he was hot stuff. I could work with him okay, and we did fine.

He had some notion that he was a doctor or prize EMT (emergency medical technician) in addition to being a police officer. He had started following the ambulances around on calls and spending too much time with them. During this briefing, Sergeant Mungo told him to stop doing that. It was not our job, and we didn't have time for it. The guy back talked to him with some cocky reply. Mungo looked right at him with a stare that would stop a clock. He said, "I won't tell you again, and if you say another word, I'll lay you out on the floor." Old-time supervision, effective, and far less paperwork. The guy never made another peep. He quit trying to play doctor too.

Most prostitutes just did their business. They were making plenty of money, but some of them got greedy. The Johns would have loads of cash from the high-paying jobs. Every guy had a wallet full or a big roll of bills in his pocket. We started getting robbery/

theft calls from the Johns. The money could not be found or proved to be the Johns', and it was the word of two law breakers against one another. Most times, the prostitutes won.

The guys just wanted what was stolen back. They didn't want a case made. No desire for a report or court action where their name might appear in the paper or being involved in proceedings that they had no time or stomach for. One time a guy did insist on the prostitute being charged. We told him the chances of her winning in a justice of the peace court were excellent as it would be his word against hers, and there was not much we could testify to. No matter. We arrested the prostitute and took the money into evidence. She went to a justice of the peace court and pleaded not guilty. We went to trial. All testified, and she was found not guilty by the judge, and the money was given back to her. The guy maybe learned not to mess around anymore, but who knows.

We had a whole bunch of illegal Mexicans in the area that had come there to work and were being hired and making a bunch of money. They would go to a store and buy a big sheath knife and carry it on their belts. Then as they hung around the bars and downtown, some of them, of course, would consort with the ladies of the night. Some of the ladies would rob them like they had other Johns. This didn't do with the Mexican. They would pull the knife and be trying to cut the prostitute up to get their money back when we got there. Of course, for an assault or attempted assault with a deadly weapon, they went to jail. Most times, we just held them for immigration out of Salt Lake. When we would have five or six of them, immigration would take them off our hands. I ended up with gobs of nice fixed-blade sheath knives that we had kept for evidence. Then when no longer needed, it was up to the officer to destroy or dispose of the items.

Several times the Mexicans would run from the scene, usually, it had gotten out onto a sidewalk or motel front. The foot chase was on. They usually gave up as we chased them down. One time one guy made it to a parking area from downtown to the J Street apartments and hid behind a trailer. I was right behind him and called him out from there. He came out, but he was still fuming. Large knife in hand, he started toward me and had intentions of using his knife. When he heard me cock the hammer on my revolver that was pointed at his chest and then yelling, "Stop, or I'll shoot," he decided he might like to see Mexico again, I guess. Most of them could speak broken English.

We had several large families of illegals that had congregated in the area. For some reason, they started feuding with one another, and for about a year, we had a good deal of shootings and knifings with them and finally one or two murders.

One time I took one of them into custody. He was going to be held with others for immigration. After about a week in jail, immigration showed and took the men away. Less than a week later, I was on some kind of knifing call by Bunning Park with a whole pack of illegals and others, and I spotted this same guy. He had already made it back from the border. He spotted me and tried to mingle into the crowd and disappear. He went with me.

Sergeant Dan was a big guy. He had been in the department for several years before I came on. He was a good cop but a horrible driver. He had wrecked and damaged numerous police cars while responding to calls, pursuits, and so on. He was probably in his early 30s at this time. He shaved his head and kept it shined up.

He was a likable guy, I thought, but a number of the guys didn't care for him. Butch especially had it in for him. I think mostly because Butch thought the stripes worn by Dan would certainly be more appropriate on his uniform.

Officers would talk about Dan and his crazy driving and warned me about him. He usually rode by himself as no one wanted to be involved in his next collision. I avoided it too, but one night at shift change, we had a call of someone siphoning gas from BLM (Bureau of Land Management) vehicles about two blocks from the police department. He saw me and asked me to go with him. I didn't want to, but he was going alone, so I, against my better judgment, got in the passenger side door.

We flew over to the large parking lot full of federal vehicles and started driving in it with lights off. Dan stopped and started backing when—*wham*—my neck and head about snapped off. *Boom*. He backed into a large power pole. He looked dazed and asked if I was okay. "Yea, yea." Almost afraid to look at the rear of the car and pole. We got out. They still made good bumpers in those days. Hardly any damage this time.

I worked with Dan quite a bit when we were both on graves. I never rode with him again. However, one busy night we kept getting calls to The Twilight—the big wild disco club on the west side of town. We went in a couple of times and solved the situation. We didn't have time for this tonight. We were terribly shorthanded. In fact, it was me and him on shift. We had an armed robbery of a convenience store, which happened often, business burglar alarms, and just call after call. Working like fiends to keep up with it all.

We got another call of a big disturbance at the disco bar again. It was packed full of young partiers. The disco music was blaring in the place. We both finally got there again, Dan and I. He said, "I am tired of this, what about you?"

"Yes, I agree." We had a city ordinance that gave us authority to close down a rowdy house—a place of constant disturbance.

He said, "I think we should close this place down for the night."

"I agree, but this will be a tall order. We are outnumbered *at least* one hundred to one, and no help available."

We went in, and the place was just wild. We were going to close it. We forced our way through the crowd and up to the DJ (disc jockey) who was in the standing booth spinning records. The Bee Gees were blaring in my ears. We told him to turn the music off and announce that the bar was now closed and everyone was to leave.

The DJ looked amused at us and like he was going to enjoy what came next. He stopped the loud tune. Most of the people dancing stopped, and about ⅔ of the place listened as the DJ said, "The police say that we have to close and everybody has to leave, are we going to do that?"

"*No*," the crowd shouted, and he joined in. Before another word could be uttered by the DJ, big Dan had the guy by his front shirt collar and yanked him from the booth, over the stand, and threw him on the floor. We cuffed him up and started to drag him across the floor as the crowd now parted like Moses experienced with the Red Sea! Dan yelled the warning that this bar was closed and everyone was to leave. We got a lot of mumbling and complaining but no more challenges. We dragged the DJ across the floor and out to the rear of a patrol car. Then with him in the car quietly laying on the seat, we returned to the bar where the crowd had gathered their stuff and was filing out the door.

Matt Keslar started in the department six months after I did. Every six months, a few new guys were being hired. The force had been expanded to probably twenty-twenty-five officers or so now from what had been around a dozen. The hiring mostly now was replacing officers that quit, were fired, or didn't make probation.

Matt, as I said, was a good guy. Absolutely dependable but quiet. He was new at this career too. We rode together in half a dozen or so fleet cars that were available. These cars were running almost twenty-four hours a day, seven days a week, and by all kinds of drivers.

The fleet car I often drove had a loose wire under the front passenger floorboard for some time before it was finally repaired. This would stop the siren if it was mashed on in just a certain way. Matt found this out by accident when we were on a Code 3 call one afternoon. After that, he took great pleasure in waiting until we were about to an intersection or coming to some traffic we had to navigate through, with the lights and siren going, he would stop the siren. We would go sailing through with only lights on. He would then throw his head back and cackle. I would be chewing him out but kind of laughing myself and glad that we had made it past the traffic unimpeded. Finally, to his dismay, the wire was repaired.

Hornet and I became very good friends. Once I had been in Alaska for a number of years, we came back for a vacation. While visiting him and his sister Mary who was a swell woman and good friend too, at their home, they wanted me to have one of Hornet's rifles. He offered me one of two. I took the vintage .30-06. It was one of the old ones and in good shape. It is a fine shooting rifle, and I have used it many times over. I cherish it as a gift from a once-in-a-lifetime friend.

I fished many times with Hornet and made a few overnight trips with him. He was tough and never complained. Had a good sense of humor. There were small things that he would need help with, but that was no problem. He had cinnamon balls on one trip and got me started eating those. Crunching them over the years rather than just sucking on them has cost me several fillings and broken crowns. Oh well, a small price to pay for such a good treat.

Hornet and I were fishing and camping at Soda Lake near Pinedale one summer. He liked coffee as much as I did. We had our camping stuff in his truck and stayed the night. We made the coffee out of the lake water. They don't call it Soda Lake for no reason. We put the powdered cream in the coffee, and it would just roll and boil. We drank it, but it was like drinking salted coffee and then some!

We were living in Anchorage years later when Hornet passed away. I just had a brief last conversation with him on the phone the day before he passed. I miss old Hornet. He was one of the few that you never run into again, and we are all at a loss for that.

The city court was held at the top of the old city hall, in the council chambers. Usually with Judge Gary. Once in a while, it was old Judge George. The building had an infestation of pigeons. While in court, they could be heard cooing in the attic, and every once in a while, a pigeon feather would come floating down to the floor.

The police department was on the main floor. One swing shift, I had been wearing my police cap most of the shift as I came and went from the building to my patrol car and so on. I was alone that shift and stopped a car in the early evening for some violation. There were two girls in the car, and they kept looking at me really funny and trying not to laugh while we conducted business. I tried to ignore them and finish the event.

When it was completed, they went on their way, and I returned to my patrol car thinking that the girls were just acting like silly girls. Then I caught my reflection in the rearview mirror. On the black bill of the police cap, right in front of the hat badge, was a big glob of white pigeon's manure. I had to laugh. Boy, was I lucky I had that hat on when the bird took his revenge on the local constabulary?

One later busy night, we had a frantic call from the Catholic priest at the north side church. He was in the rectory and was hiding upstairs. He reported that someone was breaking into the building where he was alone. Only I, Matt Keslar, and Sergeant Mark were available to respond.

The buildings faced the busy street with lots of traffic and activity this warm summer night. We found that there had been a forced entry. We were preparing to go inside when we heard someone yelling from an upper window at the front side of the building. People on the street were looking up there too. Matt and I stepped back so we could look up there from the front door. Here was this guy in only pink bikini underpants climbing out of the window and onto the roof of the building. He shouted to us, "Don't shoot, I'm the priest." We neither one had a gun *un*holstered, and I recognized his face, and indeed he was the priest. That was a little bit of a shocker! He was now hanging onto the roof in full view of the amazed crowd that had gathered and those passing by. We learned that the burglars were in the building, so we entered the building and began searching for them.

As I passed a fridge, I opened the door for a peak, and another surprise. Hardly any food items were in it, but, boy did it have a big selection of booze?

Matt and I located the burglars in an upper room. They had decided the jig was up, so they barricaded themselves into a room and would not come out. Sergeant Mark joined us now. They refused to come out, so he went to his car to get some tear gas. In the meantime, I was talking to one of the burglars through the barricaded door and convinced them to give up. They opened the door, and we took the two brothers into custody as the sergeant returned, disappointed that he did not get to deploy the gas.

The two young men were from Texas. They had left there in a stolen car and were committing thefts and stealing cars all the way to Rock Springs. We took them into custody without incident and put them into the city jail.

A few days later, they were to be transferred to the county jail, having been charged with several felonies. An old deputy that was a detective in the sheriff's department came to move the men. He was a friend of the sheriff and had seen his better days. He knew it all, though, and was one of those guys that you couldn't tell anything to. Anyway, on the way to Green River, the men overpowered the deputy. Gave him a beating, took his gun, and threw him out, and off they went in his unmarked car.

They had to be chased down by the highway patrol and recaptured some distance from there. The old deputy, who was marked and bruised from the incident, never wanted to talk about it, but he sure lost his high and mighty attitude around us "young smart alecks" after that.

Oh, and the priest. Yes, he made it off the roof without falling to his peril. Not much was said to him about it other than the normal, "just the facts, ma'am, just the facts," as Joe Friday of *Dragnet* would recite. He was always sheepish around me after that, however. He transferred to another perish the next year. I hope he is staying away from steep roofs in the dark of night. It could be hazardous to his health.

One late evening I had a brand-new fleet car by myself. I was heading to the department and just about to go onto the Elk Street overpass from the north side when a large car came toward me off the overpass. It crossed over into my lane of traffic and then veered back and went past me.

I went after the large gray-colored car as it turned and sped into the downtown area. I activated the overhead lights and called in pursuit as the car then raced from the downtown area toward Bunning Park. The car would not stop and kept picking up speed. I pursued it from the south side of the park to the north side, where it failed to continue straight ahead and crashed into my father's garage at the corner of the property where I grew up.

It was a terrific crash, and the south side of the building flew out into the roadway with all kinds of stuff from the interior as well as the car stopped about halfway impaled into the front of the building. It was a large gray-colored car, and the guy was probably doing fifty on the narrow roadway prior to the impact.

Oh great, of all the places the idiot could have found to run into, it had to be my dad's place. Dave, another officer who started in the department with me, arrived in another patrol car. We took the two guys into custody. I had the passenger who gave no resistance while Dave grabbed the driver, who decided he still had not had enough. Dave punched the guy on the jaw, and that stopped the little friction between them. The driver had a broken jaw. Whether from the accident or the punch, who could say.

I knew both men. They were troublemakers. I had gone to the sixth grade with the driver before he quit school. They had both been drinking and using drugs that night when afoot on the south side of town, they decided to steal the car and go for a ride. They had just started when we encountered each other at the overpass.

I was babying the new patrol car in the wild chase and being careful with it, but we were expected in those days to never quit. You chased by vehicle, foot, or whatever till the bitter end. While in the basic police academy in Wyoming, I remember a highway patrol captain was teaching one of our classes. He was lecturing on vehicle pursuits. He told us in no uncertain terms that in a pursuit, you pursue, pursue, pursue.

Only one vehicle ever really got away from me. It was a big highway-type motorcycle. It was out on Dewar Dr in the four-lane traffic roadways. It was late in the evening, and this guy just kept running red lights. I was getting him stopped when he spotted the entrance ramp nearby onto I-80. He jumped onto it, and the chase was on down the dark interstate. I was doing 130 with the patrol car and gaining on him. All I had to do was get him shut down or chase him to the Green River area, where I would have a roadblock set up.

Well, he apparently knew this too. He was a good rider, but this was a risky chase. The guy slowed enough to make a quick exit onto the ramp for Highway 191 south to the Flaming Gorge area, and we took off again. I knew this highway well. It had a narrow shoulder, was curvy and an open range, and I had come close several times to hitting cows or wildlife on it in my journeys. This was too much risk for a really bad thing to happen, especially to me and my patrol car. After a couple of miles down the dark highway at one hundred miles per hour, I let him slip away. That guy knew how to ride a bike for sure.

Anyway, returning to the garage crash. Boy, my dad was surprised. He didn't really whine about it much. In fact, he came out pretty good on the insurance and fixed the building himself. It is still standing to this day. The newspaper came that morning before the car was towed out and made the story a front-page item complete with the stolen car planted into the front of the garage.

Before I left the scene of the crash that night, I had the new patrol car parked in the intersection at the bottom of the hill by the garage. (Soulsby Street and J Street.) A city worker had an old city truck that was at the end of its use that he had parked at the top of the hill while putting out street barricades. It slipped the parking brake, and *whoosh*—off to the races.

I had returned to my car when I saw this city truck rolling down the hill and picking up speed. It was on course to collide with the passenger middle area of the patrol car. I could only imagine the damage that was going to be done by this large heavy runaway pickup. Doom for sure. When suddenly, for no obvious reason other than, of course, an angel getting a hold of that steering wheel, the truck moved to the right and struck the curb and chain-link fence with heavy metal poles and came to a stop. I was glad to finish the investigation at that scene and get out of there before the sky fell on me.

On a dark cold busy December night, an uninvited man in a Santa Clause suit was playing Santa in a busy chain grocery store. They let him go ahead as he was harmless and just standing near a front door, passing out candy to children and chatting with shoppers. He had been there for about an hour when suddenly Santa turned into an armed robber. He pulled a pistol and forced several clerks to empty their tills into his Santa bag. Then in a flash, he flew out the door.

The call came in, and I and two other units responded to the mall area where the traffic and activity were much. However, in responding almost to the area, we spotted a lone occupant driving away from the area, but the giveaway was that the man had on a Santa suit sans the beard and hat.

We got him stopped and disarmed. This was the *bad* Santa, of course. We held him at the scene per court decisions, under investigative detention. Several personnel from the store then came to the nearby scene and identified the man as the robber as well. The beard, hat, and bag of money were all in the car. He was arrested and taken to the city jail. I couldn't wait for spring. It would probably next be the Easter Bunny!

I responded on a grave shift to a silent burglar alarm at a closed Skaggs Drugstore, which was really like a large department store. There were several of us working, but everyone else was tied up with combative prisoners at the jail. The sheriff's department and highway patrol would usually roll it up around midnight if they could. Then ask us to take over if we could till, they could respond.

On nearing the area, I shut off all lights and parked about one hundred yards away from the south side of the store among some other buildings and approached on foot. There was no obvious activity in the quiet area, but as I crept up to the nearby doors, I saw that the bottom half of one of the heavy glass doors had been broken out. This was way too much building for even several guys to cover, but I had no choice.

I crouched near the damaged door and was peering into the semi-darkened building. All was quiet other than fans running inside. Suddenly, a figure appeared at the far end of the building near the north doors. I watched. The lone person was packing an armload of stuff and quickly heading my way. I felt pretty certain that he was alone.

I waited till he was almost to the door when I announced myself with a flashlight in his face and a pistol pointed at him. He gave me no trouble. Put everything on the floor and spread-eagle there while I cuffed and took him into custody. He was a young man, about my age. I didn't know him, but I did know his grandmother, who had lived near my family on A Street and, in fact, had babysat me once in a while. She was a sweet, kindly aged woman.

The guy had broken into the store to empty their considerable pistol display that they offered for sale. His arms had been loaded down with new pistols. Another minute or two, and he would have made his exit good. Once at the jail, I found that he was living with his grandmother. He refused to call her and tell her of his whereabouts, even though she would be sitting up and worried about him. I placed the call and had to share the bad news. What a rat he was. A thief and a self-centered goof to boot. I hope after prison, he made something of himself. Yes, back then, it was common to receive a two- to three-year sentence in the state penitentiary for burglary for the first offense.

Matt Keslar and I arrested three teenage girls from the Lander—Riverton area one afternoon that were runaways. Well, they could get in big trouble in Rock Springs in this time period. So, we took them in and booked them into jail. While booking, they were emptying their coat pockets and so on, and one of the girls had a big wad of material in one of the pockets. I pulled it out but didn't recognize anything, so I took a whiff of the material trying to figure it out. About then, the material opened up, and it turned out to be about four or five pairs of panties. Keslar laughed and laughed. He thought this was hilarious. I was more than embarrassed. Especially with the girls all sitting there in the audience, grinning widely.

That situation occurred in the fall; I believe. The next spring or early summer, I was off duty and pulled into the front of a large chain grocery store on Center Street. I was getting ready for a fishing-camping trip and dressed in rundown garb. I was making a quick stop to pick up a few items.

There was a pay phone at the front exterior of the store, and as I parked, I saw the "female Larry, Moe, and Curly from Lander—Riverton." They had tried it again. Just my luck. I went over to them. Boy, they were about as surprised as I was. I used the phone and called for a car to come to pick them up again. Jim Callas arrived in a few minutes and took the errant gals to jail. I never saw them after that. Another encounter, and we could have started having an old home week. As I say, Rock Springs would have been an exciting place for them to come to, compared to the Lander area, but the results would probably not have turned out well for gullible teen girls.

One late grave shift, I was in another brand-new patrol car and working with a female officer. We were patrolling the south downtown area. It was a cool early morning, and things had quieted down. As we turned onto a street and were approaching a local auto dealership near the police department, suddenly, from the closed and nearly dark large garage building, a new-looking car came flying out of a bay door and onto the street almost in front of us.

It began racing away from the area. We went into pursuit. The only other car out then was Neil Kourbelas', who was headed that way to help. The car would not stop and raced out of the area, going toward the high school.

We arrived in the school area with lights and a siren going right behind the unyielding car. Out of the dark came Neil at the intersection we were nearing. He had a car with a push bar on its front, and he made good use of it. He impacted the car on the passenger side stopping it and then continued pushing it sideways until it came to rest with the driver's side against a high chain-link fence at the school.

This patrol car had a siren system that had to be turned off manually. Well, there was no time for that. We all jumped from our cars with the siren blaring and lights flashing to see a large black man crawling out of the open driver's window with the obvious intent on fleeing on foot into the dark.

Neil and I climbed onto the car with lights and pistols pointed at the young man and took hold of him before more trouble could take root. The guy had broken into the dealership to steal a new car. The dealership did not have any burglar alarm system, and the criminal would have been home free except for the timing misfortune of driving out into the front of a patrol car. The new car was recovered, but it did have quite a bit of damage from the push bar, the fence, and all. I was happy to say that the new patrol car functioned just fine and never received a scratch.

One afternoon while on patrol, I was dispatched to an accident at the southeast side of town. It was a pleasant sunny summer day. A lone rider on a motorcycle had come racing into town from Highway 430, and as he came into the residential area adjoining the rural area, he was going too fast on the gentle curve and lost it. The cycle went falling over and went into a slide with him on it. He had no helmet on, and his forehead impacted with a tailgate latch on the rear tailgate of an old pickup truck parked at the curd and stopped him in place. The cycle slid underneath the truck.

I arrived and called for an ambulance. The guy was on his back and unconscious. His face was spread out like a pancake, and he had a large gash on his forehead. It would be ten-fifteen minutes before EMTs would arrive, and more and more people were coming out onto the street to watch. Deputy Haskell and another city officer arrived to help, but they wanted no part of contacting this bloody mess on the street.

I knew it was probably pointless, but I had to at least try CPR (cardiopulmonary resuscitation). Those days it was mouth-to-mouth. So, I did my duty. I noticed that each time that I gave the guy a breath, the blood would come shooting out of the gash on his forehead like Old Faithful. Enough was enough. I tried a few more, and there was no response. The guy was dead and beyond any aid to bring him back. I had to finish the investigation and go change uniforms. Just of note, I don't think a helmet would have made much difference for this poor guy. It was just a good thing that he didn't collide with somebody else and hurt or kill them. There were kids on bikes and people out and about that he might easily have been impacted. Also, I went to many other motorcycle accidents in which people were wearing helmets and were killed anyway. Some of the guys called helmets "brain buckets." "At least," they would say, "you don't have to scrape the brains up off the roadway." Only cops can really and usually appreciate such a statement like that.

When I could, I would foot-patrol malls and downtown areas. Park the car where it was concealed and not usually just walk about and check doors and typical patrol but try to blend into the area and sometimes just hide and quietly watch and listen. It was amazing—the things you would run into like that, that seldom would be found while in a patrol car. Also, people seldom would see you, even in uniform and if you weren't concealed that well, especially at night.

I would go alone if no one else wanted to, and usually, they did not, especially in cold and nasty weather. Neil Kourbelas was always a game for it, and once in a while, Dave, one of the newer guys that was well worth his salt, from Virginia. Hornet nicknamed

Dave Speed because everything he did was fast. He even talked really fast, he was a hunting and fishing nut, and I made a number of trips with him.

One grave shift, Dave and I were on foot patrol on the north side of town. It had gotten quiet, and we were just doing a typical patrol. Then a loud burglar alarm was activated somewhere nearby. Not being sure of its location, we just started running toward the alarm. Just as we ran up to the electronics shop from which the audible alarm was blaring, a young man came running out of the building and right into our arms. He was packing a stereo and a speaker set. The door from which he just exited had its front glass broken out. He was shocked and quickly admitted that there was one other culprit involved that fled out the rear door of the store when the alarm went off. They were counting on grabbing as much stuff as they could and getting away before police cars showed up. They were not expecting cops on foot and fast to boot.

This guy was new to us, but his cohort was not. He was a big guy and was a troublemaker. We put out the information on our handheld radios, and within a few minutes, one of the guys in a patrol car spotted the one who had gotten away just going into a convenience store. He was hooked up too.

For the first few years, we had no portable radios. So, you were totally on your own when you left the patrol car. We thought little of it, though, and would check in every so often by a business phone here or there in case another officer in a car needed help.

One grave shift, there were a number of people working. It was typically busy but not crazy. One of the cars had tried to stop a motorcycle that then ran on him. They were in pursuit and headed my way. I was on the north side of town in the Elk Street area near I-80 ramps. Several cars were chasing the lone rider now. As they headed toward me, the guy began turning around and was going to turn off Elk Street and try to get onto the interstate, get out of town as it were. As he made the sharp turnaround, he dumped the cycle in the middle of the road and fell off. Quickly he jumped up and was going to try to ride the cycle and keep going. He had no intention of stopping. I had no intention of letting him, so in a flash, I drove the front of the patrol car up onto the cycle, making it impossible to raise it up, and he was surrounded and tackled by several cops. There was a nearby truck stop that had a bird's-eye view of the whole thing, and they were obviously enjoying the show.

The lieutenant was not one of the older guys, so who knew what he might say or do about this aggressive but effective action. He was becoming more of a realist than a politician or an armchair cop. He just kept talking about me driving up onto the cycle. Thought it was a brilliant move and funny too. Had I not have done that, the guy would have had time to ride the cycle, and the chase would have gone on till who knows who got torn up. I didn't pay much attention to the talk, I thought it was just a typical move that we often did in those times. Certainly not brilliant.

The Townsend Club, located in a small what was once an old green-colored residence off Elk Street and just south of Bunning Park, was mostly an after-hours club that really got hopping after 2 a.m. when the other bars had to close. It had been in existence since I was a kid, maybe longer. Now it was a wild place overrun with the late bar crowd. Brawlers, dopers, drunks, fighters, thieves, perverts, prostitutes, well, you get the picture. It had a single front door and stairs with iron railings on both sides. Cars would be parked all over the residential area, and people carousing the area all night.

We would be called there numerous times, almost every night. The place would be packed wall to wall with people, and in the back rooms were the restrooms that were dirty crowded areas often with toilet water an inch deep on the floor. Fights and assaults were most common. Guns and knives often involved.

Sitting at the far interior end of the bar would be a large black man known as Dotsie. Earl Dotsie. In fact, though the small neon sign at the building's front indicated that the place was The Townsend Club, it was called Dotsie's. He surveyed his kingdom from his barstool with his back to the wall and what he said went in the place.

Dotsie was cagey. He appeared to be low-key and never had much contact and certainly no run-ins with the police. His bartenders and minions would take care of this.

Once, the city council was holding a hearing at the city hall to consider taking his liquor license away from him due to all of the trouble at the bar. This had been talked and rumored for some time, but nothing ever came of it. However, now they were holding an official meeting on the topic. They issued subpoenas to testify before the council, and I had been subpoenaed.

I arrived at the meeting upstairs of the old city hall and was seated outside the chambers. There sitting with me were Dotsie, one of the Gaviotis brothers that ran the OK bar on K Street, and Sheriff Stark. The newspaper arrived and took our picture, and it was on the front page the next day.

I exchanged a few pleasantries with the other men. I had known of all of them since I was a kid. I had no idea what I was to testify about other than what most other officers might have been willing to talk about. The general filth, mayhem, and out-of-control climate at the club.

After we sat there waiting to testify, the council was going through some preliminary procedures and may have had someone testify not in this group. Perhaps an hour had passed when the meeting was called to a halt and we were all dismissed. Nothing else was ever said about the hearing, and no more threats about the club losing its license were made. Nothing changed at the club, and it remained open for many more years.

On a swing shift, I received a welfare check call to a residence on the north side of town. Seldom did we get called to this area. It was an area "on the other side of the tracks," north of 9th Street. It was known as the other side of the tracks when I was a kid. Mostly black people lived there. Much of it was small old homes.

The check was to be made on Dotsie. I arrived and went into the home after announcing myself and being invited in by a loud male voice in the rear of the small run-down place. Dotsie lived there alone. This did not look like a place that the king of the club would have resided in. It did not give the impression of a home of a businessman who operated a lucrative establishment. Some of the floors leaned, and it had old appliances and was sparsely furnished with old furniture.

In the small back bedroom, I found Dotsie. He was wearing loud-colored silk-appearing pajamas and lying in an old bed. He was okay, just had not been feeling well. The exchange was brief otherwise.

The only other time I spoke with Dotsie was when my father (who was not the party animal he had once been) had gone to the club late at night and had fallen asleep at the bar. Somebody lifted his wallet. My mother called me just after 7 a.m. that morning when I arrived home from a grave shift. She said, "Oh, your dad got drunk and fell asleep at Dotsie's, and his wallet is gone." Could I do something?

Dotsie would remain seated at the bar while it was being cleaned and the last of the drunks were being escorted or thrown out. He would usually be there until 8 or 9 a.m. before going home.

I called the bar and told the bartender to put Dotsie on the phone for me. He answered, and I told him what the problem was. I said that the wallet didn't have much money in it, but my dad did need his driver's license and other stuff back along with the wallet and that I expected it back that morning. He grunted some as was his custom and didn't say much but said he would call me back.

Dotsie did not want to make trouble with the police. I knew that not much went on in that place that he was not aware of. Within an hour, the wallet was found. No money but intact otherwise. I went down and retrieved it from Dotsie. We didn't say much. He just mostly grunted and averted eye contact. Much to mom's relief, I took the wallet back to dear old pops. We lived on the other side of Bunning Park, almost in an eye view of The Townsend Club.

Dotsie died while we lived in Alaska. The club closed, but the old green building still stands, minus the neon sign over the front door, and it is being lived in once again as a residence.

One early morning Detective Delbert of the sheriff's department (once a city officer) had been in the club for some time when he observed a drug deal take place. He arrested a suspect and was taking the man out of the building to his unmarked police car.

The guy was an oil worker, and his brother and several fellow workers were present and gathered at the exterior front steps of the place. They were drunk and belligerent and not going to allow this black cop to take their buddy away.

As usual, the place was jam-packed and wild. Delbert kept identifying himself and warning the men to move away, but they refused and became more threatening. Delbert produced his pistol and continued to warn the men until the man's brother, as I recall, lunged forward to attack Delbert. Delbert shot the man in the head, and pandemonium ensued. The crowd backed away and let Delbert pass with his prisoner while they cursed and threatened and looked at the injured man.

The guy died, of course, at the scene upon falling to the ground, and Delbert made it to the city jail (old jail) with the prisoner. A short time later, the crowd showed up at the jail and were threatening to storm the place to take the prisoner away. They were outnumbered by armed officers and left after a while.

A big stink was stirred up once again. The same deputy county attorney and his cohort now decided that here was another golden opportunity for them to redeem themselves from the terrible bruising they had suffered from the Cantrell case and Gerry Spence. They charged Delbert with murder and prosecuted him.

I spoke with Delbert one day when he was being taken out of the old jail where he had incarcerated the guy selling drugs that led to the shooting incident, along with many others he had arrested as a city cop. Now he had spent time in the old jail himself. I ministered briefly to him and spoke words of encouragement, which he gladly received, as he was being taken down the street to a hearing before Justice of the Peace Nena.

Delbert was found not guilty at later proceedings and released. This did not take the efforts of Attorney Spence either. He was later the head of security at the hospital and eventually, after a number of failed attempts to be elected as a sheriff, returned to a patrolman position in the police department. Delbert was a good guy. I last saw him at my younger sister's funeral in Rock Springs in 2013. I thanked him for coming and chatted with him briefly. He passed away in 2019 after retiring from the police department earlier.

Though we were on different ends of the spectrum, Chief Hawk always treated me well as an officer and chaplain and would give me all assistance he could with the chaplain's division. Shortly after he became the chief, the city leased a building further down Broadway Ave for expanded police operations.

We still used the old jail and police facilities there, but his office was down the street. Without asking, he offered me the large office in the old building that was prime real estate in the place for the chaplain's office. This had been the chief's and lieutenant's offices. We took them and made good use of them. This was the same office that I had just a few years earlier stood just inside of the doorway of with Chief Muir and been sworn in at. How times change. Who could possibly know?

We stored cassette Bible and counseling tapes in the office that officers and I had donated funds to the division to, to be able to have them. As well as Bibles and books. A clothing store donated nice new winter coats to us for distribution without our asking. Turkeys were donated at cost one year that we distributed to local needy families at Thanksgiving. In fact, the newspapers took a picture of me in uniform delivering some of the turkeys to a family at their home as a chaplain. We had ample room to meet and speak with and minister to anyone at the centrally located office. There were some personnel who were not happy with the division having the best office in the building. God will supply if we just make ourselves available.

I once had a black pimp, an older guy that I had trouble with as an officer and had arrested, brought into the office one night by officers. He was crying bitterly. He needed help. His longtime girlfriend had just been murdered. He was inconsolable. I was able to minister to him, and we prayed. He left the office much helped.

We also administered a local traveler's aid from the chaplain's office. It was the duty of myself or another available chaplain, usually me, to come in when called to assist people traveling through the area that were short on funds. After a brief interview, if the folks were found to be in actual need, they would be given a voucher for some gas and food at one of the participating local convenience stores.

The amount of help was limited but sufficient. Some few travelers would thank you upon receiving the voucher, but it was more common to have people complain that they were not being given enough. My mother always told me, "Beggars can't be choosers." I guess these folks were never given sage advice like that during their rearing.

I disliked and objected to the treatment that Hawk and especially his cronies dished out to fellow officers. The older guys were held to different standards than the new officers, and it became a deeply divided agency with us and them. I was loyal to the old crew without question. Also, being a determined individual, I would not put up with much of the junk that was dished out. Still, I had to walk a very narrow line as I was a Christian and the chaplain of the department. This required me to be able to minister to and with the newer officers and leadership as well.

One by one, the older guys would be obviously singled out and tormented or put into a position of being dismissed. Sergeant Dan was one of them. Even after civil service hearings, he was terminated and should not have been. Officers became discouraged, and the quality of police service was affected and not in a good way.

A new mayor was elected, who had lived most of his life in Rock Springs, and things were changing. Not all for good, to be certain. A new city hall-jail was being built near the old city hall, and we were getting more officers, equipment, and pay, but things were not great at all. Many of the new officers, most of whom received the many promotions oddly enough, had trouble acclimating to the climate and culture. As they did, their wives and families had it as bad or worse. Some of the new officers sided on the QT with the older officers, and many of the officers got into trouble themselves or did not stay long in the department. If the new guys got in a jam, the administration would cover for them if at all possible while hanging the old guys out to dry.

I just did my job and stayed out of the mess as much as I could. Chief Hawk had me nominated at the local Jaycees awards banquet for being the Law Enforcement Officer of the Year, Religious Leader of the Year, and something else that I have long forgotten. It was a nice gesture from the chief. The banquet and awards ceremony drew a large crowd. Officer Looney, who was new, from California and just under Hawk, came to the affair with his wife in tow. He was most friendly and encouraging. This treatment was short-lived for him. He grew to have it in for me as Hawk's time was getting short. He had his eye on getting rid of his old buddy Hawk and taking over.

Looney was Jewish, and I am not certain why he decided to target me other than he thought I was too evangelic for his taste and would not play politics with him. I was one of the old crew, and maybe it was just a matter too, he just did not like me, possibly even detested or hated me despite my glowing, magnetic personality—just joking about that part of it, folks. I never really did anything to him personally, but he sure grew to hate me.

As Hawk left and Looney was an interim chief, I became a bigger target for him. We had take-home cars now and had been told to take the rear seats out of the cars and thoroughly check them for contraband, weapons, and so on prior to the shift briefing and the tour beginning.

One night at the beginning of the grave shift, I parked near the front of the leased building and took out my rear seat as I did religiously and thoroughly check my patrol car. I then went into the briefing room with the rest of the crew. We were nearing the end of the briefing when this one officer that was a favored boy of Looney's came in and said he was checking our cars as ordered. They were all keyed the same, and that surprise, surprise, he had found a baggie of cocaine under the rear seat of my car. I had failed to search as ordered. He proudly held this baggie up for all to see as he made his announcement.

A hatchet job was readily recognized, and this was one attempt supreme. I simply looked the guy straight in the face and, without any show of much excitement, said, "You did not find that in my car. I took the seat out and checked it completely, as I do every shift. So, you had better return that stuff to where it belongs." I was well known for being a straight shooter. Not bragging about myself, but this is required as a Christian and in order to try to be a good officer.

This guy, who was hoping for detective and probably had a good shot at it, just turned kind of pale. Not what they expected. I ignored him and looked back to the supervisor, who was front and center. The jerk put the bag back down to his side and quietly left the room, and not another word was said about it.

This was not an easy department to work for now. Lots of unneeded tension and trouble, and most of it was self-made internal stuff like that. One newly promoted officer shot himself at home. Some quit, some were fired. Divorce and separations were common. Most of this turmoil was with the newer people, however.

More trouble was to be with Looney, but it quieted for a bit now as he was passed over by the mayor for the chief position. He remained in the number two spot and would be chief after the new chief from Colorado only lasted about a year.

While Hawk was still a chief, we had an arsonist in town one summer. He would find out-of-the-way apartment complexes and set fire traps in which it would be difficult for the occupants to get out of the older buildings while they burned. This happened at night or during early morning hours several times that summer.

Every time we were able to arrive in time to get the fires out and keep anyone from being injured or killed, although there was considerable property damage. Unfortunately, we never caught the nut doing this, and it stopped just as quickly as it started.

One night a two-story brick apartment house on Broadway that had lots of occupants in it was targeted by this firebug. They did a good job of setting fire to the only exit out of the building, and people were trapped in it. I was first to arrive and located people trapped on an upper floor of the building that were not easily found. Upon the fire department arriving, I got them to the rear of the building quickly, and ladders were deployed, and the people rescued before anyone perished. We saved about a dozen people that night from likely injury or death.

For this, Hawk had the mayor and council give me, the firemen, and one new lieutenant that happened onto the scene but did nothing public awards for our action at a council meeting. The local paper put the story and picture of us with the nice certificates in one of the papers soon after that.

Hawk was always friendly with me. He didn't claim to be Christian and certainly didn't have characteristics of one, but he treated me well. I ran into him at the police academy in Douglas, Wyoming, after we had been in Wrangell and returned to Wyoming for a few years. He was now the chief in Hanna, Wyoming. He followed me around like a lost pup for the week that we were in class. He could not have been more friendly. He was okay, but though I held no hard feelings for him, of course, I did not like what he had allowed to happen to some good men while he was a chief in Rock Springs.

We now had to write our reports in our cars rather than at the department. They had to be hand-printed on forms. It was an effort to increase police visibility on the street. There were pros and cons to that.

Anyway, one beautiful early summer Sunday morning, I was parked on the upper end of A Street writing a report, running radar, and just watching the area. Though this is a residential area, it is the main feeder street too. It has two lanes with a center left-turn lane and is fairly steep at the top near where I was located.

All of a sudden, I saw this small car come roaring past, going downhill at about fifty miles per hour. It passed a car by going into the left-turn lane and speeded on. I took off and finally caught up to the car, not knowing what to expect. I got the car stopped and saw one lone seated person in it.

I made the approach and found one quite large woman to be the driver. I was expecting some big story, problem, or something. The woman said nothing. I asked her why she was illegally passing cars and driving double the speed limit. She just replied matter-of-factly, "I'm on my way to church!" *Wow!* I thought. She got some pretty hefty tickets to go with her to her morning service.

Another time I was parked in full view, I never tried to hide out doing traffic control, and I wasn't big on traffic enforcement, except for drunk drivers. Some of the local attorneys called me the "King of the DWIUs" as I probably arrested more than anyone in the department, and if they went to trial, I almost always prevailed in the case. I was also the officer in charge of the chemical testing equipment for the department and did the training with this equipment and for the apprehension of impaired drivers for our department as well as the local highway patrol and sheriff's department.

However, returning to my story at hand, I was on the busy Dewar Dr when I picked up an approaching vehicle driving well beyond the speed limit and coming inbound. I stopped the car. It was driven by the lone occupant, a young female.

I immediately noticed that the back seat of the car was packed with what appeared to be packaged psilocybin magic mushrooms. I asked the young woman what was on her back seat after doing the few preliminaries. She apparently had forgotten that they were on the seat in full view. She had a shocked and surprised look and stuttered that she wasn't sure. This is obviously what drug use will do to the brain!

Brain cells are killed off, I have observed this many times with drug users—duh! This was her car, and there were many more magic mushrooms than for personal use. She went to jail, and the speeding ticket was the least of her problems. She didn't understand why all the disruption to her life and activities—duh!

We now had several female officers, two out of the five were okay. There was one particular day shift, a Sunday, in fact, that I was working with one of the three that should have been in some other occupation. The other problem with her was that she was a favorite of Chief Looney and pretty much did what she wanted.

We were terribly short that day, and it was the two of us. She disappeared most of the day, and I wasn't keeping tabs on her. She had horses stabled just out of city limits with the chief and would disappear out there on work hours, only checking in with dispatch and avoiding calls.

A call came in from the Ernst shopping center, which was a large department store in the White Mountain Mall on the west side of town. The call was from the pharmacy of the store. They said that there was a suspicious man hanging out there for no reason and that he would not leave when he was told to. He was a large man and seemed disoriented or under the influence of something.

The mall was busy and packed with shoppers. So was this store. I called the female officer and told her to respond to the store as well. She was supposed to be en route. I am sure that she just remained on her portable radio doing whatever and never did show up. I arrived at the store and tried to wait for her, but the pharmacy called twice more and said the man was getting increasingly agitated and disruptive with customers and refused to leave the store. He obviously had something in mind as far as getting drugs from the pharmacy by hook or by crook.

I couldn't wait for help. None was coming. I went in and encountered the large Polynesian-looking male. He spoke broken English but understood. He was agitated and did not want to leave the store. I told him he was trespassing and not wanted on the premises and that he would have to leave or go to jail. He complied and began walking down an aisle with me behind him.

All at once, he stopped and turned and grabbed at me. We tussled and became engaged in the aisle with other shoppers trying to scurry out of the way. We were bouncing off shelves and knocking stuff over and off them. This guy was way bigger than me and wild. We wrestled for several seconds until we went to the floor and were rolling around. As we came to rest, it was my misfortune that he was sitting on top of me with my arms pinned by this heavy goof.

He looked wild and didn't intend to leave the store. He reared back with all his might and began punching at my face. I couldn't move. He threw four or five hard punches with all of his might. Had they connected, he would have done lots of damage to me. This was the only time I was ever in a position like this or ever would be.

Every punch would come to about an inch of my face, and it was as if a shield was there in place, stopping the blows. There was absolutely no other reason for it. He was not pulling the punches and fully intended to and was trying to work me over. Unseen angels were on the scene as I have had other times, keeping me from harm and danger. Read Psalm 91 of the Bible. It is true. The guy was appearing frustrated. Punching and punching and not being able to touch me. I still had the problem of this guy on top of me, weapon retention, and getting control of him. Well, God took care of that too.

It was pretty unusual for citizens to help the police in those days most of the time, you sure didn't want to count on it as often they would stand by and let 'er rip. However, two or three men standing by and seeing the fight came to my aid and grabbed the guy. I quickly sprang off the floor, completely uninjured, and got him cuffed while they struggled to hold his arms behind him. He continued to try to struggle, but I had him now. Took control and quickly marched him out to the patrol car.

Was there any policewoman in sight? No, there was not. No need to say or do anything. Looney or his underlings would cover for her and make an attack on me. She failed me several other times as well when I was stuck with her alone for help. I hold no hard feelings, of course, but people like that don't have any business trying to be a police officer. She was eventually kicked in the jaw by one of her horses and forced out of police work. The only problem was that she received disability from the city when it had nothing to do with her job. It's who you know...

I was traveling out of town preaching on Sunday mornings often now again for some of the local pastors or for churches that had no pastor. This made long days for me. Got off a grave shift usually and left ASAP for a service in Big Piney—Marbleton, or Green River. I was also put on a circuit with the Full Gospel Business Men's Fellowship and spoke for them when they were in full swing during that time. I went to Idaho Falls, Worland, and the community college in Riverton.

Steve Watt, a highway patrolman that I wrote about previously that came to our aid in my accident, was shot during this time by a bank robber, just outside of town and captured by our department. Chief Looney's son, who had some genetic illness, passed away about the same time too. These are lengthy stories, and perhaps I will write about them sometime along with so many other stories of interest and humor from my eight years in the RSPD, etc., but that would be another book in itself.

I will wrap up this era with just a few more short notes before going onto Alaska, etc. I was also solemnizing weddings for officers and had done four of them as well as funeral services for some non-police. I was keeping up two careers, hunting, and fishing as much as possible as I love the outdoors and that activity as well as camping, hiking, and so on.

My life was threatened by Butch, Neil, and Matt about this time. An engagement had been made for me to meet a girl with them and their wives, but I missed it. They made another one and said I had better show up or else! It was to be a yard picnic at Butch's house. I was busy and almost didn't go, but I felt prodded to show up, so I did. That was when I met Brenda. Glad I didn't miss that date. She went to the Assemblies of God church with her mother. Butch and Neil were attending too, but I hardly ever went there now as I was going out of town on almost all Sundays to minister or would be needed at the jail as a chaplain.

We were married on July 17th, 1982, in the Assemblies of God church on A Street that had been such a part of my life already. Just before this, I had several minor run-ins with Looney and his crew. Most of the men were good with me, but it was important for them to please the boss, right or wrong, so right did not matter.

I had served as an acting supervisor many times, and I, Neil Kourbelas, and another officer had been made investigative patrolmen under Chief Hawk when the detective division was deactivated. We served as uniformed detectives. Still took calls if we could when the patrol was overwhelmed, but generally, we were doing investigations. This continued under Looney until he was able to get his own choices into place, and then he had detectives and supervisors, almost all new people.

One Sunday in 1982, it was the Fourth of July. We were a skeleton crew with only an acting sergeant, me, and one other guy on. It was busy. The other two were new people. I had supervised them before and was able to work with them just fine, as I could with about anyone.

However, Looney was after me. I was only a few weeks away from my marriage. I was to give a talk that morning in the worship service about the holiday in uniform at the Assemblies of God church. I was taking call after call with no help from the other two. The acting sergeant was in dispatch with a female dispatcher. She was a young single woman. He had left his wife and children in town and was living with this girl. His family were nice people, and it was just a shame. Middle-age crisis, some like to call it. Stupidity is more fitting.

He was playing footsie with her in dispatch all day, the other guy was off the radio doing who knows what, and I was out there on my own, going from call to call. That morning we were told that one of the prisoners had an infectious disease and a stool sample had been taken. This would need to be taken to the hospital.

As one might imagine, neither of those two officers would do it. So, when I was dispatched to come to get the sample, I refused and was busy with calls and reports as it was. This was what Looney needed. It turned into a big nasty battle. He tried to fire me, but the mayor would not allow it. So, he gave me a ten-day suspension without pay, the next best hammer he had to use for now.

We had a police protective organization that was a quasi-union. They had filed lawsuits and fought for several of the mistreated men and policies that were being brought about. They knew that I was being treated badly and hired an attorney for me. Robert Johnson was a longtime Rock Springs lawyer. He was very good.

We took the case to a civil service hearing. My treatment by Looney was scandalous. The civil service commission knew that, but they also had to save face for this new chief, too, or that would be problematic. After the hearing, the commission cut the suspension in nearly half, and I got my back pay.

Looney pretty much left me alone after that, although at every turn, if he could undercut me, he and a few of his henchmen that hoped to continue their upward mobility in the organization would not pass up the opportunity. The attacks—harassment by the men, supervisors other than Looney—were never personal, and I got along with most of them quite well and had their respect.

There was a rabbi in the chaplain's division that had joined with several other ministers now. I tried to treat him like anyone else, but he was good friends with Looney, and he would go out of his way at chaplain meetings to openly criticize me and defend Looney. This was completely out of the context of what the meeting was about and/or what business was being conducted with the dozen or so ministers that were chaplains. I would simply downplay his attacks and go on. The rabbi just had a nasty, vindictive spirit about him.

Unfortunately, very few of these chaplains would actually interact with the officers or be available to serve. Other than me, there was one other minister that was dependable and served. The others would come to meetings and show up briefly at the department, but that was about it.

We had a late-night armed robbery on the west side of town one night by two men at a convenience store. They took off for the nearby interstate with several of us in pursuit. There were two highway patrolmen nearby, so they joined in one of their patrol cars and joined the pursuit.

The men were in a pickup truck, racing down the interstate. As the chase ensued, the men began throwing money out of the vehicle. They would not stop. The highway patrol was very aggressive in a vehicle pursuit. They got close to the pickup, and the patrolman on the passenger side of the patrol car began firing at the truck with a shotgun.

After a few more miles, the young men pulled over and gave up. We took them to the city jail, and they were booked. We now had jail officers at the new city jail. The men were from California and admitted pulling armed robberies there before coming to Wyoming.

One of the men was especially cooperative and agreed to talk with officers from California about his numerous crimes there. I made strict arrangements to have him kept apart at the city jail from anyone else and to be treated well until officers came from Orange County, California.

The day before the detectives arrived, unknown to me, Looney and his men had the man transported to the county jail and placed with his cohort in the general jail population. Of course, when I went to interview him with the Californian detective, the man would say nothing. I had obviously been deliberately torpedoed. This was a very nasty move to let these guys get off with other felonies just to spite me. He was kept in the state and charged with the felony but got off for the out-of-state stuff to my knowledge, in this life anyway.

I stayed for two more years, but the department was increasingly a disappointing mess. I heard Alaska calling. Some say I read too many *Alaska* magazines. Well, I don't know about that, but the Lord had plans for us, so we followed them. There was a time that I would not have left Wyoming or the RSPD, but those days had passed. Oh yes, I hated leaving family and friends, and there would be days that I would sorely miss Wyoming. Days in which I would ponder what I might have been doing if I had remained there. All of my siblings live and remain in Rock Springs.

I went into Looney's office to deliver my resignation letters as an officer and chaplain. He would not come out to see me. I left the letters with his secretary. I was glad not to have to see him either. His reign was short-lived at the agency before he was replaced. I have no hard feelings and wish him no ill will, but, I don't think that he ever had much success after that. He remained in Rock Springs and went into some kind of business to pay his bills, I suppose. He ran for the legislature against former highway patrolman Steve Watt and was easily defeated. You reap what you sow.

With Brett, our first child born five days earlier, we were packed up, much to my in-laws' consternation, and left for Southeast Alaska with a large moving truck, small four-wheel drive-in tow, Brenda driving her two-door car, and our black lab dog, Buck, on September 14th, 1984. It was a cool frosty autumn morning. We were ripe for adventure, but it also hurt to leave my beloved Wyoming and the many friends and family who remained there. We would be in for only what could be imagined in this very different life in the far north. No family, friends, or connections there other than the few people we had met on our brief visit to the place for a few days. Maybe this took courage, one would assume. I don't know about that, but it did take faith and obedience to the Lord. He opened the doors and opportunities, and looking back, I am so thankful that we went forward rather than take the easy way and have just stayed put where all was familiar.

10. Brett, Stephanie and little dog Licorice, with
Dad's caribou horns in Wrangell. AK

11. Our "happy children" with the Reagan's in Wrangell Drug.

12. A public use cabin in the Tongass National Forest.
Accessible usually only by boat or float plane.

13. The U.S. Post Office and Customs House in Wrangell, that also
served as the police department, jail and state court facilities.

14. Family vist in Wrangell. Beach photo taken by Ken of (left to right) Chuck, his son Randy, Jan, Tammy, Brenda, and Mom. The two little people are Stephanie and Brett.

15. Excited mountain goat hunters about to board a float plane to depart the Wrangell Airport. Randy Martin and Ken.

16. Ken's brown bear hide preping for taxidermy in Wrangell.

BOOK 3

Before this adventure began, Brenda and I were first invited in August to fly up to Wrangell to visit and interview for a position with the seven-man Wrangell Police Department. They wanted spouses to come and see the area because it was not an easy place to live, especially for the female persuasion.

It was a fishing-logging semi-wilderness town of about 3500 on an isolated island. It had little shopping other than several blocks of local small shops and stores. The island had quite an extensive road system, most of its rock or gravel roadways. The only travel to and from the island was by plane or boat/ferry.

The area is beautiful. Giant ancient red and yellow cedar trees as well as Sitka spruce, Hemlock, and smaller bull pines with lush vegetation and berry bushes. Miles of devil's club and spongy muskeg. High areas in the picturesque alpine with such views and clean, fresh air that rivals almost any location. Mountains, ocean, and quiet bays in this Tongass National Forest. There is usually 110 to 120 inches of precipitation per year there. Mostly rain, but also snow. What an adventure, but not for most people, a visit will suffice, and that not too lengthy or far off the beaten path.

We flew out of the Rock Springs airport and eventually into Wrangell on a large commercial passenger jet that was rather unique to Alaska. It departed from its terminal in the Seattle-Tacoma area onto a small runaway parallel to the ocean. Two officers were leaving, and I was to be considered for one of the spots. Brenda was eight months pregnant and large, all in the front. The stewardesses were stunned to learn what we were doing when we would enter the planes. I remember they were all young, attractive females then; they would just stare at us when we described the adventure we were on and the little fact that our baby was only a month or less away. "Alarmed" would be an understatement from the frozen looks on their faces that a baby could present itself in flight. This did not seem to make them feel really warm and fuzzy. We depended on God and never gave it much concern and certainly no worry. *No* problem. We were back home and involved in a Saturday moving sale when Brenda began feeling like the time was soon. We finished out the day, and off to the hospital late that evening we went.

Brett was born early the next morning with all of our families in the waiting room. He was cleaned up and blanketed and handed to papa first. I was in the delivery room for the event. I had seen far more gore than this at most accident or crime scenes on a nearly daily basis. I don't know what bothers anyone so much about a little mess with childbirth.

My family kept me supplied with pizza and coffee while I waited with Brenda in the room for several hours until she was moved to the delivery room. Then the feed was over, and gowns and masks were the order of the early morning.

We spent several days in Wrangell checking out the place and allowing them and ourselves to see if it would be a good fit. Housing was in short supply, and we would be able to rent an apartment that would become open from one of the departing officers. Things went well, and we were offered and accepted the job and were to arrive there within several weeks.

We had several days of long travel. The moving truck had a governor on it that kept the speed at fifty-five miles per hour tops. Going uphill and pulling the small four-wheel drive, I was often traveling at thirty-five miles per hour. Buck and I were in the moving truck while Brenda and Brett followed in her car. The battery was dead one morning in the moving truck, and one of the driver's front turn signals had been duct-taped on.

We were en route to my old sidekick, Steve Reichel, and his family. They lived in the Seattle area, where he had become involved in the irrigation business. What a reprieve when we arrived. He knew the area well. We spent several days with them.

This was not merely for pleasure, however. The moving truck had to be completely unloaded and everything packed into a metal container that would go onto a barge for shipment to Southeast Alaska. Then Brenda and Brett remained with the Reichel's a few more days while Buck, our car, four-wheel drive, and I embarked on the Alaska State ferry, *The Columbia*, named for Alaska glaciers. This was a large ferry, the largest of the fleet.

I was like a fish out of water. The adventure was intoxicating, however. Miles of ocean and sea life, all different types of people, many tourists still traveling in mid-September. Buck had to stay in the four-wheel drive, and I could only go get him out for exercise and food/water when we stopped in ports. I had no cabin and stayed on lawn chairs that were located on the aft part of the ship. This saved lots of expense and was pretty cozy and a popular thing to do among the mostly younger people, my age, and so on. There were a few tough old codgers that camped out there too.

I skipped most meals at the dining area as they were pretty pricey. This was over a three-day journey, and one of the last mornings, the weather was just wonderful. I went for broke and had a large breakfast. Several hours later, the world had turned upside down. The weather was horrible. The seas were rough, and the ship was rocking and rolling. Most people got hunkered down. I tried to, but I had to keep going outside for fresh air. I was working hard to avoid the feeling of severe seasickness that was overtaking me.

Hour after hour of this, and I was sick as a dog. I found a corner in a passageway and sat there all hunkered over. I made a sudden charge for a nearby bathroom but never made it and had to vomit in a large ashtray. This was tough stuff on a dry-land Wyoming kid.

Many hours later, it finally quit, and I came back to the world. The rest of the trip was nice again. There was a tourist from farms in Nebraska. One of the older guys sat among the passengers in the forward viewing area. He just kept repeating that he liked the land. This was all too much. Nothing but the ocean and far-off peaks. He did not like this trip one bit and couldn't wait to get back to the farm. Finally, on a Sunday afternoon, the ferry approached Wrangell. It was a welcoming sight. A little village nestled along the ocean shore below timbered, mountainous peaks. It was cool and sunny.

After docking, I was met by Officer Putz and his wife. He was on duty, and they had come to help us get off the ship and to the apartment house. Putz and the family had come from Wisconsin and had been in Alaska for only about a year at that time.

Brenda and Brett were already at the newer apartment complex at 404 Alaska Ave. Steve had taken them to SeaTac, where they boarded a passenger jet with the "Fly with a friendly face" logo on the rear of the jet to Ketchikan and then Wrangell early that morning. They were waiting there for me and the dog. Brenda was worn out.

Many chapters could be written about all of this, and maybe later more shall. Suffice it for now to just record some of the high and low points that are most easily embedded in mind.

We had arrived on September 23rd, and I began work on the 25th on a swing shift. Bill had been the other officer hired and had been there just a few days before me. He was a few years younger than me. A nice single tall dark-haired easy-going guy. We became friends. He was a hunting and fishing nut. He was from Minnesota and was looking for adventure, too, along with his yellow lab Lenny, a small truck, and an eighteen-foot boat. Arriving for the interview and taking the first position open put him in a position to have dibs on the other vacancy available for rent to newcomers. He had a place at the Old Institute about three miles out of the main part of town on the Zimovia Highway. I would have dearly chosen this spot over the apartment house. It was an old place but not in too bad of shape and much more secluded and private than our place.

Chief Bill was a big man, not fat. He had come to Alaska from California some years ago. He tired of all the silliness and sameness of the place and came to Ketchikan looking for adventure. He had been in Wrangell for a number of years now. He was decent enough, but he kept his distance in this small department between himself and the men. I got along fine with him, although some in town despised him, and he was rumored to be hard to work for. No, I had worked for a few men that were difficult to work for, and he was not among their number. Do your job, be on your toes, and no problem.

We later became working friends, and I often took his defense when people would spread silly and vile rumors about him. This did not endear me to some of the locals as they wanted it to be like the Three Musketeers with them and that not including the chief.

The lieutenant was a little guy named Dave. He smoked like a fiend and could stand still enough for ash to lengthen to at least an inch or more on the smoke hanging from his mouth. He was not overly friendly, but I got along fine with him. He was often caller Barney by the locals. That being for Sheriff Andy Taylor on the *Mayberry R.F.D.* television show. Dave certainly did fit the physical appearance of Barney, but he could be tough in a fight for a little guy. He came from Oregon and had been in Wrangell for some years. He was in the guard and had seen action in Vietnam when he was in the army.

This would now be the department. It had been reduced in size for the time being as one man was currently on disability, and it was uncertain if or when he would return due to a back injury. The chief and one man worked days during the week. Otherwise, you worked alone on one of the other two shifts as well as weekend-day shifts.

A dispatcher worked during the day shift on weekdays and also covered as a secretary, issued driver's licenses, and was a jail guard. At other times, unless the jail was occupied, you were alone. The phones had to be answered over the radio system. You were a dispatcher and lone officer. Help could be summoned by whomever you could call up, but it was discouraged. You were expected to pretty much cover whatever.

The police department was located in the old federal building near the waterfront. The old federal jail was now the local lockup. The court and customs office were upstairs with the police department. The post office was on the first floor. A new public safety building was being built. This had cost Chief Bill a good deal of grief pushing that project through along with a longtime old crusty fire chief Gordon. Lots of people didn't want modernization and added expense with the government. Only the basement shooting range was completed. The upper floors that would be a new modern police facility, jail, fire department, and court system were sometime down the road a year or so.

I didn't mind the old building. It was in need of replacement, but I started out in the old Rock Springs city hall and jail, so this was like an old hat to me. We had two marked and one unmarked fleet patrol cars. All good cars. Uniforms were French blue with dark blue shirt cuffs, and the same dark blue stripe down each leg, a regulation police cap, and a star-shaped gold-colored badge. .45 was the required firearm; mace, a large portable radio that worked like the car radio—the phone could be answered with it, a wooden baton, flashlight, and cuffs were among the arsenal on our belts. The chief distinguished himself by wearing a white uniform shirt.

Wrangell was a rough place, especially at night. A young population with four bars, several liquor stores, and an Elks club. Mostly fisherman, loggers, and mill workers. Marijuana and cocaine were very popular, and Alaska was very much the Last Frontier. A lone officer had their hands full. There were quite a few displaced people from Oregon and Washington in the area. It was a big tourist area in season, and hunting and fishing along with boats and water sports were big. Fishing derbies and big Fourth of July celebrations like we never saw anywhere in Wyoming. John Muir had visited the area and climbed onto a noted point above town for the view. Wyatt Earp had been there. The town and many areas around had Russian names due to Russia at one time owning the land. The British had been there too. Wrangell was now under its third flag, the U.S., and, of course, statehood since 1959.

Alaska had a decision from the State Court of Appeals, called the Ravin Decision. It, despite federal law, allowed Alaskans to possess up to four ounces of marijuana in their residence. Alaska's constitution also gave more protection to search-and-seizure privacy than the U.S. constitution, among other considerations. The Last Frontier, you see.

We attended the Harbor Light Assembly of God with Pastor Whittlesey and his wife. They had four young unmarried daughters from middle school to college-age living at home. Very pretty and talented young women. Pastor and family were like family to us, and we became good friends. Grandparents to our kids. He was also the part-time U.S. Customs Agent for the area. They were in their later 40s.

The church was a nice roomy modern building located on Zimovia Highway. A new high school was going to be built along with the remainder of the public safety building. For a small, secluded town, this place had a lot going for it. There was money in this area-state. My pay and benefits were a good deal better than Rock Springs, even though Rock Springs was among the better paying departments to work for in Wyoming. The Alaska retirement system I was able to lock into was far superior to that of Rock Springs or Wyoming.

People, even church people, were suspicious and standoffish to me as I was government law enforcement. It took time to build relationships with folks. That's the way Alaskans were. Mostly anti-government, wanted to be left alone and enjoy this last wild place in America. Well, I was of that mindset myself in some ways. Obviously, or I would never have come to a place like this and thrived. As I stated, it is not for most people, and few really adjust to it even if they stay awhile.

There are lots of things wild about Wyoming still, but it is a far different world than what I found here in most senses. Culture, the climate, the land, the mentality, the laws, the vast distances. You could go just a short way out of town on the island and immediately be in a wilderness. Brown bears, black bears, Sitka black-tailed deer, bald eagles, and rugged, thickly timbered, and vegetated terrain. Creeks and rivers were numerous. Muskeg ground was in spades. It was like walking on a sponge unless you broke through. Then it was thick mud and water, and there were holes that one could step into in these muskeg areas and disappear or at least go up to your waist and have great difficulty exiting from.

There was a strong native culture and influence in Wrangell and Southeast Alaska with the Haida and Tlingit natives. Shakes Island, near the Inner Harbor in town, was a historic spot. There were a significant number of veterans in Alaska, too, for the small population.

It could be forty degrees, and hypothermia could easily set in even if you were dressed well for an outing. Once becoming wet, oh man, you couldn't sit around much, or a chill would overtake even a hardy person like myself within a half hour or so. The cool, wet breezes would push it to the limit.

The ocean water was cold all of the time. If you ended up in the drink, rapid extraction was crucial. Hypothermia would set in within twenty to thirty minutes. So regular flotation devices were very limited. You may stay afloat, but in the water too long—one was a corpse to be recovered if possible. Full-body float suits were the best for surviving the frigid waters once immersed.

I was not big on the ocean or seafood for the first few months, but I acclimated to it and soon found it to be a watery highway to adventure on nearby islands and the mainland that was only several miles to the east of Wrangell Island.

Seafood, I discovered, was really good. I bought a small four-teen-foot boat to start with. Then I had a much superior nineteen-foot cabin cruiser. A boat was a must. The boats were usually kept in a slip at the harbor. That was really handy. You just went to the boat with your stuff. Loaded it up and took off from the harbor. Within minutes, we would be near town fishing for halibut and salmon. A crab pot was kept in the water at the boat slip. We would catch all of the Dungeness crab that we wanted. Shrimp were caught in deeper waters along with crab too. We ate seafood like we would deer and antelope in Wyoming.

Still, there was much hunting and fishing on the island too. A vehicle was necessary. We kept our boat in the Shoemaker Bay Harbor near the old Institute. There were harbors right in town, too, but these spots were nearly impossible to get for a boat. The harbors were operated by the city and overseen by a harbormaster. We were required to provide law enforcement service to the harbors. Quite a few of the boats in the harbors were used as residences as well, and commercial boats were harbored there.

There are two high and low tides in Alaska daily. They are extreme. The ramps to the harbors could be very steep at a low tide. When landing a boat on a shore or out away from the shore, this was a constant concern if you didn't want to be left high and dry or have damage to your vessel. If one was in the water at tide change, caution was a must if you didn't want to be pulled out to sea or taken somewhere where you had no intention of going. Tide books were like the Bible, and I had to quickly learn about long-lining and coast guard buoys and navigational aids. I took a coast guard boating class during the evenings for a week. It was really helpful.

I was missing Wyoming but surely enjoying this new land. I have never regretted moving to and living in Alaska. The Lord sent us there twice. We spent nearly twenty-five years there and were every bit Alaskans. Financially it was a boondoggle for us. The friends and experiences could never have come about, even with extended trips there.

Pastor Terry Whittlesey was a good friend and help to us always. He had a slanted view of Chief Bill but overcame that after some time of being around me. Brenda had moved her heavy piano to Alaska, and the first two places we lived in were on the second floor. That thing took four to six healthy men to move up tight, cramped stairways. Terry always recruited the manpower for us. Of course, the church had no piano player till we came too, it was reciprocated to them. Not only that, but I had my ministry credentials transferred to Alaska, and so Terry had a spare speaker. During our time there, I served as a board member, treasurer, teacher, and guest speaker. I also did the wedding reenactment for Terry and his wife, Diane, the request of the family. I took that as a high honor for such dear people.

Mention moving Brenda's ton of piano, and people would nearly turn pale and head for the nearest exit. She finally sold it when we moved from Wrangell and bought a manageable keyboard. That saved untold chiropractor bills for poor slobs that were being talked into moving the heavy monster, and that was usually up steep stairways.

I was working a graveyard shift a few years later. It was dark, around 6 a.m. I was parked in a turnout across from the church building on Zimovia Highway. I was sitting quietly observing the few passing vehicles and the quiet area when Pastor Terry drove into the church parking lot and parked his little truck near the front door. He had come to make a quick check of the building before going on to the customs office.

He had not noticed the patrol car, even though it was obvious. Without thinking, I immediately had an idea, although I did not think it would work. As he fumbled with keys at the darkened front door, I picked up the microphone for the car PA system, and in a drawn-out authoritative voice, I said, "Terry, Terry, this is the Lord." He seemed stunned and began looking skyward. I was howling to myself. If only I had this on video. Suddenly, the jig was up as he slowly spun in a circle while looking upward, he spotted the patrol car. He glared and then waved me off and went into the building. I had gotten him good. He laughed about it later that day. He had a good sense of humor and was just a regular guy and a wonderful pastor. He was a longtime Alaskan, having come from Washington State and also pastoring at another Alaskan town too.

At the church, we made some good friends besides the Whittlesey's. Randy Martin and family. Randy became a lifelong friend. He worked at the logging mill when we met. They were from Oregon. He is a hunting and fishing nut.

Irene Ingle was a dear aged woman. She had lived in Wrangell for many years, and the library is named for her. Her friend, another spunky little old-timer, was Limpe. They were both widows. Limpe and her middle-aged son lived in a small house. The son ran a small tourist shop and was an artist. He was part native (Tlingit-Haida).

One Sunday morning, Pastor Terry asked me to come in uniform and make some verbal presentation that I have long since forgotten the content of. I was seated alone in the front pew area of the church. Seated behind me was Limpe.

It was close to the time to start when I felt a little tap on my left shoulder. I turned to see Limpe looking intently at me. She didn't recognize me, and she said, "Are you with the coast guard?"

"No, Limpe. I'm a police officer."

There was a brief pause, then she said, "I hope you don't pinch (arrest) me," and she giggled.

I just had to laugh and say, "Probably not."

There was only one state trooper in the nearby area at Petersburg. We had a fish and wildlife trooper on the island, but we seldom saw either. When calls came in from out of the large city limits' area, we had to respond as no trooper would be available. Officers in Alaska had statewide jurisdiction. However, the city was wild about having our patrol vehicles ran all over the island and using our personnel when the state should have been there. Even so, we went. We eventually had trooper credentials, so this made the city feel better about liability.

Officer Bill and I had to attend a two-week officer's course at the Trooper Academy in Sitka in January-February 1985. The class was full of new city officers from Ketchikan to Barrow that had certification from other states and now had to be certified for our new home. Officer Bill had been a park officer in Minnesota. A basic trooper academy was ongoing at the same time. The troopers were all business there, and the place was run like a military installation with a captain heading up the outfit.

They had no food service, however, so meals were served at the nearby Sheldon Jackson community college in their cafeteria. This was in a nice wooded area within a short walking distance from the academy.

Bill and I had gone over there one afternoon for lunch. Seated at a far end of the building by himself was an older man wearing a gray sweater. I paid little attention to him. Bill said to me, "You see that guy sitting over there? Yeah, I think that is James Michener."

"Nah," said I.

He said, "Ya, I think so. Let's go see."

So, we interrupted the guy's meal, and indeed, it was the famous author, Michener. He was very cordial and asked us to be seated and join him for lunch. He was there doing research for his book *Alaska*, of course. I was surprised. He was curious about our lives and didn't talk about himself.

This was the second famous author for me. I had met and had dinner in my last year in Rock Springs with Larry McMurtry at a local inn and dining room. McMurtry met with Cantrell and what was left of the old graveyard crew. He was going to write a book that would possibly become a movie as well, about Cantrell and the Rock Springs boom days' events. This never came to fruition, however, because of a hair-pulling between McMurtry and Attorney Jerry

Spence, who wanted to be the main character in the story rather than Ed and his officers, as I have been told. Anyway, two authors in unlikely places. Not bad, however, more was to come.

In our last year in Wrangell, as I recall, we were busy painting our house exterior. It was a very nice day when some friend stopped by to tell Brenda that Ronald and Nancy Reagan had been touring Alaska and they were due to stop by themselves with secret service, of course, in town shortly. Bush was now president, but this was exciting news. Would they just look the town over from the boat, or would they actually come into town? Suddenly, the town was abuzz.

We hurriedly cleaned up and went downtown. Within minutes, a small high-dollar vessel docked near the Stikine Inn, and here were the Reagans walking up and down the main street of Wrangell. They would pop in a store here or there. They were absolutely friendly to the crowds. Giving autographs and having pictures taken of folks wanting to be photographed with them by all takers. They would visit and answer questions except for "Who would win the next election, Bush or Clinton?" They wouldn't commit to their former vice president as being the winner, and a good thing too. Clinton gave him a thrashing.

I spoke with them and shook Reagan's hand where I met them with no one else at their side on the sidewalk just after they came out of the local drugstore. We took our camera, and Brenda got a picture of Brett and Stephanie (our son and daughter) standing with the Reagans in the drugstore. The kids didn't grasp the opportunity here. They didn't look really interested in the picture, now they laugh when they see it. At the time, the kids felt like they were just having a picture with two old strangers in sweaters and common wear. No crowns, flying banners, honor guards, or trumpets. Oh pooh!

I had an 8×10 of the photo for myself as well as for our kids of the event made. I have hung it in offices where I have worked since. Many times, people have studied the picture and, in surprise, asked who the kids were and how they got a picture like that with the president. They are even more surprised when they find out where the out-of-the-way location was.

I met and visited with Governor Walter Hickel and his wife while passing through a larger Alaska airport one afternoon with my family. We were all seated in a waiting area, waiting for flights. I told my wife that the elderly couple seated over from us being largely ignored looked like former Governor Wally Hickel. She didn't know. I went over and introduced myself. He and his wife were very friendly and glad that I spoke with them. I think they were glad to have a little recognition from someone. He, of course, also served as a secretary of the interior under Nixon.

Many years later, while working in the Atwood Building in Anchorage, which was state offices, I worked on the fifteenth floor. The floor above us was the Anchorage Governor's Office. I rode the elevator and waited in the lobby for it oftentimes with Governor Murkowski and Palin. Palin was a very nice person. She would visit with us just like any normal Alaskan. She had no security detail and drove her state vehicle herself. Murkowski was loud and spoke down to his staff in front of everyone else. He was arrogant. We ignored him. He was just that way, but having been in Washington DC for too long before returning home and becoming a governor didn't help matters either. The couple of staff that accompanied him would chase after him and cower as he came and went into the state building from his large dark chauffeured SUV at the front doors. What a disgusting job that would be.

I was chosen by Chief Brent, the successor to Chief Bill, to be the escort/security officer for Governor Cooper when he came to Wrangell for the day to attend various meetings and events. Cooper was friendly and told me that I could be a state trooper and encouraged me to get busy becoming one. He sent autographed pictures of himself for both of my children after his visit. He had one security man with him. There was one anti-government guy, a big young long-haired wild-looking guy that we had to separate from the governor after he gave a speech at a luncheon at the Stikine Inn. The guy charged up to the governor and started verbally harassing and questioning him. Otherwise, the trip was just a good experience. Cooper was a plant from way down south and only served one term and left the state.

When going to Juneau for training, testing, and grand jury, I always liked to go take a walk and peek of the governor's mansion up on the hill and the old federal building that was now where the legislature met.

I had been in Wrangell several weeks when I had just completed a weekend-day shift. Officer Bill was coming on the afternoon shift. He received a call of a man acting suspiciously at a small trailer house in a small dumpy sort of a trailer court a few miles out the Zimovia Highway. He asked if I would go along.

We found the trailer in the court, which was hanging onto the beginning of a hillside just off the highway. We knocked and were summoned in to find a lone male sitting at a small kitchen table in the run-down, dirty trailer.

He had a small AM/FM radio in front of him with the back off it. He was holding a can of spray lubricant and would spray it into the radio and then stare at it intently while mumbling to himself. We looked at each other. We had never had contact with this man. "What are you doing?" The guy would spray the radio again and then began telling us that it was full of spiders. Big ones! He kept his eyes on the radio.

Obviously, this guy was on LSD, too much marijuana, mental issues, or something. There was not a spider to be seen. But you could not convince him otherwise. Now we had a problem here. We had a local hospital with two no-nonsense doctors. An older woman that gave me my police physical and a gruff middle-aged male that was also a part-time commercial fisherman and drinker. He had been an army doctor in "Nam." He was a surgeon. They would have little patience for this character, especially the surgeon. The hospital was pretty good for a small town. They delivered babies and did surgery there. It also housed long-term aged care. They were not really equipped to house mental patients, however. No rubber rooms.

We had one mental-health guy in Wrangell. He usually would come to the jail when we did an emergency hold on someone acting out, harming themselves, etc. Almost always, within a short time, he would declare them okay, and they could be released! A miracle worker! He was a little more than strange and unusual himself!

We watched the guy and talked to him for a few minutes. He was harmless, just messed up. Well, truth be told, there were some strange people up here. We didn't have enough facilities to hold all of them, they were had to be put somewhere. Too many drugs, booze, and cabin fever.

Not anything else was heard of the "lubricant spray" man until about two nights later. Officer Putz was working a late shift and called me at home for help. It was dark, late, and rainy. An elderly couple had called, very excited they were. A male was at their front door knocking and trying to open the locked door.

The residence was close to the trailer court where the "lubricant spray" weird man had been. I threw on civilian clothes, a duty belt, and a police jacket. We flew out the road and found the guy just as reported. He was still yelling and pounding on the door. We took him into custody without any trouble and booked him into jail.

The poor guy had only been in town for a few days. He was staying at the trailer with a friend who wasn't home much. He had come to Alaska to strike it rich from Idaho. So far, things were looking bleak for him.

I went on duty that afternoon as the chief and his wife, the day dispatcher, and another officer finished up and were leaving. The Idahoan inductee was the only prisoner lodged in the jail now. He had not been a problem so far but was getting antsy.

Working with me that day was dispatcher/jail guard Delores. A heavyset woman in her early 50s. The Idahoan man didn't wait long till after things quieted down for him to start demanding coffee. Delores told him she would get him food and drink at the dinner serving, which was soon. He didn't like that. He started shouting from his cell that he wanted coffee. His demands echoed through the tiled hallway and into the dispatch-office area.

I was in the building and went back to see what could be done. He was pacing in the cell and told me very forcefully that he wanted coffee. "Well, this is not a restaurant, and you'll get coffee with dinner, so calm down." I went out and shut the single door between the office and the jail. Minutes later, all Hades was breaking loose in the cell.

This was an old jail. It had worked fine until the Idahoan dude showed up, though. The cells had old metal bunk beds. He had taken it apart and had one heavy metal rail from the bed, swinging it like a bat. He was beating on the bars and walls of the cell and shouting like mad.

He would not stop now, coffee or not. I told Delores to call help. We were going to have to get in the cell and take him down. She began calling. Got ahold of Lieutenants Dave and Putz. They both lived out the road, so would be in ASAP.

I checked on the lone prisoner again. He had beaten the ceramic toilet to pieces, and water was everywhere now. The post office called from below the jail. They wondered what was going on. They were getting flooded with water. I got the water turned off and tried again to calm him, but nothing doing.

I went back out in the office with the door shut to reduce some of the noise and waited there with Delores, who was starting to look worried. "My God," she said, "he can't get out of there, can he?"

"No," I assured her. "With those bars, he can't get out."

Well, the bars of the jail were heavy, and he didn't affect them one bit. Unknown to me, however, was that the tiled walls were old and easy to break apart with the metal bar. He knocked a hole through the wall and was able to exit the cell. Go into a janitor's closet and exit that via the flimsy unlocked door.

Suddenly, the door between the jail and the office flew open, and here came Mr. Idaho, walking right toward the seated Delores. I was standing just off to her side near the door that exited into the hallway to the court. She leapt from the chair and vaulted over the four-foot-high counter like a pole vaulter and threw open the double doors opening to the hallway and disappeared in a flash. I didn't know that a large, heavy woman could move that fast.

I watched this in the blink of an eye while getting ready to draw my .45. The guy started toward me as I positioned myself confronting him. *Great*, the thought ran through my mind, *a few weeks in Alaska, and I have to kill a guy.* I would have no choice. He was my size, of similar age, and wild. I could not take the chance of having my weapon get into his hands, and clearly, a one-on-one with this wild man would have been dicey at best. I could not let him go past me and exit the building where who knows what could happen. I had time to pull my weapon and shoot him, but he turned and walked into an interview room area, shouting that he was going to get coffee. I drink lots of it myself and have many friends that do too. I never since or afterwards saw anyone want coffee that desperately, though.

Keeping the distance, I followed him. He had stopped between the office and the interview room where there was a small coffee pot, and there he was getting his cup of coffee. About that time, Lieutenant Dave came in, and Putz followed seconds later. "Where is he?" I pointed to the area. We approached him as best we could in the small, cramped surroundings. The floor with about an inch of water on it, the fight was on. His coffee flew out of his hand, and it took all three of us to get him down and cuffed. Then we dragged him out of the water onto a dry carpeted office area and held him on the floor while he thrashed and struggled and yelled.

Volunteer firemen began arriving too. Apparently, Delores ran into the court office that was still open when she fled the police department and had them put out a call for all help that could come. We kept the wild man on his back on the floor while the female doctor was summoned and started pumping him full of a sedative. She couldn't believe how much of the drug it took to quiet him down.

Finally, we tied his legs, and with him out of it, he was put on a stretcher and transported to the hospital. Secured to a bed, an officer with him all night, and the doctor monitoring him and keeping him heavily sedated.

What a wreck he had turned this old federal jail into! Probably the only or one of the few escapes from it in all of its long history. It was a few days before I could get Delores to laugh about her escape over the counter.

The prisoner/escapee was kept sedated, and we took him to Ketchikan by small plane the next morning. He was to be returned home to Idaho, where his family was, and told never to come back, or he would face considerable charges and expenses for the damage.

All in all, it worked out well. A group called C-FOG (Citizens for Open Government) had been formed in Wrangell. They hated the chief and the longtime fire chief as well. They were opposed to the new public safety building. Thought the jail and all was overkill. This quieted their pleas to the town. It was obvious that the jail and old building had outlived their safe and efficient use.

In February, not long after I came back from the academy in Sitka, our son was not feeling well. He was about five months old. We treated him with over-the-counter and home remedies. He seemed okay but just kept not being as lively as one would expect. He was fussy and not sleeping well. We took him to Dr. Schirmer, the female doctor. A very nice Christian lady she was.

She thought he had some cold or flu and kept things low-key, thinking that these new parents were just overly concerned. We followed her advice, but the symptoms continued and worsened. Then he became really sick.

There was a bad strain of infant meningitis around Southeast Alaska at that time, and he had picked it up. This was before there was a vaccination for this disease. It turned into a nightmare for these young new Alaskans.

We kept him at the Wrangell hospital for several days, but he grew sicker despite their valiant efforts. We had to catch an afternoon flight, weather permitting, of the jet going through and get him to the Children's Hospital in Seattle. We did this, and they sent a nurse along with us. An ambulance met us at the plane and off to the hospital.

Brett was now under the treatment of pediatricians that had special training for these types of illnesses. However, he was very sick. I stayed for several days and had to get back to work once that it looked like the worst was past. Pastor Terry, the chief, many of the townspeople, and my co-workers were helpful and supportive of us in this rough time.

Families and friends were praying day and night for us and our little guy. Steve Reichel showed up at the hospital and helped all he could. Brenda's mom and dad flew up in their own plane to be with Brenda and Brett. Several weeks, and they finally were taken to the airport by Steve and sent back home to Wrangell.

After being home for several days, things did not seem right with Brett, and soon, he had a relapse. Very, very sick. It did not look good. Children died or had results of retardation, blindness, deafness, and all kinds of terrible things over this. We later learned of some that resulted in nearby communities with such tragic results.

It was onto an afternoon jet again. One flight came north in the morning en route to Petersburg, Sitka, and Juneau, and then in the afternoon, it returned south on the same path and onto Ketchikan and Seattle.

Brenda and Brett went to Ketchikan and were in the hospital for several days there. Things seemed to look up but then not so good. On to the children's hospital again. After another lengthy stay repeated, Brett seemed to be over the relapse.

My family returned home. Brett was a happy baby but looked skinny. The hospital sent him home with a large glass bottle of phenobarbital. He had some seizures, and the doctors said that these would continue throughout his life unless he was on a daily dose of the drug. We gave it to him by eyedropper. He hated it, and it made him nauseous.

A couple of days passed. This had to stop. We were not going to settle for this situation. We agreed that I was going to pour the drug down the toilet and there was to be no more of this attack by the evil one (Satan) on our child and home. That took faith, which God honors, and it is the only way to please Him, the Word of God—the Bible—tells us.

Our son continued to get his health back and never took another dose of phenobarbital. He never had a seizure, and he had no effects ever from all of that attack on his health.

I had a dream one night. Not a regular dream or a too-much-pizza dream but one from God. I dreamed that Brenda, who was now pregnant again, had a little girl. The little infant had red hair. I told this to Brenda. Well, red hair didn't run in our families.

We had now rented a two-family house at 8.5 Mile Zimovia Hwy. It was a newer home perched on the side of a steep mountain just off the gravel road. The beach was on the other side of the roadway. It was a beautiful spot. The view was out onto the Zimovia

Strait on the west side of Wrangell Island. To the west of us was a beautiful view of Wornoski and Etolin Islands with their high timbered mountains. I would stand on the deck late in the day and listen to wolves howl nearby. It was a secluded area with bald eagles on the beach and large Sitka spruce trees covering the area.

We had lived there only a short time when it was time to take Brenda to the hospital. She had everything in the car. I drove her in. Yes. Dr. Schirmer was going to keep her. It was time. She told me her bag was in the car, but I guess I was a little rattled. I drove clear back to the house before I realized that the bag was in the trunk. Quickly back to the hospital I went. "Where you'd go?" Brenda asked. I downplayed this slip and mumbled something, but she and the nurse knew that I had been hit with the new daddy bug.

Brenda's mother, Dee, had come up to stay with us till Brenda had the baby, then we were all going south to take her home and have several weeks of vacation. Later that sunny afternoon, a little red-haired girl arrived. Stephanie Jo. This was the summer of 1986. That whole month of August, it had not rained. One dry sunny beautiful day after another. It was dusty now. When we left on the jet in early September for the trip south, it began to rain. It rained the entire time we were away, and when we returned later that month, it was still raining. Ahh, back to normal weather!

Before we left for vacation and just a few days after having a new baby home, I took all of us out on our cabin cruiser. It was calm sunny weather. We went clear out past Elephant's Nose—the north tip of Wornoski Island—and into a hole between it and Etolin Island. I had caught some big halibut and skates here.

The halibut started in. I had two poles in the pole holders and was on the open aft of the boat. The family was sitting inside the cabin with the door open, enjoying the quiet area. I had one pole in front of me and one to my rear.

I heard a loud snap behind me, and when I quickly turned, I saw that the pole was going over the side of the boat, mount and all. I made a lunge for it but off to the deep went a good halibut pole and heavy reel. A large halibut undoubtedly had grabbed onto it and pulled the whole mounted rod holder loose from the boat and took everything.

Often when we were out fishing, anchored up in a good spot like this, we would have whales breach around us. On occasion, a large log ship from Japan would pass by—headed to the wood mill or a state ferry. Eagles and seagulls were all about.

We rented the house at that location for close to a couple of years. In icy winters, the driveway was not passable. Nothing but ice. Brenda nearly went over the edge of it one day with her car sliding backwards toward the cliff with the highway below it. That would have been a terrible disaster. I was out shoving some snow away from the place and stood helpless, watching her along with little Brett in his car seat, heading for the edge of this cliff. For no obvious reason, the rear of the car stopped at the icy edge. Angels at work again! I don't doubt it, and you shouldn't either!

I kept Buck the black lab on a chain at the front of the home. Sometimes the bottom of the house was occupied, but often, we had the place to ourselves. I was going to work that afternoon and let him off the chain for a short time while I put on my uniform.

I went out a few minutes later to call him as he wasn't around. I found him at the bottom of the driveway. He had gotten onto the road edge and been hit by a vehicle. He was dead. We were devastated. That was a hard day to go to work on.

I wrapped him in a blanket and placed him near the house. The next day we took him onto the beach below the house. Much of the ground was frozen except for the beach. I dug a hole while Brenda and Brett looked on and placed my Wyoming buddy into it. "I will miss you, Buck." This country was hard on pets as well as people.

We purchased a home, our first at 405 Zimovia Hwy. This was in town and only one other house over from the newly completed public safety building. That would make it nice to walk to work. This house was the home of the police officer that had been disabled and never returned to work. They moved and sold the home to us. We lived there until moving back to Wyoming in 1992 for three years.

I was running around with Officer Bill and then the Martins. Hunting and fishing when not by myself or taking the family out.

Brenda's folks came up to see us in spring. Bill and I took Lenard, Brenda's father, out on Bill's boat fishing. The weather was great. We went out one day, and the fishing was a little slow, but I caught my first big king salmon while we were anchored fishing for halibut.

Oh, it was a nice fish. So, we put him on the heavy cord and tied him to the back of the boat after a bit of more slow fishing. We decided to try another spot. I asked Bill if the fish would be okay there. "Oh ya, no problem." I wasn't really comfortable with this, however, as we sped off to another location.

We arrived at another spot and got all set up to fish. I checked on my large king salmon and found that the back half of him had been chopped off by the boat's motor. It was kind of funny, and Bill and Lenard had a half-smirk on their faces, but I was not too happy about this. Always something with Bill.

The next day we were out fishing for halibut. All three of us caught our limit in nice big fish. While pulling them on board with a big gaff hook, Bill got one on board that was overly active. The big fish was flopping around really bad on the floor of the boat. Bill took the gaff and started pounding the fish on the head to kill him. As he reared back and forth with the hook, holding it by the wood handle, he was hitting the fish with the blunt end of the metal hook. The sharp end was catching the rear of Bill's coat with each strike.

Bill was wearing a new feathered-down coat that his wife had just bought him. (Bill married a woman from Minnesota, Susie. A really nice young woman.) Lenard and I stood in shock behind Bill, watching him swing wildly with the gaff. We were both silent, wanting to shout at Bill, but it would have done no good. He was in a frenzy. The fish was going to lose. Big rips were being torn in the coat with each strike of the sharp metal hook contacting the shell of the garment. Goose feathers were pouring out of the coat and floating all over the boat. Bill was oblivious to this; he went right on with all his attention on the fish. Finally satisfied that he had killed the large halibut and stopped the wild flopping of the fish, he rose up and turned toward us. He looked puzzled as white feathers were all over the place. We told him what happened. He looked like he could vomit and not from seasickness. "Really?" he said as we told him how the jacket was ruined. I felt bad for him, but there was a little satisfaction in all of this for me over the careless handling of my chopped-off first king salmon.

My family came up to see us, minus my father, who had passed away from premature death brought on by himself. All the early past years of wild living had caught up to him, and he refused to leave them in the past and enjoy life. We received a call around 3 a.m. on December 7th—Pearl Harbor Day, in 1989. A call at that hour that awakens one out of sleep is usually not good. I answered the phone, expecting it to be the police department calling for assistance. Instead, it was the sad voice of my mother. Dad had gone out in a car south of Rock Springs and ended his life late on the 6th, eight days before his sixtieth birthday. He never cared to come to visit us in Alaska and seldom left home now. I had talked to him several times about getting right with God, and he always said someday he might. He passed up many chances to do it. Did he finally get things right, even in a darkened state of mind?

My family came during the Fourth of July activities. We had a grand time. I arranged a tour flight for all of them one afternoon in a small plane that flew over the area. Then I took them out in two parties on our boat for halibut fishing. My sister Jan was definitely not suited to the ocean. The water was like glass when I had her and my other sister Tammy out together. We caught some nice fish and had a great day in the sunny calm conditions. Jan was not one to complain, but she had been nauseous the whole trip. Once back at the harbor, she vomited up her socks. Then had a laugh about it. She was cheery in most conditions. Tammy had done fine but knew that Jan was feeling sick on the water. She dared not tell her clueless brother about it, though, or Jan would have pitched her overboard.

Brett was just a little guy when I started taking him out on easy day hunts with me. About two he was. He learned to sit patiently for hours if we needed to watch the area for bears or deer. Usually not in the best of weather either. We would usually go out in the four-wheel drive. It had developed a quirk of the headlights going off on the rough roads. I would have to fiddle with the light switch on the dash until they came back on.

On one trip, it had gotten quite dark on our way home, and we were probably twenty miles out of town. The lights quit working, and I could not get them to come back on. It made driving very treacherous on the narrow, curvy mountain roads. Traffic was very light, but it was really risky to meet an oncoming vehicle with no lights.

I messed and messed with the switch, and the lights refused to work. Brett was watching all of this and said, "Why don't we pray and ask Jesus to fix the lights for us?" I was surprised at this and agreed, although I didn't put a lot of stock into it and hated to see him disappointed.

We prayed a simple prayer for the four-wheel drive's lights, and then I tried them. They came on without hesitation. We owned that vehicle all of the years we were in Wrangell, at least another five or six years from that time. We used the vehicle all the time and had it in the rough country continually. I sold it when we moved to Wyoming in 1992, and those lights worked perfectly all of that time.

My dentist in Wrangell was like most residents there, a hunter and fisherman. He was telling me on one visit to his office and while I was in the torture seat being worked over about a remote forest service cabin between Wrangell and Petersburg that he had gone duck and goose hunting to and had seen brown bears as well as black bears around the beaches. The cabins were nice. Dry and heated and could be rented for several days for a nominal fee at that time. We used them and the free-use shelters many times on outdoor trips. This particular cabin was not easy to access, and the area was near a glacier. It could only be accessed at occasional high tides by boat or floatplane, and the mouth of the Stikine River had to be crossed. This could be a tricky maneuver in itself.

Later, as I contemplated this information, I was finally able to get everything lined up at just the right time and made a lone trip to the cabin to bear-hunt. I had Wrangell Air fly me in. I had the cabin for three days, as I recall. It was a beautiful area with big meadows of muskeg, heavy timber, sloughs, high mountains, and the LeConte Glacier just around the corner. Iceberg calves were floating about in the ocean bay out from the nice little cabin.

The weather was not bad but turned worse and became rainy and socked in after I arrived that afternoon. I had to wait till the next day to hunt since I had flown in, so I just checked out the area near the cabin and settled in.

The next morning, I crossed the nearby slough and went into the openings to the north of the cabin. I had a 7mm Magnum rifle with 175-grain federal ammunition. Not the best bear killer, but I had confidence in the gun. I had only been out about five minutes when I walked smack into a large brown bear facing me about one hundred yards distant. He was out feeding in the grass and spotted me at the same time as I tried to conceal myself at one small lone tree in the opening. He was not afraid. This was not the setup I had hoped for. I was more than nervous and got the shakes, buck fever. The bear turned sideways to me. They do this in an effort to show their size to whoever they think they need to in order to try to avoid an encounter.

Well, this was not what I had in mind, but I didn't come here to just look. I took good aim on the bear and fired. The shot hit his front shoulder, which was a preferred shot. It raised the large animal off the ground a few inches and rolled him over. He came up on his feet and ran like a racehorse. Fortunately for me, he ran away from me and out into the opening. If he had charged me at this speed, I would have been hard-pressed to stop him, I feel quite certain.

The bear ran and then slowed and turned back sideways to me. He was now walking toward the timber. He was now about 150 yards away. I fired again. He went down on his belly but got back up again and walked into the heavy timber.

I was never able to locate the bear. Boy, I hated that. Now I wish he would have come at me instead of running off. I spent the rest of my time trying to find that beautiful large animal but sans bear. There were moose in the area and lots of ducks and geese on this spring trip.

I had a great time except for losing that bear. I returned there several more times with Randy Martin for a backup shot. He carried an 8mm Magnum, and I now had a .338 Magnum with 250-grain federal premium cartridges. I was able to get a really nice male brown bear on the slough just a bit over from where I lost the first bear, and then I also got a really nice male black bear on the beach north of the cabin. These were all spring hunts, and the bears had prime hides. I helped Randy shoot his brown bear one, on fall south of Wrangell Island. It was a pretty bear, but the hide was thin compared to the spring bears.

We took Randy's aluminum boat into the cabins usually, but on the trip where I shot the black bear on the beach, we had Wrangell Air fly us in. Dan, the pilot, had been flying for years and had now seen his better days. His son had flown me in on my first failed bear hunt. He was an excellent pilot in his 20s. Dan, the father, had flown Randy and me in on a goat hunt near Tyee Lake. He was still doing well flying then, and we both got goats. That is some rugged hunting and not for most.

On this black bear trip to the cabin, the flight in was nice. Dan showed up several days later to pick us up as scheduled. The weather was nice, and we loaded the plane with my large black bear hide that we had caped and the meat in meat packs. Loaded up all our gear, and we took off across the bay.

The plane was going pretty fast past jagged rocks sticking up in the bay, but when Dan pulled the gear to get us airborne, we settled back onto the water in the floatplane. He took off again and repeated this act.

Randy and I were looking at each other and thinking, *What the heck? We don't have that much weight to have this problem.* Dan looked at us and said, "Which way is the wind blowing?"

"You've got to be kidding. Who's the pilot here?"

He kept looking around and checking a rope hanging from the wing and finally figured out that he was not going into the wind. He turned the plane, and we began racing out of the bay. This time, when he pulled the gear, we rose up with hesitation and off toward the Wrangell Airport. Boy, oh boy, no more flying for us with the older Dan. His son was named Dan also.

The first time we flew with old Dan, he was a good pilot. Randy Martin and I flew to Upper Tyee Lake to begin our first goat hunt. The weather was good. This was a new country to us. We each had a registration—goat tag. Which meant we had purchased our twenty-five-dollar hunting license, and then everything else was free except for a brown bear tag. There were no drawings to have to hassle with. You simply went into the fish and game and got whatever tags you desired. Very nice.

We were flying by high peaks when I spotted a nice open area up high where goats were nearby. I said to Dan, "I wonder if we could land over there," as I pointed out the area I liked.

Dan chuckled and said, "Ya, one-time." Okay, bad idea.

He landed us on the high lake, and we asked him where he thought we had to take off to on foot. He pointed out a high mountain and said, "Try that." I think he had no idea of where to go any more than we did. However, we had seen a good-size herd of goats up on the tops of those areas as we flew in. They were hanging around snowfields.

Off we went on the steep, thickly timbered, and vegetated mountain. We had our rifles and about forty-five-fifty-pound packs. Everything we needed scaled down as much as possible to stay for a number of days. In fact, if bad weather set in, we may be here for who knows how long before we could get back down and the plane could return. We had made arrangements with Dan for the pickup in the afternoon several days hence.

After hours of climbing, slipping, and struggling, we got to the tops and made camp. Beautiful country. We could see in every direction. Mountains, lakes, glaciers, ocean bay far off and below us. We were at the beginning of the mainland. This was wild country. No planes flying nearby and no one around for many miles.

The hunting was slow. The goats apparently scattered when the plane flew by them. We hunted until we finally spotted a lone goat standing out on a glacier crossing between a deep ravine below. We were about 500 yards below the goat. Randy decided to try for the goat. He asked me to shoot as well. The mountain area was steep, and we were looking skyward to make the shot.

We got really good and steady. He fired, and the goat was hit but remained standing. I fired, and the goat was hit again. He reeled and fell off into the deep ravine. We watched as it bounced off rocks and brushed on the way down, the good part was that it was moving closer to us as it tumbled along.

The goat came to rest in the ravine, and we were able to climb down and access him. A nice nanny. Nice horns about eight inches in length. The coats were not as nice as they would be in the late fall, but this country was not accessible then for the most part, and if it was, it would take major time to hunt it. Time that neither of us had with jobs and young families.

We were thrilled. We gutted and skinned the goat. Then deboned it and packed the meat into bags, which were loaded on our packs. The meat bags were true Alaskan items. Not the stuff sold at sporting goods stores. They were not used but still very durable old bedsheets that our wives had sewn into bags. I still use them in Wyoming. They are far superior to those for purchase. The weather remained pretty good, and we continued to hunt out of our small high camp once we got situated with the goat there.

Hunting was slow again, and I had not had a chance for one. We were down to our last day when we got up as it barely got light that morning. Randy spotted a lone goat high above us on a steep vegetated slope. I was not passing this up. Once again, it was a shot of above 500 yards up a steep, high ridge and slope. We got situated again, and I fired. The goat was hit. Randy fired, and it was hit again and disappeared, tumbling down the slope.

We scrambled up the slick mess. We couldn't afford to lose traction and go sliding down the slope as it ended in a steep drop-off into a canyon and ravine below. This slope was covered all the way up with green slick leafy growth. Finally, we got to the goat lying dead in a rocky spot on the slope. We took care of it and carefully got back to camp. This had to be a rush deal as we had to have everything on our backs, got off this mountain, and be at the lake for pickup this afternoon. Interesting, however, was the fact that my goat took a terrible fall and lost one of its horns. Randy's goat took even a far worse fall in rocks and a glacier area and yet had both horns intact. Not to worry, this was a common problem for goat hunters in this country that was easily remedied by the taxidermist I chose in Sitka. Randy and his wife taxidermized his goat.

We were moving like madmen to get camp packed, the goats on our packs, and get down to the lake. Hours of going in that direction, and we were both worn out with over one-hundred-pound packs and rifles. Muddy, beaten by brush. Scarred by falls onto rocks. Full of devil's club thorns and wet with sweat and the moisture from the wet brush, we got to the lake area. There was one more steep drop-off that was covered in trees and brush. *Get to the bottom of it, and we are there.* Randy heard a bear below us. We were covered in goat blood and had all of this fresh meat on our backs. We yelled, and the bear, which we couldn't see, seemed to leave.

The logical thing would be to keep going and look for a better way down to the lake if one could be found. Time was short, and we were exhausted. We decided to take our chances and just step off the bank and free-fall to the bottom through all of the brush and trees. It was hard to say with certainty really how far down that was or what we would hit on the way down. Loaded heavy, I stepped off and flew through and past trees, limbs, devil's club, and brush like a jungle. Then I hit bottom. *Thunk.* Randy did likewise. We made it. No bear appeared, and only about a half-mile further on the slopping area, and we would be at the lake.

Joy, when we got there. We did it, old buddy. Completed a tough hunt in a wild country with minimal supplies. Best yet, we got goats. Dan flew in shortly afterwards, and off to the airport we went. Our clothes were tattered from the trip. We were full of devil's club thorns and many cuts and bruises, but we were two happy guys. Two goats to have taxidermized by Randy and his wife and lots of good goat dinners in-store.

Randy was with me when I got my brown bear that I mentioned previously. We had gone to the area with his boat for several days. We had spotted the bear along grass flats at the far back area of the slough. There were big bear beds in the grass flats. Five to six feet in diameter where the tall grass was smashed down, and a bear had lodged there. We had to be cautious not to jump a bear in one of them as we crept along, trying to close the distance on the bear we spotted.

Randy climbed up a small tree as we neared and was able to spot the bear again. He was alone, probably a big male, just at the edge of grass and trees. We crawled in. I had to crawl over a small ridge in front of us to be able to get a prone shot at him.

As I crawled, I could just see the top of the bear as he fed on grass. My knee barely hit a brush that only made a slight sound, but that bear jumped and was in the timber in about two hops. I had no chance to shoot. I moved back just a bit and joined Randy. We set up by trees where we were somewhat concealed and had a good view of the area.

The bear knew something was there, and he didn't like it. He began roaring and knocking over small trees just out of our view. This went on for about a minute. This, too, is a very wild country. No one in the area for many miles. Bears, large brown and black alike. Goats on the peaks above. Sitka black-tailed deer, and a few moose. This, too, is the edge of the mainland. We were staying in the nearby forest service cabin, which was like a mansion in this setting. Especially compared to camps when one is goat-hunting the high country.

There was not a breeze, and the bear went quiet. Then there were no birds making a racket or anything else. It was like time stopped, and it was deathly quiet. We sat like statues watching. Suddenly, the large beautiful bear stepped out of the thick timber to the edge and stood there looking back and forth. He appeared ready to battle whatever may have disturbed his afternoon feeding.

He looked right past us in our camo clothing and concealed as we were. I wait until he took another step out into the opening. Couldn't let him return to the timber. Then, at about fifty yards, as he was broadside to us, I fired my .338 with 250-grain ammo into his left front shoulder. He fell over onto his left side and lied that moaning loudly. Randy then, as we had agreed, fired too and shot him through the upper back. Within a few seconds, the bear was quiet. Wow, this was not rabbit hunting. What an adventure.

After calming down, we were finally able to skin the bear and pack the heavy bloody hide back across the muddy slough and go the mile or so along the grass flat back to the cabin and boat. We had a great time. Hot dinner and coffee on the woodstove in the camp, and it was not raining.

Brown and grizzly bear meat is not usually eaten by humans. That is the only big animal I have taken that the meat was left. We ate all black bears over the years. Not to worry, however. The meat did not go to waste.

Early the next morning, we snuck back to the area where the carcass was left. Randy still had his bear tag, or if a large black bear was on the meat pile, that would work too. The large Sitka spruce and cedar trees were full of bald eagles as we approached the spot. We came around the little bend by the slough, and we were in for a surprise. No bears, but the area all around the carcass was tramped down to mud. It had been grass of about six inches high or more. There was not a speck of meat left on that entire carcass, and the gut pile was nearly gone. The bald eagles had a late dinner and breakfast that was hard to beat, thanks to hunters.

Once again, as with many of my Alaskan animals, Randy and his wife taxidermized them at cost for me. That was a bargain. I was a licensed gun dealer, so I would try to reciprocate for Randy and order guns, ammo, and equipment at cost for them. Still, the low-cost taxidermy saved me buckets of money.

One early June, Randy and I took his boat and our wives and went to the cabin area again, where I got the brown bear. It was a late black-bear-hunting/camping trip. We had nice weather and stayed for two days at the cabin. The grass was knee-high, the bugs were getting bad, and the bears had gone off to mate in areas further from the beaches and grass flats.

We cruised out into the bay one afternoon. The bay had numerous calves from the LeConte Glacier afloat in it. There was one particularly large iceberg calf floating, and Randy pulled the boat up to it and told me to keep it alongside the berg. It was impressive. He then, to my displeasure, jumped onto the floating berg and stood there for a few minutes while we laughed and warned him to be careful at the same time.

We filled a cooler full of chunks of the bergs before going home. We kept them all summer in the freezer and would put small chunks into our soft drinks. They would fizz like a seltzer type of tablet until they disappeared. Company really enjoyed this icy treat.

Randy and his family heard so much about Wyoming from me that they moved there in 1992 just before we left. We had many more adventures in Wyoming together, and we are fast friends to this day, even though he has remarried. He is a friend that stuck by us through all times and just a fun guy to go with. Didn't complain and was always ready for an adventure, regardless of the toughness that it may present. He is a few years younger than me but had injured his knees playing high school football. He had several operations that set him back, but once healed up, he would transverse the ruggedest of the country right along with me. Believe me, the Alaska country is not for road hunters, those who like to just get out and have a pleasant hunt, or those who prefer nice weather or are picky with their equipment. This country is more than hard on guns. Bring a good gun, and you are sure to go back home with something that only once resembled a fine weapon.

The country was hard on other equipment too. Tent zippers would rust. Blued rifles, which were still most commonly in use, would turn rusty overnight if not constantly watched and cared for. Clothes, packs, and other rifles were beaten up traveling the rough, thick vegetation and then in boats with the ocean spray and water. That really would deteriorate stuff. Rain, snow, and wind. Devil's club and thornbush. Mud and muskegs. Randy fell into a deep hole in a muskeg on one of our deer hunts on Wrangell Island as we hunted apart. We had driven out the road in his four-wheel drive and then took off in separate directions. It was November and pretty damp and cold.

I returned to the vehicle later that morning to find that he had just arrived there a few minutes earlier. He was wet and muddy. About frozen. He had gone through the muskeg without warning as he crept along looking for deer. He went up past his waist and, for a long time, thought he might not be able to get out. Finally, he did and stumbled back to his vehicle where he had the heater going full blast and was trying to thaw out. What fun! His rifle was wet and covered in mud.

A favorite thing about Southeast Alaska was to go out into the brush or, while being out there, pick the large luscious blue- and salmonberries. I would often sit in the late summer or fall while hunting, while watching an area taking a break, just eat them by the handfuls.

The berries grew prolifically. The bears loved them, and they gave the meat a nice taste. We would go out and pick buckets of them. Brenda would make wonderful jelly and blueberry muffins. We had a little black poodle, Licorice, and a black lab, Buck, that the kids had bought with some of their permanent fund money one year. The dogs came as puppies from the Lower 48. The poodle was a tough little critter and would give the lab a run for the money. We would take the dogs with us, berry-picking. They would eat the berries without the leaves off the branches on their own.

Deer hunting began on August 1st. For the first couple of months, a hunter had to take a long high hike—climb into the alpine areas of the mountains. It was nice up on the top if the weather wasn't too fretful. I became spoiled hunting this country. There was no requirement or need to wear hunter orange as you very seldom saw another person, even at your own party. Once we split up to hunt, we seldom would see each other again until meeting on a beach, at a vehicle, or some other designated point. There were no cell phones or way to contact each other, and tracking in this country was nearly impossible. It was certainly important not to get turned around or injured.

Later in the hunting season, as the rut began for deer around November and snow and bad weather pushed the animals lower, there was no need to go up high. Bears and often deer were on the beaches or near them.

Randy Martin, I, Brett, and once Randy's son would go to Berg Bay in December to stay in the forest service cabin there and duck- and goose-hunt. This, too, was on the mainland on what was called the back channel. It was the Blake Canal on the east side of Wrangell Island. Wild country. I saw my first brown bear on the grass flats there. I had gone there in a boat one spring with two men from our church that worked for the airlines. We were mostly just running around looking the country over. We were slowly motoring along the bay when out of high grass, a large bear stood up about fifty yards away. I was glad we had not walked up on him. He looked like he was ready for trouble. We left him alone. He was a fine-looking creature, but he did not care to be disturbed.

The days were short in December and not usually really pleasant weather. We would come into the warm cabin that had a lantern and was heated by an oilstove after being out hunting all day, cold and damp. That was like heaven. Randy would cook deer steak and corn bread on the stove with loads of coffee.

One year the snow was five-foot deep there. Another year was wet and rainy. On one trip that only Randy and I had gone, it was a slow hunting, but I had shot two mallard ducks. We went back to the cabin to take a break for the late morning. The ducks were still flopping around on the shore after I shot them, and they fell, so I twisted their necks, and we put both into a backpack that Randy was wearing.

We arrived on the trail and boardwalk at the cabin about twenty minutes later, and Randy was going to hang the ducks up outside. When he emptied the pack, both ducks sprung to life and started running around. One headed for the area under the cabin that was nearly inaccessible to us. We sprang into action quick once over the shock and got one with a boat oar, and the other just had to be man-handled. Not one Lazarus but two!

I had a number of bad or risky boat rides, as you might imagine. We were careful with the weather as the water could churn up in a very short time and the tides always complicated things too.

Most boats would have a smaller kicker motor in addition to the main motor in case it failed. Only a fool ran around without flotation devices, flares, good VHF radio, and so on, and then it could still be risky, and you were on your own most of the time. The Coast Guard were appreciated in this country with their rescue boats and helicopters. At times someone had a medical emergency. The weather would not permit any kind of travel to get out to advanced medical care. Usually, the coast guard could get in for a medivac with their large copters out of Ketchikan or Juneau. Their rescues of ships, boaters, hunters lost or injured on land, and so on are legendary.

One particular boat ride that I did not like was on the back channel only a few miles down the channel. It was a nice spring day. I had taken Brenda and the kids out, and we were trolling for king salmon. We had been out for several hours when out of nowhere, the wind started. Clouds poured in, and by the time we had our poles reeled in, the kicker (small outboard motor) pulled up, and the large outboard motor going, the water was bad. We had to move at a low speed and hit the waves head-on. Water often going over the cabin from the crashing waves. The wind got worse as we rounded Wrangell Island and passed by the airport. If the motor failed, we could be in big trouble, and other possibilities loomed as well.

I stayed calm, but I did not like this with all of the family on board. After a long torturous ride, we were able to pull into the Inner Harbor, where I was hoping to tie up and wait out this mess. Once there, there was nowhere to land the boat. We could not stay in the harbor; water was rolling in too much. I didn't want to head to our boat slip at Shoemaker Bay, about four miles south of here, but I had no choice.

Out into the violent wind and terrible ride again. After a long time of praying to get there and fighting to keep the boat on course, we made it. Boy, I kissed the ground when we got tied up in our slip. I kissed the ground other times too, but I didn't mind it as bad if the family was safe at home.

I went commercial fishing one time with a Christian friend, Chad, young, very competent fisherman. His wife, nephew, and I went out for the twenty-four-hour opener on halibut. The weather was good. I had not commercially fished before, so this was on-the-job training. Prepping equipment and then going out and laying miles of line, attaching hooks very carefully and rapidly as the line fed out. Buoys were put out, and then we would return to the different sets and check them. Pulling in the line and placing the fish in the boat's hold. Reset the lines and keep going. There were few breaks, and it was all steady work but good work.

When the time limit was up, we had to have all lines in, and we had a pretty good load of halibut. Chad—a nice thirty-eight-foot vessel. Then we were all tired but had to take the fish into Wrangell and unload and sell them at one of the local processes. I made a little over a thousand dollars for my share in that twenty-four-hour time period. I used most of my money to buy Brenda a Mother's ring that she wanted at the Schirmer's Jewelry shop in Wrangell. Bill Schirmer was a large talkative man. He was the brother of Dr. Harriet Schirmer. We had also bought a station wagon from them and numerous pieces of jewelry. Bill and his wife operated a high-quality jewelry shop until they retired and moved south.

Randy Martin and I went out another time with Chad on his vessel. He was going to put out shrimp pots and work on his boat at a cabin-dock area he had just south of Wrangell Island. Once again, the weather was great. We were to help him with the pots and then use his skiff to roam the beaches for bears while he stayed on his boat and worked on it.

We had a great time and saw a mama (sow) brown bear, she was large and beautiful with two playful cubs prancing around by her. This was on the south end of Wrangell Island. Good thing we were out in the boat about one hundred yards. She gave us a look like any closer, and she would show us what for. She was a powerful-looking animal. They remained walking along the open beach as we cruised slowly by. That is a sight I will never forget and miss seeing, although I had close encounters with grizzly bears later in northwest Wyoming while sheep- and elk-hunting. Wolves too. We had a great trip and came back with a large share of fresh shrimp.

I ran around some hunting and fishing with Brian. He had grown up in Wrangell. He was a hunting and fishing nut. He was a commercial fisherman as well as a grade-school teacher. He was pro-law enforcement. He was a good Christian man. He had married pastor Terry's oldest daughter, who was our friend as well.

He introduced me to Bob, a retired teacher who had lived there many years. Bob was single—never married. He had a nice cabin of his own at the mouth of the Stikine River. He took the family there one day that I had to work, but I did go there another time with Bob,

Brian, and Steve, a friend of Brian. We duck-hunted and got a bunch of mallards. The weather got worse as the day went on. We had a nasty ride back in Bob's open boat. A cold, wet, drenching every fifteen-twenty seconds from the crashing waves and rain for about forty-five minutes. It was a great trip, though.

There were low-class, criminal people in Wrangell, as bad as you would find in any large city. Drug addicts, alcoholics, child molesters, thieves, no-goods, and perverts. But there were many fine people, too, and we made lifelong friends there.

Chief Bill promoted me to sergeant and also made me assistant jail administrator along with Lieutenant Dave. Things were going pretty well on the job, and we stayed busy with our five to six men. We had a call one night of a shooting in the restroom of the Stikine Inn. This was a good-size nice two-story restaurant, bar, and hotel. A commercial fisherman in his 40s and a logger in his late 20s or so had been after the same woman that had been the fisherman's steady girlfriend. The woman was playing both guys but had been favoring the logger. The fisherman had enough.

The logger was using a urinal when the fisherman walked in and shot him with a .30-30 rifle. His life ended quickly before he could enjoy finishing his bladder concerns. The bar had seen the fisherman come in with the gun and called the police. The officer on duty sped there but, not certain who the fisherman was, just noticed a vehicle leaving the bar area quickly as he arrived. The people inside confirmed for the officer that the person racing off was the murder suspect.

The officer remained on scene to try to aid the victim and secure the area. The chief and I responded off duty to the Inner Boat harbor, where the fisherman docked his live on vessel. We suspected he had raced off to it. We arrived within minutes but too late. The fisherman had boarded his vessel and taken it out a few hundred yards into the open water. He set the boat on fire and shot himself. It was all recovery and investigation of a murder-suicide then. It was raining like mad.

Another time we had a longtime resident that lived in his boat in the harbor area in town that had been reported to have molested a young female relative. The chief called the man and told him what the allegations were and asked him to come in for a visit about this. The man agreed and said he would be up with an hour or so.

Not too long after this, we had a report of a single gunshot in the harbor area. The guy had gone to a nearby gun store. Bought a brand-new pistol and ammo and returned to his vessel and shot himself.

Some fisherman got into a brawl in one of the bars one night, and one of them gouged the other's eye out with his fingers. From small incidents to serious crimes. Alaska had no shortage in even the smallest village.

Chief Bill decided to retire, and maybe he had listened to me too much, but he ended up in Newcastle, Wyoming, a few years after retiring, where he became their chief.

Brent was the new chief. He was a very large, loud, and vulgar-talking individual. He would berate his mother, who had survived his father, in front of female and male employees and loudly curse her and tell of his hate for her and other women. Call her the vilest of names.

I worked okay with him and could have had a good deal of upward mobility in the agency had I catered to him, but I could not abide much of his logic and actions. I had relinquished my promotion.

He was able to network well with the troopers and get good undercover people that resulted in many search warrants, arrests, and confiscation of considerable quantities of cocaine, marijuana, and other illegal substances. We filled much of the new jail with suspects several times that had felony arrest warrants for sale and/or possession of drugs. Took down one large sophisticated marijuana grow operation that was being operated by a young guy near his home where, in addition to his own children, he and his wife had several other foster children, and he was a little league baseball coach. Most of the grow operation was in a large metal building by his home, however, when we searched the residence as well, we found a room with marijuana being hung up and dried out, too, where the kids had access to.

Chief Brent asked me to be the school resource officer, which was a fairly new concept at that time, especially for Alaska. He sent me to Drug Abuse Resistance Education (DARE) training in Mesa, Arizona. I began my new assignment that summer. Had a nice office, worked all weekdays except for evening meetings with local groups and occasional drug training on weekends for EMTs and fire personnel that I would instruct. I wore a suit and did very little enforcement then.

There was resistance to having a police officer in the schools at first from the new liberal female school superintendent. After I met with several local community groups about this resistance, in a matter of days, the doors were opened wide to me. I enjoyed this. I worked primarily with the fifth and sixth graders to start but then expanded the classes to junior high and lower elementary grades. I also later began teaching the NRA gun safety classes to elementary students. This was well received.

Part of my job was public relations with the community by attending events, writing weekly articles for the *Wrangell* paper, interviewing with radio station KSTK, and raising funds for materials from the Elks club and others.

I did this for over a year but then decided to turn it over to Officer Putz and return to enforcement work. I later did DARE and Eddie Eagle classes in Klawock schools while still involved in enforcement or administration work as well.

We had nice black and red DARE T-shirts that would be given to the public, teachers, and graduating DARE students. Chief Brent wanted one. I had to specifically order an XXX-Large for him, and it was tight when he wore it.

He and I went to the grand jury, this was common in Alaska for felony cases, the district attorneys did not just file a charge like in Wyoming. They had grand juries operating constantly and would issue charges once a person was indicted by the jury. We usually had to Sitka or Ketchikan, and it was often a two-day trip.

On the one trip that Brent and I made together to Sitka, we had lunch at a fast-food joint. He had an inflated ego. We ate, and, of course, he had two trays of food to my one. We finished and were getting up to leave. I was gathering up my empty food and drink cartons, like any decent customer does, to dispose of them in the garbage can. He said, "Just leave it," and left his mess all over the table. I ignored stupid stuff like that from him.

I made one hunting trip with him in his open boat up the Stikine River. A wild and beautiful place. We were going to Twin Lakes to hunt-bear in the spring and stay at the forest service cabin. I had my rifle and one pack. He had boxes of food and unneeded junk. He brought a big but needed bottle of talcum powder with him. He would pour a bunch of it down the rear of his huge undershorts at night before going to bed. He said if he didn't, he would end up with the red rear end. This was hilarious. He did not appreciate my howling.

We had left the harbor in town a bit early and got stuck on the mudflats in the river mouth. We had to wait for the tide to rise before we lifted and went on. While waiting, he deiced to put more boat oil and gas in his fuel tank. He did this and then took this empty plastic jug that had contained the oil and tossed it in the water. I said, "Don't do that." He just laughed at me as the litter was carried off by the tide.

The trip was okay otherwise, but I did little socializing with him as we just didn't mix. He had no interest in spiritual life, and I didn't push it on him at all, but we were like oil and water in our lifestyles.

He promoted new people over me that were in line with his logic, even though we could work together okay. That was alright. I didn't want to get in with him any tighter as it would not have worked.

I stopped a vehicle one Sunday afternoon on Zimovia Highway. For speeding. It was the older Church of God pastor. I didn't know him too well. He was a nice guy, but I was not one to show favoritism. I wrote him a speeding ticket. He didn't balk about it.

To my surprise, this got around town that, yeah, Weimer even wrote a ticket to Pastor Dave. Not just the bar crowd and Joe Blow. Dave contacted me later and asked if I would preach on a Sunday morning for his church when he had to be out of town. He invited me other times as well, and we got along just fine. He was a good example of how to take a pill that was not sweet to the pallet.

Gold operations—mining—started up the Stikine River and were based out of Wrangell. This brought even more activity to the area. One time on the back channel, the two guys I mentioned before that worked for the airlines and I had been out in one guy's boat again, and we pulled into a bay on the island where the guy wanted to show us an old place that he had found.

There was an old deserted cabin there, and sluice boxes ran down the slope. The old guy would go into town and buy his supplies with gold. He was now long gone from here. There were other old cabins around in secluded places in this country that were always interesting to wonder onto and inspect. Lots of history and places where some pretty tough people had once lived.

I was at training one winter in Fairbanks at a class that was attended by cops and district attorneys. One of the deputy attorneys that I worked with from either Ketchikan or Sitka was there and had a car. The weather was terrible. Ice fog so thick one could barely see. It was twenty-five to thirty below at lunch break. He didn't want to eat at the hotel restaurant we were at. He was a large bearded man. Nothing doing but that he talked several of us into going with him to dine on fast food.

We eked our way there and had lunch. Then on the way back, we were stopped at what could just barely be seen as a red traffic light. *Boom*, we were rear-ended by another car. We didn't dare get out and take our life into our hands.

Everybody stayed seated and were pretty silent, for three cops and a district attorney as the driver from the car that had run into us approached. The person couldn't be seen until they were right up along the driver's side of us. It was a state trooper sergeant in a patrol car. Campaign hat and all. He had not seen our car or light until the crash. No more going out for lunch in this stuff for me when perfectly good meals could be had at the hotel. It was so cold that everybody just left their unlocked vehicles running while going in for lunch and shopping. Probably not too big of a risk. Car thieves couldn't see to find a car to steal anyway in that soup.

I investigated a home burglary and was able to charge two young guys with a felony. In the process, I recovered most of the property that had been taken from the home that belonged to a middle-aged couple. The property that did not have serial numbers had to be identified by the victims. The young guys swore that all of the property we recovered came from the victim's home, and there had been no other residential burglaries recently.

We had the victims come in to identify the property recovered. Included in the property were a number of pretty graphic adult toys. The couple were obviously embarrassed but kept stone faces as they assured us that all the property was theirs except for the sex toys. Putz later had one of the battery-operated toys loping along on a table in the interview room. He could be a mess. Funny at times but very different.

Putz was a portly cop. He was often seen to be consuming a bag of potato chips. Then he would open the bag up and lick the insides of it, telling us that the oil and salt were very healthy for a person. He really was convinced of this.

While Chief Bill was still a chief, he got aggravated with Putz consuming 70 percent of anything the guys brought from home to share with the department, cookies and such. The chief put together a big platter of crackers with spread on them. The kicker was that the spread was some real cheap nasty canned dog food, of which he added a little mayonnaise.

He set them out and warned everybody except Putz. Putz would grab a few every time he came in the office until they were nearly consumed by him. Putz didn't believe it when he was told about it the next day. He said it couldn't have been, they tasted good. Didn't seem to bother him!

We had an EMT/EMS class to attend in the fire department for a few days. During one late morning session, teams had to practice putting someone on a backboard and making them ready for transport, completely secured to the board so they didn't move. Putz was in my team, and he was all too happy to be the victim. He laid on the board cracking dumb jokes while we took vitals, treated and secured him to the board. We were about done, and it was time for a lunch break, so we were the final team to finish. Everybody left but this last team. We finished. With a short powwow (conference) of everybody but Putz, we picked him up and sat him upright in a corner on the board. Then with him making disparaging comments about our lack of having a father when we were born and anything else, he could shout out while whimpering, "Come on, you guys get me off of here," we turned off the lights and left the large training room, shutting the door as we left for lunch, laughing to ourselves all the way out. He looked like an angry helpless mummy on that backboard. We came back after a short lunch and freed the "mad mummy." He took it pretty good.

Cruise ships and state ferries commonly docked in Wrangell, the ferries on a regular schedule. They were a pretty good way to travel at a reasonable cost if you had the time. Passengers would disembark from these vessels and walk the very short distance into the downtown area. This would bring big numbers of shoppers and pedestrians into the streets and shops, restaurants, and bars. Especially the cruise ships. The sidewalks would be full of people, and they would be all over the street, too, to the point that one could barely drive. Most would not move out of the way of vehicles either. They were too occupied with all of the unusual sights, sounds, and smells of a real Alaskan town.

Garnet Ledge was just north of Wrangell Island. It had been donated to the children and local youth out-of-doors group in Wrangell by the owner. The donation was for the purpose of the youths digging out the beautiful dark garnets and selling them to the tourists. The kids would be lined up with tables at the docks when the ships came in, selling garnets and other trinkets. Our kids did this too one summer, and a good deal of money was made by the youths every summer with this venture. The tourists, especially from the cruise ships, loved to visit with the kids and parents nearby while inspecting the goods and making many purchases. We still have one coffee can of the garnets that we kept when we moved from Wrangell.

Pastor Terry would have to check in the cruise ships with customs, and he would often hold an afternoon service on them when they were docked on a Sunday. He then asked me and Brenda if we would like to do this too. We did hold services on the ships several times. I would give a short message from the Bible, and Brenda would play some hymns on the ship piano. The people that attended from the ship loved it. We had the kids with us, and the older people loved to dote on them and visit with us. They were so curious to inquire about our life in Alaska, and we were always happy to answer their many questions and tell them a few short tales. The services only lasted for about twenty to thirty minutes, and then it was visiting until the ship's horn would sound within a few more minutes, and we had to be off as the ship would be moving on to the next port. Those vessels were always impressive. Huge.

Chief Brent had a trooper buddy and some local FBI buddies of his come, and we did SWAT-type training on old houses nearby. Petersburg sent some of their people over too. It was pretty good assault training with tear gas, flash-bangs, using Mini-14 rifles and a fully Auto 10mm machine gun. All the other goodies too.

The FBI agents were pretty good. The trooper was arrogant and a know-it-all. We had one exercise in the indoor firing range in the new public safety building, this was a very nice range. It was made to shoot from the firing stations toward the target areas. This trooper had the guys there at the time line up and fire at targets in the darkened area near concrete walls at the sides of the range. The range was not designed for this. I told the idiot that this was a stupid idea. Nothing doing, this was part of the deal, so about five of us went through his course of firing our handguns at the nearby silhouette targets in front of concrete walls. Dummy apparently was not told at the trooper firearms instructor course that ricochets occur in a situation like this. Common sense obviously is not as common as one would think either.

I could hear projectiles ricocheting off the walls. We were near the end of the course when I felt like a bee was stinging me on the middle of my forehead. We got done. I knew that a part of a lead bullet had hit me, but there was no blood and only a small cut in the middle of my forehead. I could feel a piece of lead under my skin. That at least stopped any more of this screwy idea with other shooters waiting to go through the exercise.

I had to go to the clinic the next day. The projectile remained under my skin and was painful. It was not coming out. I went to see Dr. Davenport. He was a good guy. He was commercially fishing when not at the hospital or clinic. He was a large, burly man in his 50s with a full beard. Rough but very likable.

He got me laid down on his office table and was going to remove the projectile while cursing someone so stupid to have people firing at a concrete wall. His phone rang about the time he was ready to dig out the thing. He had no receptionist. He excused himself and stepped to the nearby phone. Talked to someone for just a minute about some crucial health concern and then told them, "Okay, I've got to go to *de*lead Weimer." I had to laugh. A little digging, and out came the chunk of lead that had split off a bullet after striking the wall and ricocheting. Good thing it didn't aim for an eye.

I was still keeping a good supply of hot cinnamon balls on hand that Hornet had got me started with in Rock Springs. They were great to chomp on while out on a cool, wet bear or deer hunt, fishing, and so on. I would leave one on Chief Brent's desk every so often. He couldn't help himself; he would eat it. Then he would cuss me for doing that, he had such heartburn and indigestion that he suffered the rest of the day.

One swing shift, a drunk in a big pickup truck drove through a part of a fence, yard, and house that was the longtime home of the parents of my friend Brian. The house was located on a corner near the post office. The truck was badly damaged and did tremendous damage to the home. Brian's mother was home alone when it happened. She was reading a book. Poor woman thought the house was coming down on her. Brian had grown up there. It always amazed me that the public by large thought that drunk drivers were just good old boys and girls and did not do much harm.

The guy drove away and hid the vehicle. Brian was upset, and together he and I tracked the guy down. He was from out of town. Off to jail with the menace.

A lot of Alaskans had the same opinion of someone using marijuana and going out in public too. Over the years, I saw many people maimed and killed while under the influence of the hallucinogen. It is a gateway drug that leads to other drug use, and it is just another tool of the devil to entrap people in chains, bad habits and harm their physical body in the process. I never touched the stuff when it was popular in high school.

One sunny afternoon a little girl was crossing the main street downtown near the drugstore when she was run over by a young guy driving a large pickup truck. He had been smoking a bunch of marijuana that day and didn't get stopped in time to avoid her. His life was ruined. Criminal charges were severe, but he was his own worst executioner. He could not live with himself. He was found a short time later in a remote cabin where he had gone to moose-hunt. He had ended his young life by hanging himself with a rope from a cabin rafter. He had to silence the torment that could not be undone by man.

With many years in enforcement and ministry, a person learns a vast amount about people and those all around you. This has pros and cons. Sometimes there were things that came to light about others that I wish I never knew. I would recall what Ed Cantrell had said to me and other young cops in my early Rock Springs days. Painfully he would tell us, "Sometimes you can know too much." It was obvious that if he could have, he would have erased some of those memories and a plethora of information.

Years later, now, as I record these memories that are all still fresh in my mind, I think of the many that I have worked and lived with. Many were rare jewels that are all gone now. I am more the richer for having had the opportunity to meet and know them. I miss them. There are getting to be fewer and fewer like they were, and someday they will be gone.

Chief Bill had relocated to Wyoming and was now the chief in Newcastle. Located in the beautiful Black Hills section that is in Wyoming adjoining South Dakota. I was feeling the urge to get back home, even though I liked being an Alaskan and had experiences that never would have taken place had I not ventured there.

I was tired of Chief Brent and some of the characters he was promoting that were merely yes-men. We got along fine, but he was no Ed Cantrell or Lieutenant Overy. The Lord was preparing us to leave, and we put our home up for sale, which turned into another story. It was eventually sold, and we moved to Newcastle, lock, stock, and barrel, as they say. I liked this area of Wyoming as good or better than any in the state. I thought this would be a really nice area to retire in someday. Very nice country. Mild *dry* weather lots of the time, nice people that are few and far between. Country that is relatively wild but easy to get around in compared to parts I've spent my days in. Nice timbered country but large open areas of grassland and some sage too. The best turkey hunting in the state, but yet there are good numbers of whitetail and mule deer, antelope, elk, rabbits, predators, and sage chicken among the wild kingdom. Nice dry tent camping on public land. No halibut, king salmon, or brown bears. The giant Alaska moose is in short supply. The good highway system is great. Very little boat or airplane travel will be needed.

Once settling there, I went through the hiring procedure and joined my old friend Chief Bill in the police department. Many adventures and unusual events occurred. There are makings for another fine book sometime. We remained there for three years. We returned to Alaska then. It's a hard place to leave or stay away from, but so is Wyoming.

We went to the wild and large remote island called Prince of Wales in Southeast Alaska. Spent five and a half years there employed in the police department and serving in the local church in various ways. Then to Anchorage, where I worked as an investigator for the State Medical Examiner's office and the State Department of Commerce for the Professional Licensing Division. After a bit more than ten years, the kids were on their own, and I retired, and we, as you might guess, returned to Wyoming. Alaska had changed a great deal in the past ten-twelve years, and Wyoming had some too. Has anyone found the perfect place to live in this life? I think not.

Without reservation, I proclaim that Jehovah God is good all of the time. Rain or shine, thick or thin, He never has failed. His Word, the Bible, is entirely true and is the manual to base your life upon. If you have never accepted Jesus as your personal savior, Lord, and friend, don't delay another day. Call upon His name. The name of Jesus is the only name—the only path to God. Repent of sin, receive

Him as the risen Lord and live for Him the rest of your days. You'll be glad you did. It is an eternal decision, and once this life is over, your decision is irrevocable forever. God has nothing but good for us if we will just speak His promises, believe them, and receive them. Quit speaking doubt, sickness, and failure. Fear and everything bad and evil come from Satan. Satan, the devil, hates the human race. A born-again Christian need never fear the evil one. He is defeated. Just resist him as Jesus did as a man. The devil needs to fear the child of God, not vice versa.

I really wanted to locate in the Newcastle area, but we ended up on the northwest side of the state in Powell, Wyoming. We had a new home built and didn't intend to leave there. A farming area that appealed more to Brenda than me at first. Once I made good friends and learned the area, the pheasant, deer, and rabbit hunting lured me in. Within forty to seventy miles, there was good fishing and wild country with mountain goats, sheep, elk, wolves, and grizzly bears. Antelope and coyotes in the prairie to the south. We cut Christmas trees just east of the border of Yellowstone Park and once saw a black wolf cross the road there, on a trip to the park with friends. We lived about seventy miles from the park.

There are many stories to tell of sheep and elk hunting among wolves and grizzly bears, catching a bigger trout from a lake than what game and fish were aware of being there. Being hit by a car going around sixty miles per hour while jogging. Making a simple decision while helping a friend on a hunting trip that led to broken ribs and a separated shoulder. Oh, that was fun! *It is sure good, I must say, to be Found and Not Lost. I've tried both, so I know for certain.*

Six and a half years later, the Lord had different ideas and mostly to my liking too. We were to relocate to Upton, Wyoming, in Weston County, only thirty miles from the county seat at Newcastle. Here I plan to remain till Jesus returns or our days come to an end. However, as an old friend of mine would often say while try'`--` `-o` look mysterious and wise all at the same time and yet kee/ chuckle controlled, *"One never knows, does one?"* "No" was t/ reply, one never knows!*

About the Author

Kenneth Joe Weimer (Ken) was born in Rock Springs, Wyoming, in 1955. Rock Springs was not the typical Wyoming community. His middle name derives from his grandfather Joseph (Joe). Ken was raised and attended school in Rock Springs with his three siblings. Though the family was unchurched, Ken met the Lord and was born again around the age of twelve or thirteen.

He graduated from the Rock Springs High School, began law enforcement and ministry careers there. He was married and had his first child in Rock Springs before relocating to Alaska.

Ken earned a diploma from the Berean School of the Bible, is a graduate of the Wyoming Law Enforcement Academy and the Alaska Public Safety Academy. He served in many varied capacities in law enforcement for a total of thirty-five years in Wyoming and Alaska. He worked for several years prior to entering law enforcement in labor jobs and professional security work.

He has served as well for over thirty years in public ministry. He is an ordained minister, public speaker, and teacher. He is an avid outdoorsman, hunter, and fisherman, as well as often biking and hiking. He detests using anything but a tent for extended outdoor trips.

He is the father of two adult children and a grandfather to five grandchildren. Having retired from law enforcement, he now resides in the beautiful Black Hills, northeast region of Wyoming, living in the town of Upton with his wife Brenda and their two dachshunds. There they founded The Cross Ministry, of which they are active in street ministry throughout the area. Ken also has served as a Rapid Response chaplain with Billy Graham Evangelistic Association since 2016.